The Immigrant Heritage of America Series

The Immigrant
Experience in Wisconsin

By La Vern J. Rippley

Twayne Publishers • Boston

The Immigrant Experience in Wisconsin

La Vern J. Rippley

Copyright © 1985 by G. K. Hall & Company
All Rights Reserved
Published by Twayne Publishers
A Division of G. K. Hall & Co.
A publishing subsidiary of ITT
70 Lincoln Street
Boston, Massachusetts 02111

11212070

Printed on permanent/durable acid-free
paper and bound in the United States of
America.

Library of Congress Cataloging in Publication Data

Rippley, La Vern J.
   The immigrant experience in Wisconsin.

   (The Immigrant heritage of America series)
   Bibliography: p.
   Includes index.
   1. Minorities—Wisconsin—Politics and government
2. Wisconsin—Politics and government.   I. Title.
II. Series.
F590.A1R56   1985   977.5   84-19820
ISBN 0-8057-8424-1

For my brother
Charles L. Rippley
of
Waumandee, Wisconsin

Contents

About the Author

La Vern J. Rippley's paternal ancestors immigrated with the name <u>Rieple</u> from Unadingen near Donaueschingen in Baden, Germany, around 1855 and settled in Buffalo County, Wisconsin, near the small community of Waumandee. Today the county remains largely German and Swiss, and the German language lives among older inhabitants. His maternal grandparents arrived with the name <u>Rucinski</u> from the Silesian town of Poppelau (presently Popielów, Poland) in southeastern Germany around 1886 and settled in the Trempealeau County Polish-speaking community between Arcadia and Independence, Wisconsin. Born at Waumandee in 1935, Rippley took an M.A. at Kent State and a Ph.D. at Ohio State University, following study with a Fulbright Fellowship at the University of Munich. He taught for three years at Ohio Wesleyan University before accepting a professorship at St. Olaf College in Northfield, Minnesota, where he has served as chair of the department.

Rippley is the author of <u>The Columbus Germans</u> (Baltimore: Fuerst, 1968); <u>Of German Ways</u> (Minneapolis: Dillon, 1970, 1973); <u>The German-Americans</u> (Boston: Twayne, 1976; Lanham, Md.: University Press of America, 1984). He has translated <u>Excursion through America</u> by Nicolaus Mohr (Chicago: R. R. Donnelley, 1973); he translated with Armand Bauer and edited <u>Russian-German Settlements in the United States</u> (Fargo: Institute for Regional Studies, 1974); he edited and supplemented <u>Research Possibilities in the German-American Field</u> (Hamburg: Buske, 1980). Rippley is also the author of over 100 articles in historical journals and is editor of the <u>Newsletter</u> of the Society for German-American Studies.

Foreword

Professor Rippley's work stands by itself as a well
researched and penetrating insight into how multiethnicism shaped the political climate of the State of
Wisconsin. More generally, it illustrates the broader
problem of building a unified political entity out of a
wide variety of ethnic groups. It seems to me that
Professor Rippley has gotten to the heart of what makes
our state and our nation unique: diversity in unity.
   The problems inherent in a multiethnic political
system are very significant. The integration of disparate cultural and religious groupings into a viable
community is extremely difficult. Professor Rippley
illustrates this fact in his examination of immigrant
Wisconsin. He outlines the political and the geographical facets of the various ethnic groups in the state
and shows us how these influences have shaped Wisconsin's politics throughout its history. The most out-
standing insight contained in Professor Rippley's work
is that Wisconsin's unique political character is in
part attributable to its multiethnic heritage. Professor Rippley has made important contributions in both
the political history of the state and more generally
in the study of multiethnicism.
   The work itself is a "synthesis" of the histories of
the various immigrant groups in Wisconsin as they
slowly, but surely, merged to form a single political
entity. Appropriately, Professor Rippley begins with
the formal establishment of Wisconsin as a state in
1848. Even at this early date, Wisconsin was a
patchwork of discrete and insular ethnic communities
only loosely associated under the leadership of an
American-born minority. The Civil War produced the
first major crisis which strained the traditional
political loyalties of the different ethnic communities. Professor Rippley skillfully traces the
divisions within and among the various groups over the
course and conduct of the war.
   In his examination of the post-Civil War period,

Professor Rippley focuses on the relationship between religion and ethnic loyalty in determining political affiliation and he concludes, surprisingly, that religion was as much a factor as ethnicity. Professor Rippley's chapter on the "Wisconsin Idea in Progressive Politics" is a fascinating look at how the state's unique political character was manifested in both an individual and a movement. The individual was Robert "Fighting Bob" La Follette and the movement was progressive politics. Progressivism was a populist-oriented movement which in Wisconsin found a great deal of support due to immigrant dissatisfaction with both of the "traditional" American political parties. To this day, Wisconsin politics maintains this nontraditional bent.

According to Professor Rippley, the First World War was an important turning point for the "hyphenated" Americans in both state and national politics. On the one hand, World War I presented foreign-born Wisconsinites, especially those from the Central Powers, with some difficult choices. Loyalty to the Old Country conflicted with obligations to their new home. Adverse national sentiments against these people presaged those directed against the Japanese-Americans twenty years later. On the other hand, the period from 1910 through 1920 saw the acceleration of the Americanization of these groups, at least superficially. Indeed, the Second World War produced much less ethnic division as a result of the United States' actions. The German-American "bunds" were short-lived phenomena and the "America First Committees" were characterized more by ideological, rather than ethnic, orientation. Ethnicity was still an important force, but it was limited at this point primarily to the ballot box.

The Cold War opened a new chapter on immigrant politics with the waves of displaced persons coming to the state after the Second World War. At first these people adopted what Professor Rippley refers to as the "suitcase mentality" as they looked toward the eventual return to their native countries. Their influence on state and national politics was limited. But with the consolidation of Communist rule in Eastern Europe, these groups began to exert more influence. Professor Rippley's analysis of the transition from the Cold War politics of the Eisenhower years to the new ideas of the Kennedy Administration provides an important

Foreword

perspective on the changing attitudes of Wisconsin's
immigrants. His work concludes with some timely
thoughts on how the most recent new arrivals, the
Hispanics and the Southeast Asians, may eventually
contribute to the changing political character of the
State of Wisconsin.

William Proxmire
<u>United States Senate</u>

Preface

Unique among all states of the Union, Wisconsin has two
ethnic villages that seek to commemorate in living form
the many ethnic peoples that settled the state. The
larger of the two is "Old World Wisconsin, an Outdoor
Ethnic Museum," developed by the State Historical
Society in cooperation with the State Department of
Natural Resources. A project in historic, cultural,
and environmental preservation, the outdoor museum is
situated just south of the town of Eagle on Highway 67
between Janesville and Milwaukee. It is easily reached
from Madison, Whitewater, Watertown, and other southeastern Wisconsin cities (1). The other ethnic museum
has an indoor design, the "European Village," within
the Milwaukee Public Museum at 800 West Wells Street (2).
    Old World Wisconsin was slow in evolving. In 1944
Fred Holmes published a book entitled Old World Wisconsin in which he discussed the state's immigrants. More
than a decade later in 1956 Hans Kuether proposed re-
creating an outdoor Pomeranian village near Lebanon
that would feature the half-timbered construction
styles of his native northeastern Germany. Although
Kuether's hopes never saw fruition, he did correspond
extensively with staff members of the Wisconsin State
Historical Society, especially Richard W. E. Perrin,
who had written much about the architecture of the
immigrants. It was Perrin who developed the idea for
Old World Wisconsin. It would be a multinational,
multicultural outdoor museum on a site that could
accomodate genuine pieces of ethnic architecture and
house the artifacts that the immigrants themselves
brought to pioneer Wisconsin. Eventually the Old World
Wisconsin Committee of the Board of Curators for the
State Historical Society selected a tract of land
containing 576 acres in the Kettle Moraine State
Forest. With the help of foreign governments whose
people would be commemorated as well as state and
federal funds matched by private donations, Old World
Wisconsin took shape in time for widely publicized

activities in the Bicentennial year of 1976. Although many of the projects will not be completed for decades, the open-air museum (unique to America but familiar in Sweden, Germany, Romania, and other countries) today functions prominently in the network of historical sites in Wisconsin.

The Milwaukee European Village opened its year-round indoor exhibit in December 1979, following plans developed by a committee established in late 1974. From frequent contacts with Wisconsin's countless immigrants came the idea of reproducing a village with structures for thirty-two ethnic types. Homogeneous clusters lend harmony to the composite. In the group for the British Isles are homes for the Welsh, Scottish, and Irish. Close by are the Lowlanders—Belgians and Dutch. Beyond them come the Scandinavians with representations for the Norwegians, Swedish, Danish, and Finnish followed by the Estonians, Latvians, and Lithuanians. Next are the central European cottages, one for Polish, another for Czechoslovakians. There is one east European cottage for Russians, another for Ukrainians, one for Jewish, and one each for Croatians, Hungarians, Serbians, Romanians, and Bulgarians. The Mediterraneans are each represented by a modest structure for Greek, Italian, French, Spanish, and Portuguese peoples. Finally in the central area are the German, Austrian, and Swiss structures, the latter being a clock tower. Authentically planned and executed, the village has trees that are artificial, artifacts that are genuine. For special occasions the homes are enlivened by real people, costumed and outfitted with the tools and instruments of early settlement. Since most of the immigrants to Wisconsin came from rural villages, the exhibits portray the simplicity as well as the hopes for a better life that typified most of the newcomers.

In present-day Wisconsin annual festivities are bound up with ethnicity. The Norwegians celebrate May 17 (Independence Day for Norway) as perhaps nowhere outside the mother country while the German Sommerfest draws over 100,000 visitors annually to Milwaukee. Milwaukee maintains public grounds and schedules ethnic festivals so that the year conveniently rewards each of its interested groups. The state bureau of tourism is also helpful in identifying and promoting the many outstate celebrations that unwind throughout the summer months.

Preface

It seems appropriate, then, that a volume in the
Twayne series be dedicated specifically to this vi-
brantly ethnic state. This book is not, however, a
current-day festival of nations. It is not about the
Old World in Wisconsin either. Nor is it about person-
alties and leaders who, from Wisconsin ethnic elements,
sprang to greatness in civic, religious, or military
life. There is only information about the state's
nationality groups at various stages from their time of
arrival to the days of their assimilation, generally
speaking between 1850 and 1950. Specific groups are
never treated in isolation, with a chapter for this one
and another for that one. Instead the status of each
is presented more or less during the time in which
their ethnicity thrived. Many statistics are presented
to demonstrate the size and significance of the nationalities at various times. Space is not available to
describe their specific cultures, maintenance of
language, dress, religion or Old World life-styles. A
good deal of attention is paid to politics in the
belief that the American nation as an experiment in
government was a dominant factor in the attraction of
immigrants to the United States and to Wisconsin.
Political loyalties and election results are frequently
analyzed for their deeper meanings about ethnicity for
the state and the nation.

On the whole the research contained in the book is
not primary. All available printed sources were consulted, however, and a synthesis was made. Often a
conflict arose as to how much local information was
crucial and which details could be dispensed with.
Very often community histories and family genealogies
were too far removed from the more general topic to be
included. The same holds true for the thousands of
local church histories that were consulted. Names were
excluded for the most part if they had only local
influence, but included if their importance extended
beyond the immediate region and held significance
statewide. Most published material as well as M.A.
theses and Ph.D. dissertations can be discovered in the
notes. A selected bibliography appears at the end.

The term "ethnicity" and its meaning are always a
problem. One can be ethnic by pedigree, adoption,
nation of origin, place of birth, language spoken,
marriage to another ethnic person, and even by free
choice of association. For the sake of variety, the

term "nationality" group sometimes substitutes for "ethnic" group. But this term is just as difficult because the nations of Europe were in great flux as to boundary throughout the period of immigration to Wisconsin. Germany was constituted of many German-speaking lands following unification in 1871. Poland officially did not exist, or was described as Prussian-, Russian-, and Austrian-Poland. Switzerland, of course, has three official languages. Czechoslovakia incorporated two or more nations (Bohemia and Slovakia first and foremost) after the Versailles Treaty in 1919. Scandinavians are often lumped together but constitute three closely related languages and cultures (Danish, Norwegian, and Swedish) and one not so closely related (Finnish). I have chosen to call "ethnic" those people who had a non-English immigrant status, either directly or after several generations. Included, therefore, are the Irish. Excluded certainly are the British descendants from New England and New York State, of whom there were many in Wisconsin, often with the street name of Yankees. Likewise, I have not paid more than passing attention to the British immigrants themselves, although by any definition they would be a "nationality" group if not an "ethnic" one strictly speaking. For the most part language is presumed to define a cultural group and it is a primary factor in deciding to which ethnic group a person belongs.

The chapters in this book are divided by themes with some overlap because ethnicity is tightly bound up with religion, politics, conflicting value systems, and much more. Even more so, the peoples from a general cultural area had vastly different backgrounds, e.g., a German from Pomerania or Prussia has a special linguistic dialect and a different religion than one coming from Bavaria. Poles from each of the three sections mentioned above were very different, especially as a result of the influences forced on them by their conquerors, yet all were Poles and in the United States wanted to be nationalistically identified together. At the same time, they fought heated battles with each other inside the ethnic community. The complexity of these issues inevitably lends a confusion that in the final analysis mirrors the reality of the ethnicity question itself.

This volume is designed to provide a broad survey for a general audience. The author is well aware of the scope that some scholars would expect or prefer. In making this study, the author became intensely aware of the countless monographs that could be written about individual topics on the immigrant heritage of Wisconsin, and it can only be hoped that many of them will be undertaken and eventually published.

La Vern J. Rippley

St. Olaf College

Chapter One
Immigrants in
Territorial Wisconsin

By the time Wisconsin attained statehood in 1948,
American-born lawyers and businessmen clearly held the
reins while foreigners, and to some extent southerners,
did the work. Such was the case in the lead region
around Mineral Point after 1832 when some 7,000 Cornish
miners were attracted to southwestern Wisconsin.
Before they moved on or were assimilated they had
erected lasting trademarks of their homeland in the
buff-colored, limestone cottages, which still charac-
terize many townsites, especially Mineral Point. For
an understanding of immigrant life in territorial
Wisconsin, however, we must shift from the southwestern
corner, where Mineral Point was the heart, to the
southeastern quadrant, where Milwaukee had begun to
develop into a throbbing artery. The city began as a
trading post of the American Fur Company under the
direction of a French-Canadian, Solomon Juneau (1).
From the outset Milwaukee had geographical advantages.
As with most cities that were founded before railroad
days, Milwaukee lay along the water. Not just Lake
Michigan but the Milwaukee, Menomonee, and Kinnikinic
rivers, all three of which share a common estuary with
the lake. Milwaukee's harbor made it famous. Except
for this one inlet, the shores of Lake Michigan are
too smooth for the construction of a harbor.

Like the rest of Wisconsin, Milwaukee was subject
to land speculation. After the crash of 1837 and its
subsequent depression, Milwaukee businesses gave
increasing attention to immigration as a means of
bolstering markets for goods and services. Building
canals, harbor, and merchandising facilities created
high demand for labor, which in turn meant construction
to house the laborers. In 1848, when the first statistics on the background of its residents were tabulated,
immigrants constituted over half of Milwaukee's population. They increased to roughly two-thirds of the

city's 20,000-plus population two years later (2). Of
the 12,000 foreigners in the city in 1850, over 7,000
were Germans followed by 2,800 Irish, 1,400 British-
born, and a total of 1,200 Canadians, Dutch, Norwegians, and Swiss. But most newcomers did not remain
in the city. "A vessel load lands and in a few hours
their effects are loaded upon wagons, and the whole are
moving for the interior," reported the <u>Milwaukee
Sentinel</u> (3). Those who remained in Milwaukee were
craftsmen and professionals or people who had no means
to buy land. This pattern prevailed through the decade
of the 1840s and shifted only when the 1848 Revolutions
in Germany sent intellectuals and professionals into
Wisconsin, types of individuals who were more at home
in the city than on small farms.
     Irish settlers began arriving in Milwaukee in 1835,
at first from eastern states but then directly from the
Emerald Island. In 1839 Milwaukee already had its
first Roman Catholic church with English services,
indicating that the Irish were well established. Many
Irish moved to Milwaukee from Fall River, Massachusetts, where the cotton mills closed as a result of the
panic of 1837. A later influx of Irish resulted from
the annual Irish potato famines beginning in 1845.
German immigrants also increased after similar famines
coupled with political upheaval occurred in Germany
from 1846-1852 (4). Protestant Scots-Irishmen, some of
Huguenot origin, settled near Whitewater in Koshkonong
Township (5). A fascinating Norwegian activity in
early Milwaukee was shipbuilding (6). Norwegians were
not only skilled ship carpenters but also excellent
crewmen for operating Great Lakes vessels. Beginning
in 1845 and continuing until the 1870s, Norwegians
plied the Great Lakes during the shipping season, then
switched to yard work when ice closed the harbors (7).
     Milwaukee was the point of entry for nearly all
immigrants. A Dutch settlement dates from 1846 and
bore the name of Dutch Hill. Later on, members of this
community moved to Sheboygan County to acquire fertile
farm lands and timber tracts (8). Germans occupied the
lowlands near the Milwaukee River in what was the First
Ward while the Irish settled the lowlands stretching
southward from Wisconsin Avenue to the Menomonee River
in the Third or Irish Ward. Anglo-Americans occupied
Yankee Hill, dominated the economic and social activities of the young city, and supplied the first thirteen

mayors of Milwaukee (9). At this time Know Nothingism
reared its head in New England—a movement that wanted
to keep out the foreign born in order to preserve
America for the Americans. On Milwaukee's streets one
did occasionally hear the slogans "Damn the Dutch" and
"To Hell with the Irish," but for the most part Yankees
hired immigrant laborers and seemingly all thrived in
mutual cooperation. Wisconsin in 1850 had nearly
200,000 natives compared to 107,000 born abroad (10).
Of the foreign born, approximately 48,000 were English-
speaking, 59,000 non-English. Of the English-speaking,
half were Irish, a few were Welsh and Scottish, many
were Cornish.

Beginning in 1842, there were two Irish Catholic
organizations in Milwaukee, the Total Abstinence
Society and the St. Mary's Charitable Society. An
Irishman named Timothy O'Brien was prominent in city
politics (11). There were Irish communities also in
Iowa and Green counties, most of them associated with
lead mining. Brown County around Green Bay likewise
had many Irish in Territorial days as did Ozaukee and
Sheboygan. Irish also lived in Dane, Jefferson, Dodge,
and Columbia counties. They tended to congregate in
townships they had named, such as Erin, New Dublin,
Emmet, Clyman, and Lowell. Counties west of Lake
Michigan once harbored Irishmen who were then pushed
westward by incoming Germans. In Dane County the Irish
held farms in Burke, Westport, and Cross Plains townships as well as in Medina, which was an Irish Protestant community. The capital city of Madison also had
an Irish settlement. Wherever the Irish went they
quickly showed their talents for political action,
giving rise to the comment in Wisconsin that "the
Germans owned it but the Irish ran it." Irish born
members attended the state constitutional conventions
and were represented in the territorial legislature.
At the close of the territorial period, Wisconsin had
21,043 natives of Ireland (12).

English immigrants in Wisconsin territory by 1850
totaled 18,952, slightly less than the Irish. Widely
dispersed, they concentrated in the southwestern
counties of Lafayette and Iowa in the lead region.
Englishmen made three attempts to settle in closed
colonies: One in Racine County, another when the Staf-
fordshire Emigration Society in 1846 planted a colony
of potters in Columbia County, and a third at Mazomanie

in Dane County. The latter had some 600 members in
1850 (13). Wisconsin's territorial population also
included three Welsh communities. One was in Columbia
County north of Madison where they clustered around the
village of Cambria. It extended eastward into Dodge
County at Elba and Fox Lake, and annually celebrated
the musical eisteddfod. Other Welshmen settled in
Genesee township in Waukesha County and expanded into
Delafield. They also scattered throughout the lead-
mining counties of Grant, Lafayette, and Iowa (14).
Scotsmen in Wisconsin numbered 3,527 by the 1850 census
(15). They settled in Milwaukee and in townships that
bear the Scottish names Caledonia, Dover, and York in
Kenosha and Racine counties. More numerous were the
Cornish. The maritime English County of Cornwall with
its archipelago of islands extending westward into the
Atlantic was widely recognized for the mining of tin
and other metals. These miners were skilled in ex-
tracting last bits of ore in the most efficient ways
possible. When news about the rich lead fields of
Wisconsin reached Cornwall in 1827, a wave of immigration was triggered and lasted twenty years (16). The
Cornish in Wisconsin numbered about 7,000 in 1850,
after which many left in search of gold in California.
Mineral Point and Dodgeville each had over 1,000, and
the towns of Hazel Green, Linden, and Shullsburg, 950
or less. The balance were scattered in Platteville,
Benton, Cornish Hollow, British Hollow, Jefferson, New
Diggings, and smaller places. Cornish men were active
in the territorial legislature, in education, and later
in the Union army (17).

German Old Lutherans arrived in Wisconsin territory
in 1839 and bought lands for a colony, thus aiding the
city in the depression that resulted from the panic of
1837. Shortly thereafter they purchased a larger tract
of land in Washington County, northwest of Milwaukee,
and established a church of their faith (18). For
centuries two Protestant churches, the Lutheran and the
Reformed, had existed in Prussia under a tolerant
monarch. A Prussian Reformed Church member, King
William III, confident of his prerogatives under the
divine right of kings, in 1817 forced a union of the
Lutheran and Reformed churches, thus denying his people
not only a political constitution but also freedom of
religion. When this "Union" became a royal edict in
1830, anti-union Lutheran congregations resisted, first

in Silesia, later in Pomerania, then in the eastern
provinces of Prussia. When the state tried ever more
zealously to enforce the Union, Lutheran groups left
Germany, some for Australia, others for North America,
where they founded the Buffalo Synod. One group sailed
from Saxony to New Orleans, then up the Mississippi to
found the Lutheran Church of the Missouri Synod near
St. Louis. After the arrival of the Wisconsin
Lutherans in 1839 the Prussian king's successor,
Frederick William IV, in 1845 made a "general conces-
sion" granting recognition to the anti-union Lutheran
congregations (19). Constituting the largest group of
religious dissenters in Wisconsin, these Old Lutheran
Germans soon expanded to Ozaukee County, where their
nucleus was around Cedarburg, and Washington, where it
was Kirchayn and Freistadt, while farther west in Dodge
County they selected the biblical name Lebanon (20).
Other Old Lutherans heading for Missouri moved farther
up the Mississippi to establish a large settlement at
Potosi in Grant County. Although some engaged in
mining in the early days, they soon displaced Yankee
farmers. Relatives and friends from Germany gradually
joined them so that Grant County by 1870 had over 3,500
citizens born in Germany (21). Bohemians also settled
for a time near Muscoda in Grant County but most
eventually moved on, many to Nebraska and farther
west (22).

By 1845 a quarter-million acres of farmland report-
edly had been sold to Germans. They came by way of the
Erie Canal and the Great Lakes, sweeping into eastern
Wisconsin counties, among them Manitowoc, Sheboygan,
Calumet, Outagamie, Waukesha, Jefferson, Dane, Green
Lake, and Marquette. During the ice-free months, some
1,200 Germans landed weekly at Milwaukee (23). Most
Germans clung to the soil. A minority were engaged in
manufacturing, particularly brewing and tanning.
Almost all were conservative and joined the Democratic
party. The 1850 census reports 38,000 Germans, 12
percent of the total population of Wisconsin. In
Milwaukee County, however, they numbered 10,000, 32
percent of the total. By contrast the Dutch numbered
only 1,600 when the 1850 census was taken. In 1845,
Dutch immigrants moved to the southeastern townships of
Sheboygan County and, after a Dutch Catholic missionary
had paved the way, into Holland township of Brown
County (24). By and large the Dutch engaged in dairy

farming although some supplemented their incomes by
lake fishing.

Both French- and German-speaking Swiss immigrants
came to Wisconsin during the territorial period. The
French-speaking arrived early either directly from
Switzerland or by way of the Selkirk settlement along
the Red River in Canada and worked in the lead mining
region of Lafayette County. Some German-speaking Swiss
went to Fond du Lac and Sauk counties, but most concentrated in the southern counties where they established
the solidly Swiss town of New Glarus and Monroe in
Green County (25). The Canton of Glarus in 1845
decided to cope with its overpopulation by paying
emigrants' passage and buying them land in New Glarus.
In 1850 there were some 1,200 Swiss in Wisconsin.

The largest and most prosperous settlement of
Norwegians in early Wisconsin was not the early colony
of Muskego in Racine County, where the first Norwegian
newspaper in the United States appeared, but in Dane
County (26). Situated on lands adjacent to a creek of
the same name, Koshkonong became the parent colony for
Norwegian settlements throughout the United States
(27). Koshkonong expanded westward to include Stoughton and eastward into the townships of Albion, Chris-
tians, Deerfield, Dunkirk, Pleasant Spring, and Cottage
Grove, as well as along the Jefferson and Rock County
line around Lake Koshkonong. Soon a daughter settlement was founded in northern Dane County in the
townships of Vienna, Windsor, and Bristol with some
extensions into Burke and Westport. After the strong
influx of Norwegians into this area following 1846,
Norway Grove, De Forest, Morrisonville, and neighboring
towns became Norwegian strongholds. Gradually these
centers funneled Norwegian settlers into western Dane
County, where they took up residences in the townships
of Blue Mounds, Primrose, Perry, Vernon, and Springdale
with a commercial center at Mount Horeb, still known
for its strong Norwegian character. Smaller Norwegian
settlements evolved in the lead-mining region near
Wiota. There was a settlement in Jefferson County
called Skaponong, and others near Elkhorn and Delavan
(28). The Columbia County townships of Hampton and
Otsego were also populated by Norwegians. Offspring
from Koshkonong later settled in counties farther
north, especially Waupaca, Waushara, and Winnebago.

When the 1850 census was taken, there were already 8,600 Norwegian-born in Wisconsin, and eventually Wisconsin came to be considered the home of all Norwegian immigrants in the United States. The primary nationalities represented in territorial Wisconsin were the British, Germans, Irish, Norwegians, and Swiss. Other immigrant groups arrived after statehood, among them Armenians, Belgians, Bohemians, Danes, Finns, Greeks, Hungarians, Icelanders, Italians, Latvians, Lithuanians, Poles, Russians, Swedes, and others. After Wisconsin achieved statehood, there was considerable effort at the official level to attract these immigrants. One factor in territorial Wisconsin's amassing a large foreignborn and New England population lay in the opening of the Erie Canal. Completed in 1825, it facilitated transportation to Wisconsin until well into the 1850s (29). The receiving point was the harbor of Milwaukee, whose population increased from 1,700 in 1840 to over 20,000 in 1850 and doubled to 45,000 by 1860. Visiting Milwaukee in 1843 Margaret Fuller commented,

The torrent of emigration swells very strongly towards this place. During the fine weather, the poor refugees arrive daily in their national dresses all travel-soiled and worn. The night they pass in rude shanties, in a particular quarter of the town, then walk off into the country--the mothers carrying their infants, the fathers leading the little children by the hand, seeking a home where their hands may maintain them. . . . Here, on the pier, I see disembarking the Germans, the Norwegians, the Swedes, the Swiss. Who knows how much of old legendary lore, of modern wonder, they have already planted amid the Wisconsin forests. (30)

Only in the lead region were there Americans born in the southern states, who in 1850 numbered a mere 5,400. Because the lead region attracted both white and black southerners, Wisconsin's black population was concentrated in this area during the territorial period. Some came as slaves of military personnel, others as freemen or runaway slaves. There never were any slaves outside the lead region, and by 1850 there were no longer any slaves at all listed among the 635 blacks in

Wisconsin. After 1850, the concentration of blacks
shifted to the urban counties along the eastern sea-
board of the state (31).

Wisconsin's territorial population was uncharacter-
istically youthful. In 1840 over two-thirds were under
thirty. None of these early arrivals was a refugee
from religious persecution, except for the Lutherans.
Nor was political turmoil a major factor in their
coming. George Adam Fromander typifies their spirit in
his letter of 1847 written from Jefferson, Wisconsin,
to Johann Balthaser Koenig of Arzberg, Bavaria.

> We are all well and live very happily together. We
> do not care to be back in our unhappy Germany. . . .
> Hunting is permitted for everybody in places not
> fenced in, even on Sunday in the country. Hunting
> is forbidden in town during church hours. . . .
> Women are highly respected in this country. They do
> not work in the fields and may be quite genteel.
> Whoever wants to make the trip need not bring a
> great deal except a supply of shirts and woolens.
> Do not bring tools of any kind, nor extra shoes, for
> the German ones are not worth carrying across the
> sea. No matter what you need or want, it is much
> better than in Germany. . . . I do not advise a father
> of a family with many little children to move to
> this country unless he has money, for things are not
> as they were a few years ago when you could have
> cleared a piece of land. Now if a man wants land,
> he must be able to pay for it. (32)

In his January 1947 letter Fromander touches on all
aspects of immigrant farming in territorial Wisconsin.
He concludes with greetings to friends and neighbors,
"Good night, all you friends! Germany is a vale of
tears." Johann Balthaser Koenig and his family agreed
and set out for Wisconsin, bearing with them the
Fromander letters.

Chapter Two
Regional Development of Urban Ethnic Centers

Wisconsin has five physiographic regions characterized according to climate, water transportation, floral cover, quality of soil, and economic resources. These five regions also divide Wisconsin into five population provinces (1). The most populous region is southeastern Wisconsin, which slices from Green Bay southwest to Madison, including Dane and Green counties, and was the first to be populated. The second to attract settlement was the Lead Region in the Southwest, i.e., the counties of Grant, Iowa, and Lafayette, all lying south of the Wisconsin River. The third is the Western Upland, a slice of land lying adjacent to the Mississippi from the Wisconsin River north to the lower St. Croix River, including St. Croix County. The fourth is the Central Plain, which incorporated primarily old Glacial Lake Wisconsin. Lying in the heart of the state, it exhibits sandy soil and poor access except for the Wisconsin River, which bisects it. The final region is the Northern Upland, characterized by its granitic dome overlaid with thin, poor soils, which produced the White Pine and, together with the Central Plain, was the last to develop.

In 1850, practically all of the state's population was in the first two districts, from Green Bay down the Fox River Valley to Prairie du Chien. In the next decade, region three acquired the greatest percentage of new population. People spread northwestward in 1870, forming a V-pattern of concentrated settlement on both the eastern and western edges of the state. The census of 1880 shows little change in the V-pattern except that pockets of settlement began in Marathon County and along the Wisconsin Central Railroad Line (now the Soo Line). It was built from Stevens Point in Portage County through Marshfield in Wood County northward to Ashland on the Chequamagon Bay of Lake Superior. The towns of Abbotsford, Medford, Prentice, Park Falls,

and Mellen developed while the line, was being completed
in 1877 as did a string of rural settlements inland
from the railroad line (2). By 1900 newcomers had
pushed inward from the V-pattern closing off the
Central Plain. In the vast Northern Upland there was
still plenty of room, much of it economically unviable
for dense settlement. Two decades later, in 1920, the
V-pattern still prevailed. Since then, population in
these regions has declined.

Across the lower tier of the Northern Upland a chain
of cities arose. In the west were Eau Claire and
Chippewa Falls, both sawmill centers fed by the Chippewa River (3). Farther east lay Marshfield, an important hub of railroad lines that were laid to supply
lumber to the city's mills. A sawmill and stave, hub,
and furniture factories, as well as boiler works,
attracted settlers. In the center, Wausau also thrived
on sawmills, veneer plants, and finally paper mills.
Stevens Point and Wisconsin Rapids were less prominent
as sawmill centers but prospered on wood products and
paper milling. Smaller cities in the lower tier also
lived on lumber: Menomonie, Antigo, and farther north,
Merrill, Tomahawk, and Rinelander. At the two upper
corners of the Northern Upland two cities developed as
fishing and transportation centers. At the eastern
corner is Marinette. Around 1900, lumbering attracted
many Europeans but once the timber vanished, a harbor
dock was constructed to promote fishing. Paper mills,
box factories, knitting mills, glove factories, and
granite works attracted Germans from Russia and Poles
to available jobs. Opposite Marinette at the top of
the state lies Superior, which was recognized early as
a potential shipping center. In 1861 Captain George G.
Meade, later commander of Union forces at Gettysburg,
came to survey the harbor, but railroad connections
were delayed until 1881, when the Northern Pacific
finally laid a spur into the city. Late in the nineteenth century Norwegians, Finns, Germans, and Poles
flocked in to service the lumber and shipping industries. Only after the discovery of ore in the Gogebic
Range did large numbers of eastern Europeans arrive.
After the turn of the century, thousands found work in
the grain elevators, warehouses, and on the docks.
Then as now, the city suffered from boom and bust as
the freighters on whom the economy of the area depended
were held up by a massive freeze lasting four months

every year. The Finns in particular moved out to farms
in the forest cutover.

Finns initially came to a small town called
Montreal, near the Michigan border, in 1887. Here they
worked in the Iron Belt, which extends southwest of
Hurley. At one time four immigrant boarding houses in
Montreal housed 200 Finns. Gradually they left the
low-grade iron-ore fields for farms and jobs in the
ports of Ashland and Superior. Finns also arrived
about 1887 in the Amberg area of Marinette County,
where they quarried granite for Milwaukee´s structures.
At Redgranite in Waushara County they toiled likewise
to produce building blocks for Milwaukee and Chicago.
When both the quarries and the ore were exhausted,
these nonrural Finns also sought jobs in the shipyards
of Superior and in Ashland, where coal, iron ore, and
railroad work were plentiful. They soon discovered that
harbor duty was seasonal, forcing many to seek winter
work in the pineries of Douglas and Bayfield counties.
In this way the Finnish colony of Superior survived and
increased. As late as 1940 there were more than 500
Finnish-born residents in Superior. In the metropoli-
tan areas of Milwaukee, Racine, and Kenosha in 1940
there were only 359 Finnish-born residents, most of
whom worked in the large factories and tanneries. The
vast majority arrived in the 1920s after deserting the
Upper Peninsula of Michigan, northern Minnesota, and
the logging areas of Wisconsin for a better existence
in the cities (4).

In the Central Plain, there never were any cities
but several immigrant strongholds grew up in the
Western Upland, notably La Crosse. At the center of
the so-called Coulee Region, La Crosse bestrides three
rivers, the La Crosse, the Black, and the Mississippi.
The French stopped here to trade with the Winnebagos
and named the site "Prairie La Crosse" in memory of the
game they saw Indians playing, which reminded them of
French la crosse. When the Winnebagos were removed to
Minnesota in 1848, white settlers streamed in and La
Crosse became a county seat. On the heels of Yankees
from New York, Ohio, and Vermont, Germans and Norwegians supplied labor for the burgeoning sawmills,
making La Crosse a woodworking center for the Black
River pineries. With the advent of the Milwaukee Road
in 1858, the city quickly developed into a railroad and
barge shipping complex, the largest between Dubuque to

the South, Milwaukee to the East, and St. Paul to the
North. In 1880 La Crosse was the second most active
manufacturing city in the state and until 1895 a major
lumbering center. As a result, Germans, Irish, and
Bohemians flocked in and started clubs, shops, and
Roman Catholic churches. Almost immediately a Catholic bishop was appointed to establish the Diocese of La
Crosse. Simultaneously Norwegian Lutherans built
churches and in later years so did the Polish, Syrians,
and Greek Orthodox. Many German Sängerfeste (singing-
society competitions) were held in La Crosse and the
oldest Norwegian singing society in the United States
was organized here as the Normanna Sangerkor in 1869.

Madison, in the southeastern region, was never known
as an immigrant stronghold. When the Federal Writers'
Program published its Guide to the Badger State in 1941
the authors wrote of Madison "the foreign-born constitute less than 9.5 percent; natives of foreign parentage constitute 29.5 percent. . . . The largest national
groups are German and Norwegian and Italians comprise
the next largest divisions. Italians and Negroes
constitute the only distinct and homogeneous groups
(5). Madison was steadily in flux due to its floating
government and student populations. Throughout the
nineteenth century, however, Madison was consistently
between 10 and 15 percent German and Germans always
amounted to from 42 to 45 percent of the foreign-born
population. The Irish were in second place with
between 6 to 13 percent of the total, 27 to 37 percent
of the foreign-born population (6).

Manitowoc was quite different. In succession a
lumber center, a fishing town, and a shipbuilding
center, the city was the commercial hub for Manitowoc
County. It arose out of a land boom in 1835, enjoyed
an early influx of foreigners and experienced the
political turmoil and crop failures of the late 1840s.
After 1850, the Germans, Norwegians, and Irish flocked
in, followed by Bohemians around 1855 and many Poles in
the 1860s. Throughout the balance of the nineteenth
century Manitowoc thrived although shipbuilding
declined after the switch from wood to steel about
1890. Malting and grain-related industries kept the
economy alive and during World War II shipbuilding
revived when submarines were assembled in the yards.

Racine is well known for its once-high percentage of
foreign born: as late as 1930 only 37 percent of the

people were of native-born parentage. Religious
congregations served some fifteen nationality groups,
Germans and Danes accounting for the majority. Foreign-
language newspapers thrived and comparatively uncommon
groups such as the Welsh preserved their ancient tongue
by means of a society in Racine. Bohemians and Poles
were very numerous and active. In 1905 Racine had the
highest percentage of Danes in any city outside
Denmark. One out of every three Racine Danes had his
passage prepaid, testimony to the fact that such firms
as Case Farm Implement and Mitchell Fish Brothers hired
Danes to the exclusion of other nationality groups. In
Racine they lived in the Fifth Ward on the city's west
side, where Danish Lutheran churches and, from 1900 to
1921, Danish Luther College served their intellectual
needs. Fraternal organizations included Dania and the
Danish Brotherhood. There was a hospital as well as a
home for the aged. Native and German-dominated city
governments made little headway Americanizing the Danes
of Racine (7).

South of Racine lies Kenosha. Best known in recent
times as the home of American Motors Corporation,
Kenosha began as a city in 1834, when the Western
Emigration Company, organized in Hannibal, New York,
sold shares at $10 each to prospective pioneers. The
company's agent, John Bullen, in 1835 saw possibilities
for a port city where the Pike Creek split, thus forming two outlets a mile apart on Lake Michigan. Soon
New York families laid claim to the area but bankruptcy
of the Western Emigration Company led to the formation
of the Pike River Claimants' Union in 1836. Pike Creek
now changed its name to Southport and attracted citizens who quickly established newspapers, a literary
magazine, and free public schools. In the early 1840s
the federal government allocated appropriations for
improvements of the harbor and soon Irish, German, and
English immigrants began arriving in substantial numbers. Following the Revolutions of 1848 in Germany, a
significant number of German intellectuals discovered a
haven in liberal Southport, where they founded lyceums,
established lecture series, and participated in the
controversies of the day. Liberal social doctrines
were advocated and antislavery sentiment was universal.
In the late 1850s the citizens, workers, and seamen of
Kenosha united to operate an Underground Railroad station. Over the next four decades the harbor was

eclipsed by both Milwaukee and Racine to the North and
Chicago to the South. Kenosha did not again compete
favorably for immigrants until the 1890s, when the
Chicago Brass Works, Simmons, and, in 1915, the Nash
Automobile Company were established. As a result, the
only major non-English immigrants in 1885 were the
2,000 German-born. By 1900 the German-born reached
3,000 followed by the Danes with 703. By 1910 Kenosha
County included 1,740 Russians, ethnic Poles who worked
in the new plants, many Italians, and smaller numbers
of Lithuanians and Bohemians. Between 1900 and 1920
eastern and southern Europeans poured into Kenosha with
the result that by 1930 immigrants and their children
accounted for 62 percent of the county population.
Mostly factory workers at the outset, these so-called
New Immigrants by 1930 were establishing small retail
businesses.

When they arrived they found the city allocated to
ethnic enclaves built by the Old Immigrants: Germans,
Scandinavians, Irish, etc. Yankees occupied the lake-
front south of the main business district. Germans
held the district north of Pike River along 6th and 7th
avenues, an area known as "Over the Rhine" or "Little
Germany." Gradually the Germans also developed settlements to the West and South. When the Irish came in
the mid-nineteenth century they settled east of Sheri-
dan Road between the Germans and the Yankees, extending
west beyong the business district. Scandinavians, who
arrived somewhat later, moved southwest of the city
center. Norwegians, Swedes, and Danes lived in harmony
along Roosevelt Road and east of Lincoln Park between
60th and 75th streets. Smaller groups of Swiss, Dutch,
and French Canadians squeezed in among the Germans,
Scandinavians, and Irish but seldom within Yankee envi-
rons. New Immigrants often took up residences vacated
by the earlier immigrants who sought better neighborhoods in the suburbs. New Immigrant neighborhoods also
developed around major factories. Italians lived on
the west side around Nash Motors. Poles first clustered south of the MacWhyte Company and later around
Nash Motors and American Brass. The Lithuanians
settled among the Poles while the Slovaks moved east
along 6th and 7th avenues north of the central business
district. The Russian community was along 17th and
18th avenues. Czechs, Yugoslavs, Greeks, Armenians,
Ukranians, and Hungarians settled on the north and west

sides or near the industrial plants (8). All of Wisconsin's cities were sited with reference to water, either on the Great Lakes or major rivers, the Mississippi, the Wisconsin, or the Chippewa. Madison lies amid four major lakes. The four cities still to be mentioned—Green Bay, Appleton, Oshkosh, and Fond du Lac—lie on great bodies of water, Lake Winnebago, the largest inland lake in Wisconsin, the Fox River, and the Green Bay. Green Bay's capacious harbor facilitated manufacturing that attracted immigrants. Descendants of the French and British welcomed a steady influx of Yankees and French Canadians, who comprised the 1850 population. Between 1870 and 1900, large numbers of Germans, Belgians, Polish, Dutch, and Irish laborers streamed into the city. When Catholic Belgians in the vicinity began defecting from their faith, Green Bay's Bishop Sebastian Messmer in 1893 appealed to Berne Abbey in Heeswijk, Holland, for volunteer priests who could speak both French and Flemish. Out of these initiatives grew the Premonstratensian Abbey of Norbertines at De Pere, which operates St. Norbert College and ancillary institutions (9). But Green Bay was not the magnet for immigrants that southern cities were. In contrast to Kenosha, which had 12,714 foreign-born in 1920, Green Bay had only 3,565. Racine had 16,199, Superior 10,764, while Milwaukee had a whopping 110,000. Since Green Bay and Kenosha were of roughly equal size, let us pursue the comparison further. In 1920 Kenosha harbored 1,889 Germans and 1,509 Polish-born while Green Bay had only 838 Germans and 327 Poles. Green Bay was home to 790 Belgians while Kenosha had only thirteen. Green Bay had only 220 Danes, despite the proximity of New Denmark Township in the county, while Kenosha had over 830. This number was exceeded in 1920 only by Racine, which provided homes for 3,635 Danes. Milwaukee, with its enormous attraction for the foreign-born, did not have as many Danes as did Racine and Kenosha.

Appleton, at the opposite end of the Fox River from Green Bay, lies on Lake Winnebago. Because the Fox River drops some thirty-eight feet within the city limits at the point where it spills from the lake, developers in 1854 established a paper mill, a cabinet factory, and flour mills powered by the swift waters. When dairying replaced wheat as the major agricultural commodity in Wisconsin, flour milling diminished and

paper manufacturing became the mainstay. Although
immigrants filtered into Appleton to take jobs in the
mills, Appleton, like Green Bay, was not distinguished
by attracting large numbers of any nationality except
Germans. In 1920 there were 1,700 German-born followed
by 145 Austrians and 106 Czechs, all of whom spoke
German. Immigrant Appleton's claim to fame was the
birth of the Hungarian Jew Harry Houdini (1874-1926),
whose given name was Ehrich Weiss. Starting out by
picking locks his mother kept on the pantry, Ehrich, at
the age of nine, performed magician acts for circuses
in Appleton. At twelve he ran away from home and soon
moved with his family to New York City.

Oshkosh, lying at the estuary where the upper Fox
River empties into Lake Winnebago, was a camping site
for French explorers and fur traders. In 1818 the
French established the village of Butte des Morts as a
stopover on the Green Bay to Prairie du Chien route of
fur traders. Following a treaty with the Indians in
1836, the village was renamed Oshkosh in honor of the
Menomonee chief. Not only river traffic but two steam
sawmills provided Oshkosh lumber, wagon and carriage
factories, a foundry, and boat building works. By 1859
the first railroad reached Oshkosh and on its tracks
came Yankees, Germans, Irish, English, and some Welsh
settlers, most of whom worked in the pine lumber industry making shingles, sash, and door products. In 1875
the city was destroyed by fire when the sawdust and
slab waste accidentally iginited. Downtown "Sawdust
City," as the people referred to it, was then rebuilt
with stone and brick. After the turn of the century,
the city turned to diversified manufacturing: Oshkosh
B'Gosh overalls, axles, trucks, and matches. The largest nationality group in Oshkosh throughout its history
was the Germans. In 1920 there were nearly 3,000
German born. The second largest were "Russian born,"
Germans from Russia who totaled 483 in 1920 (10). In
the same year, immigrants from Poland tallied 262, many
of whom came from Volhynia and belonged to the German-
speaking community. The Russian-German settlement was
closely knit. Conditioned by approximately a century
of life along the Volga, where they had been invited by
Catherine the Great in 1763, these Germans began leaving Russia for the United States in 1874 and arrived in
large numbers annually after 1875 until the beginning
of World War I in 1914. The Russian-German settlement

in Oshkosh is on the southwest side of the city along
the Fox River between Lake Butte des Morts on the
North, Highway 44 on the South, and Highway 41 on the
West. Established in Oshkosh in 1899, the community
consisted primarily of Lutheran Volga Germans who first
settled in Pine Island, New York, but moved later to
Wisconsin (11). By 1930 there were 400 families, mostly members of the Zion Lutheran Church, which still
serves their needs. Adjacent to the Russian—German
area is the "High Holder" district of Catholic Germans
from the Empire.

The largest Russian—German settlement in Wisconsin
was at Sheboygan, where at least 550 Volga German
families lived in 1930. Over 2,000 individuals born in
Russia, presumably all Germans from Russia, lived there
in 1920. At the same time, Racine had 1,584 Russian-
born, most of whom were ethnic Germans, not Jews, for
they were members of the Lutheran faith (12). Russian-
Germans in Oshkosh usually worked in the lumber mills.
Those in Racine at first worked beet fields around
Kenosha and Racine, and only later gravitated to the
cities. In subsequent years many moved to permanent
work in North Milwaukee. Fond du Lac, at the base of
Lake Winnebago, had no large ethnic groups except for
the Germans. There were 1,411 born in Germany in 1920,
over 50 percent of all the foreign born. Like Oshkosh,
Fond du Lac thrived on the lumber industry, where the
foreign born found work.

We come finally to Milwaukee, Wisconsin's giant in
terms not only of population and industrial might but
also of ability to attract immigrants. Scholars have
argued that the more successful the individuals in a
city the more likely they were to remove themselves
from the ethnic community in which they originally
lived (13). Supposedly, when class divisions appear as
a result of successful economic achievement, internal
unity of the ethnic group is undermined and assimilation of the individual is accelerated. In the case of
Milwaukee, the opposite may well have been true. Seemingly, the more heterogeneous and widespread, the
easier it was for an ethnic group to maintain unity.
Among the Germans and Polish of Milwaukee and to a
lesser extent also among the Italians, the Irish, and
the Jews, there was stratification, but there was also
the power of each group to perpetuate itself (14).
Often the groups were large enough to generate their

own employment, maintain their cultural institutions,
such as the theater, musical organizations, and especially churches, and to produce the leadership necessary for the growth of these societies. Milwaukee has
thrived ever since its inception by French-Canadian fur
traders, Jacques Vieau and his successor, Solomon
Juneau. When Vieau relinquished his trading activities
to Juneau about 1819, development toward an American
community began (15). Town platting got underway by
1835 and in 1840 permanent settlers began purchasing
lots from absentee speculators. Commercial foundations
were laid during the mid 1840s, banks and factories
opened, and three newspapers commenced publication, one
being the German-language Wisconsin-Banner, founded as
a weekly in 1844. Beginning with Lutheran dissenters
who arrived in 1839, the stream of Germans increased
sharply, reaching 1,400 weekly during the summers of
1843 and 1844.

For the period from 1836 to 1860, Kathleen Conzen
offers a superb examination of the immigrant situation
in Milwaukee. Specific chapters treat economic conditions and the move of immigrants into the professions.
Most immigrants, however, made their livelihood by
working with their hands. For the Germans and the
Irish during the 1850s, the road to success lay in
mercantile pursuits. In youthful Milwaukee, the Irish
were attracted to the grocery business. Germans were
more diversified--dry goods, liquors, real estate,
drugstores, lumber, and a bank president. The Germans
were also grocers, tobacconists, clothiers, and store
managers. Few were wealthy enough to engage in manufacturing, exporting and importing, heavy tools, ma-
chinery, or building materials. After about 1860, this
pattern changed dramatically (16). Along the road to
success the Germans recognized by 1854 that they would
have an advantage if they owned their own banks. Thus
the Germania Bank was but the first in a long line of
successful German banks, all of which faced the usual
economic crises that periodically afflicted banking in
the United States. In upper-level professions, the
Germans were not well represented at first. There were
no German-speaking lawyers unless they came to America
at an early age and received their law training in the
English-oriented system that prevailed in the United
States. German immigrant physicians were more numerous. Eighteen of the fifty doctors listed in the

1860 city directory had German names. Among the
educated class, it was the doctors, all trained in
Germany, whose names appeared most frequently in
political and social activities in early Milwaukee. As
a result of their large numbers and strong representation at all levels of society, the Germans became a
stratified society with representation at all levels of
the economy. Consequently, they provided employment,
recreation, and services to their countrymen. Theirs
was the chance to develop into a self-sufficient
foreign-language community.

The prerequisite for such a community, as Conzen
indicates, was that the immigrants concentrate geographically (17). In 1860 the Germans on the east and
south sides were segregated from all other ethnic
communities within the city. Despite the fact that
Germans on the west side shared the area with other
groups, they still remained ethnically homogeneous
between 1850 and 1860. German social organizations
differed from those in the English-speaking sections of
the city. For instance, the German tavern was more
than a vehicle for socializing (18). In non-German
taverns the practice of standing and drinking on the
run did not fit the German's preconception of a place
to sit, talk, and learn about the new environment. The
tavern thereby fostered community. Closely associated
with this institution was the German preference for
folk music and dances. At dances, the young met
friends, found mates, and learned about politics, all
within the confines of a German-speaking community.
High culture--the theater and concerts--was readily
available for the learned and socially sophisticated of
the German community. With the arrival of German
intellectuals after the Revolutions of 1848, Milwaukee
developed so rapidly as a city of German high culture
that for a time it was known as the German Athens.
There were also literary and Freethinker organizations
that met regularly to discuss politics, socialism, and
other matters perceived as indispensable for utopic
life in the Unites States.

One of the most enduring of the German organizations in all of Milwaukee was the Turnverein, or
gymnastic society. As the century progressed Turner
societies were so active that a national training
seminary for gymnastic instructors was established in
Milwaukee. The Turnverein found the center not only of

physical training activities but, because of its close
association with its Freethinking founders, the hub of
intellectual life for the German community. In
addition the German community abounded with mutual
benefit societies, the precursors of insurance companies and in some cases of neighborhood savings and
loan associations (19). Until the turn of the century,
whole sections of Milwaukee looked like a nondescript
city in Germany. In his history of Milwaukee, Bayrd
Still remarks that many public buildings might have
stood in Strassburg or Nuremburg. Ornate residences
reflected the German Renaissance while beer gardens and
eating places recalled Berlin. There was the famous
Schlitz Palm Garden, Toser's on East Water, and "Ma"
Heiser's at Jackson and Ogden. German amusements were
commonplace, ranging from skat, the singing societies,
the German theater at the Pabst, and on Sundays the
music of Strauss and others played by Christopher
Bach's orchestra in the west-side Turnhalle (20).

After the turn of the century, the New Immigration
made itself evident in this Wisconsin city. The newcomers were especially well represented by the Poles,
who by 1910 were in possession of the entire southwestern section of the city. To the Second Ward came
the Czechs and Slovaks. The Second and Sixth wards
attracted many Russian Jews. South of Michigan and
east of Broadway the Italians developed their compact
community. By 1910 there were 70,000 Polish speaking
inhabitants in Milwaukee and of the twenty nine Roman
Catholic churches in the city, seven served the Poles.
There were 100 Polish societies and organizations, five
Polish newspapers, and three Polish libraries. The
first Polish family in Milwaukee was that of Anthony
Stupinski, who arrived about 1844. Other Polish families, with names like Nitchka, Febrowitz, Lotskinschy,
and Maskowitz, followed the Stupinskis (21). Mass
immigration from Poland resulted, however, only after
the failure of Poland to achieve independence following
the Franco-Prussion War in 1871 (22). Many Polish
citizens left their homeland for religious reasons,
specifically Bismarck's Kulturkampf, which was designed
to lessen the control of the Catholic Church over the
Polish peasantry. Once in the United States, they held
tenaciously to their ethnicity by means of their Catholicism and their Catholic social organizations. Led
by their clergy, they energetically formed parishes and

built churches, maintaining exclusive control through
choice of pastors and use of Polish for church affairs.
Bishops of dioceses reluctantly concurred with their
wishes, and in spite of German prelates, the Poles
succeeded in having their Polish parishes and Polish
pastors (23).

The Poles who came to the United State had a motto,
"An iron peace is better than a golden war," but they
seldom applied this rule during their nineteenth-
century buildup in Wisconsin. In Stevens Point, in
Green Bay, and especially in Milwaukee they lived in
harmony and shared leadership that became the pride of
all Polish Americans. But, when their iron peace
crumbled, the result was a fratricidal church war that
cast a dark shadow over Milwaukee's Polonia in the
early twentieth century. Milwaukee in 1890 had an
estimated Polish stock population of 30,000, which
reached 58,000 after the turn of the century. By 1920
an estimated 90,000 to 100,000 first- and second-
generation Poles lived in Milwaukee. According to the
federal census of 1900, 88 percent of the Milwaukee
Poles traced their origins to the German Empire, a
pattern that was applicable also to the remainder of
Wisconsin. By contrast, the Chicago Polish community
was 39 percent from Russia, 36 percent from Germany,
and 25 percent from Austria (i.e., the three regions of
administrative control following the partitions of
Poland in the 1790s; Poland achieved its autonomy only
after the Treaty of Versailles in 1919) (24).

Besides churches, the Milwaukee Poles in 1874
founded the Kosciuszko Guard, which became Company K of
the Wisconsin National Guard. In 1886 they built
Kosciuszko Hall, which served as their south-side
meeting site. Following the election to public office
of August Rudzinski in 1878 the Milwaukee Poles steadily
supported the Democratic party. The first Polish
assemblyman went to Madison in 1887 and in the same
year the first Polish state senator was elected from
Milwaukee. Starting in the 1870s, Polish immigrants
moved into the south side, in what is organizationally
known as the 14th Ward, where, around the turn of the
century, fully 80 percent of the resident families were
of Polish stock. In 1905 the ward attracted attention
for housing industrial workers and unskilled laborers
with large families: there were more children of
school age and a higher percentage of children in the

14th Ward than in any other in the city. In the same
period the ward had the highest death rate in the city,
reflecting the wretched infant mortality incidence that
was associated with poor health conditins and bad water
supplies. Nevertheless, through struggle and a compromise of living standards, Poles in the 14th Ward eventually had a higher percentage of home ownership than
prevailed city-wide, indicating that their sacrifices
of space and comfort, coupled with a willingness to
rent portions of their homes, had paid off. Owning a
house was made possible because the laborers shared it
with a second family in order to realize the income
necessary for loan repayment. A kind of self-help
prevailed, fostered by the Church, which kept the
community within a well-defined area and created a
spirit of mutuality. As we shall see in chapter 10,
this situation had political consequences far into the
twentieth century (25).

Like the Poles, the Czechs in Milwaukee were organized according to Catholic parishes, the first specifically Bohemian parish coming in 1865. By 1878 the
Bohemians also had fraternal associations and schools,
as well as Bohemian-Hall, the primary cultural center
for Milwaukee's Czechs, which stood on Twelfth Street.
Singing and benevolent societies, fire insurance companies, and building and loan associations sprang up
under Bohemian leadership toward the end of the nineteenth century. Heavy industry attracted some 5,000
Hungarians to Milwaukee after the turn of the century
and Italians soon followed. Unable to pursue trades
they had learned in southern Italy because of the
language barrier, the Italians came via the Sicilian
colony in Chicago to join the ranks of common laborers.
In 1915 about 75 percent of them were working in foundries, coal yards, and in the giant firms of Allis-
Chalmers, Falk Manufacturing, and the Rolling Mills of
Bay View. Of the 9,273 Italians in Wisconsin in 1910,
4,788 resided in Milwaukee, mostly in the Third Ward.
Because they took in many boarders like their Polish
neighbors, overcrowding resulted in deaths from tuber-
culosis, pneumonia, and rheumatism. Sicilian farmers
by heritage, the Milwaukee Italians escaped factory
life by founding small businesses and dominating the
city's fruit trade. In time they also built their
churches, notably Our Lady of Pompey at 419 North
Jackson Street, now demolished (26).

A comparable pattern evolved in the cities of Racine and Kenosha, although in the latter Italians took positions with the automobile companies and the iron works. Of all the Italians in Wisconsin, consistently over 85 percent were southern Italians. The few northerners were said to be socialists and anarchists who were feared and mistrusted by industrial employers. Estimates of Wisconsin's Italian stock population for the 1960s range up to 100,000, with the largest bloc of about 25,000 in the Milwaukee-Waukesha area and another 20,000 in the urban district of Kenosha-Racine. There were perhaps 4,000 in Beloit, another 4,000 in Hurly and Iron County, and 2,000 in Madison by the mid-1960s (27). Everywhere in Wisconsin the Italians found solace in Catholicism by way of numerous lay societies. Since most had come to Wisconsin for economic rather than religious reasons, many saved their money and eventually returned to the homeland. During the fifteen years prior to World War I, the Italians were the largest immigrant group entering America, but in the same period at least 1.5 million Italians also left the United States for their country of birth. During the two decades following World War I, fully 40 percent of the Italians who had come also returned after only a few years (28). By contrast, the Germans and the Irish were the two groups least likely to return to their countries of origin.

Beginning in approximately 1872 Slovenian settlers came to Milwaukee. Another colony formed in Sheboygan about 1889, in Cudahy in 1894, and in Kenosha in 1897. It was the Milwaukee-West Allis area that attracted the second-largest (after Cleveland) settlement of Slovenes in the United States, numbering perhaps 25,000 naturalized and American-born citizens by the 1940s. Some 2,600 lived in Sheboygan, where they worked in the industrial centers. Tired of work in the confining factories and mines, Slovenian farmers beginning in 1907 bought forest land in Clark County and established some 200 farms near the rural village of Willard, southwest of Greenwood in Hendren Township. About 100 additional Slovene farmers settled near Marshfield, Fairchild, Owen, Phillips, and Ashland (29). The Slovenes organized numerous fraternal societies, of which the South Slavic Benevolent Union, founded in Milwaukee in 1908, and the Slovenian Catholic Union, founded in Joliet, Illinois, in 1894, are the largest.

In 1926 the Slovenian Women's Union of America was
organized in Sheboygan. Slovenian churches were established in Milwaukee in 1904, in West Allis in 1907,
in Sheboygan in 1909, and in Willard in 1912. Both
Sheboygan and West Allis had Slovenian parochial
schools. Milwaukee also harbored thousands of Jews who
settled in the area bounded by Walnut, Chestnut, Third
and Eight streets. In due time there was also a Greek
community in the 3rd ward and, farther away, a bloc of
Austro-Hungarians in the former predominantly Irish
16th ward. Scandinavians clustered in the 17th and 23rd
wards with the Scots, and eventually Mexicans flooded
into low-cost areas adjacent to the central business
district. World Wars I and II caused extreme crises in
the "European City" of Milwaukee, a topic for a later
chapter.

Regardless of how or during what period Milwaukee is
studied, the dominant fact remains that it was a <u>German</u>
city. in 1880, 35 percent of the population was German-
born, and Germans comprised fully 68 percent of all the
foreign-born. In 1920 there were still 39,771 German-
born living in the city, 46 percent of all the foreign-
born. By 1930 that figure, instead of waning, increased. The Poles stood in second place but in 1920
Milwaukee had only 23,060 born in Poland, 21 percent of
the foreign-born. If one considers the stock population, the Germans vastly exceed the Polish in Milwaukee. The other sizable foreign-born populations in
1920 were the 5,906 Austrians, who sided ethnically and
linguistically with the Germans; the Hungarians, with
4,803 foreign-born; followed by the Czechoslovakians,
with 4,497; the Yugoslavs, with 4,164; and the
Italians, with 4,022. Greece and Norway had less than
1,900 each in Milwaukee in 1920. The Germans came
early and settled almost everywhere, giving the city as
late as 1950 the most substantial German stock population in the United States. Perhaps understandably,
German settlement patterns are co-terminous with the
overall growth of Milwaukee, the largest numbers living
in the North and Northwest (30). At its peak in 1900,
German stock represented fully 70 percent of all
Milwaukeeans. When the Poles began arriving in large
numbers after 1890, the vast majority were Kaszubas,
i.e., Polish ethnics from the West Prussian and Pomeranian regions around Danzig. The evidence suggests
that these "German Poles" were attracted to Milwaukee

by the Germans already there. Ruhr industrialists
vigorously recruited them during the 1880s to work in
factories and mines. Once displaced from rural
villages, thousands of Poles departed, first for the
German Ruhr, then across the Atlantic to the "German
City" of Milwaukee.
Unlike the Germans who spread out in Milwaukee, the
Poles huddled together on the near south-side in close
proximity to the heavy industry along the Menomonee
River. Here they could travel on foot to work in the
steel and flour mills, in the meat-packing centers, and
in the breweries and tanneries. A small colony settled
in the Northeast near the Milwaukee River but never
identified with the southside Poles. (More about this
in a later chapter.) Polish churches also are concentrated in south central Milwaukee, where in 1926 there
were fourteen Polish parishes, compared to only two in
the Milwaukee River area in the North (31). A recent
study of Milwaukee focuses on the factors of economic
and social existence that fostered expansion of the
industrial base (32). Another analyzes the role of
travel distance to work as it either fostered or
hindered the maintenance of ethnicity (33). Until the
mass arrival of Polish immigrants after 1890, the
British and Americans were traveling farther to work
than the Germans, Irish, Scandinavians, and others.
After about fifty years in residence, however, the need
for immigrants to remain within their local neighborhoods had diminished. Although still maintaining
separate ethnic identities, the foreign-stock populations gradually moved beyond the ethnic community and
found better-paying occupations. In 1900, Poles
traveled the shortest distances to work. This limited
their range of social contacts and retarded their
assimilation, their chance to earn higher incomes, and
the opportunity to acquire higher social and economic
status. In Milwaukee, spatial differences between
living and working mirrored the socioeconomic level of
the inhabitants and strongly affected the process and
the rate of assimilation.
  During the early decades of the twentieth century,
however, there were still two distinct non-English
ethnic communities in urban Milwaukee: the Germans and
the Poles. Each community was homogeneous. German
attorneys and doctors lived with German factory and
garment workers. Polish doctors, clergy, and managers

lived next to Polish blue-collar workers. As time
passed the following hypothesis proved true: the more
skilled the workers, the higher their socioeconomic
status, and the farther they traveled to work. Yet
Poles and Germans did not automatically disperse. They
continued to associate and identify with their ethnic
brothers even after an electrified street railroad
system made life in the suburb a viable substitute for
the ethnic neighborhood. Thus the Germans remained in
the Northwest, the Americans in the Northeast, and the
Poles in the near South. Sheer numbers and density
enabled each group to maintain broad socioeconomic
spread within each community. Because these communities continued as complete and rounded social units,
assimilation was postponed. Each nationality had its
own churches, theaters, shops, recreational facilities,
schools, and professionals to care for the people in
their own language.

In summary, Milwaukee was a haven for immigrants.
The city's foreign-born increased at every enumeration
from 1850 until it reached a peak of 111,456 in 1910,
after which a slow but steady decline occurred except
for a brief spurt between 1920 and 1930. By 1950 the
foreign-born were down to 63,450 and down further in
1970 to 39,576 (which figure leaps to 63,000, however,
if the industrial suburb of West Allis is included with
Milwaukee). Milwaukee ranked consistently between
tenth and fifteenth in total population among cities in
the United States but always ranked higher than tenth
in numbers of foreign-born. While the foreign-born
comprised 63 percent of the total population in 1850,
this percentage amounted to only 30 percent in 1910, 10
percent in 1950, and 5 percent in 1970. Throughout its
history, Milwaukee, always sheltered a greater proportion of immigrants than was characteristic for the
remainder of Wisconsin or the nation (34). Until 1895
Milwaukee's foreigners came from northern and western
Europe but by 1920 New Immigrants from southern and
eastern Europe were in the majority. At every enumeration from 1850 through 1970 the Germans were consistently the largest single nationality group. Its size
also increases dramatically if one incorporates the
German-speaking populations from Austria, Bohemia,
Switzerland, and, after 1919, from Yugoslavia (the
northern territories of which were for years German-
speaking as a result of Austrian control). At its

highest peak, according to the state census of 1895, there were 59,432 German-born Milwaukeeans, although the highest German percentage of the total foreign-born occurred in 1860, when Germans accounted for 70 percent of all foreigners. Milwaukee's German element was the sixth largest in the nation in 1890, the fourth largest in 1910, and the third largest in 1940. Following the Germans, the Milwaukee Irish were for several decades the second-largest foreign-born element until 1890. Then the Polish element increased rapidly and from 1890 onward ranked continuously second only to the Germans. Milwaukee also ranked consistently high in numbers of Czechoslovakians, Yugoslavs, Hungarians, and Austrians. The state census for 1905 reported Milwaukeeans by their country of birth as follows: Germany (51,600), Poland (German section 14,482, Russian section 3,459, Austrian 539), Austria (2,397), Russia (2,209), Norway (2,096), Ireland (2,085), Bohemia (1,934), England (1,868), Canada (1,719), Hungary (1,317), and Italy (1,242) with a smattering of less than 1,000 each from many other nations.

When mentioning Milwaukee in later chapters with reference to politics, the progressive movement, the Socialist period, as well as churches, schools, and civic organizations, we will inevitably be concerned with the strong German and Polish populations and their characteristics. Much of the flavor was dissipated by World Wars I and II but a noticeable foreign character persists to the present.

ee

immigrants and Politics: The Civil War Period

Sooner or later immigrants from Europe had to participate in the political life of Wisconsin. Since the
Germans were the most numerous and the earliest non-
English group, we begin with them. Despite their
strength, the Germans never accounted for anything like
a majority of the total population. In 1860 there were
277,000 foreign-born in Wisconsin, constituting 35.7
percent of the total state population. The foreign-
born numbers increased during each succeeding decade,
but their percentage of the population as a whole was
never again as high as it was in 1860. The 38,000
Germans in 1850 amounted to 36 percent of the foreign-
born. In 1860, although they numbered 124,000, they
constituted only 15.4 percent of the state's population
and, like the foreign-born as a group, they increased
with each decade but never again held a percentage of
the population as high as in 1850. What added to the
strength of the German element was its concentration,
which enabled it to maintain its language and culture
(1). Concerned about proximity to markets, the Germans
settled permanently and rotated crops rather than base
all of their income on wheat (2). They were also
active in the crafts and skilled trades, while adhering
almost unanimously to the Democratic party (3). Settlers from New England, by contrast, were conspicuous
for their social customs, puritanical observance of the
Sabbath, temperance legislation, the promotion of Protestant religious instruction in the schools, and support of the Whigs. Whigs showed antipathy toward
immigrants. Democrats, on the other hand, cultivated
the foreign-born. Often rejected by the Yankees, the
Irish took comfort with non-English foreigners in the
Democratic party. Democrats urged that foreigners
exercise political rights and privileges immediately,
whereas Whigs thought foreigners should prove their
American loyalty by a long wait for citizenship.

Wisconsin came into the Union in 1848 just in time
to participate in the presidential election in which
General Zachary Taylor (who had been endorsed by the
Know-Nothing party) triumphed over the Democrat Lewis
Cass. Cass carried Wisconsin in part because of Wisconsin's liberal constitution, which granted suffrage
to the foreign-born after only one year's residence in
the state. The effect was that the foreign-born were
in a position to control elections. When Know-Nothingism was at its peak in the nation, the Democrats at
their Wisconsin convention in 1855 passed a resolution
"very strongly denouncing Know-Nothingism, and declaring the nomination not binding if procured by the aid
of Know-Nothings" (4). Later that summer Republicans
also repudiated the Know-Nothings, proclaiming that
"the fundamental principles of the Republican Party are
based upon the equal rights of all men; that those
principles are utterly hostile to the proscription of
any on account of birthplace, religion, or color . . ."
(5). In the elections of 1855 Know-Nothings nevertheless supported the Republicans, leaving the impres-
sion that the Republican party was tainted with Know-
Nothingism. In subsequent elections, the Democrats
continued to use the charge of Know-Nothingism against
the Republicans as a means of holding both the Germans
and the Irish loyal to the party that had long enjoyed
the reputation of being a friend of the foreign-born.

But, the newly arrived German Forty-eighters (6)
ralled around the Republicans. Their greatest
champion, Carl Schurz (7), spoke at Albany Hall in
Milwaukee in 1859, articulating the view that Germans
were opposed to slavery and found the Republican party
in the strongest position to bring about freedom for
the slaves. The particular issue against which Schurz
aroused his colleagues was the fugitive slave law,
which had been twice declared unconstitutional by the
Supreme Court of Wisconsin, but which had been reversed
by the United States Supreme Court (8). In other
matters Schurz and his countrymen could best be
described as Jeffersonians. They held true to the
principles of the Democrats in matters of liberty and
equality for all, including the rights of foreigners
among the native-born. During the 1850s the German
Forty-eighters tried to create an image that they were
a German wing in the Republican party. As new arrivals
in the United States they claimed, with some justifica-

tion, that they were free of the charges against other
Republicans who had formerly belonged to the Whigs or
Know-Nothings. Whigs were accused of promoting the
puritanical Sabbath, the prohibition of liquor, and the
old aristocracy, which did not sit well with the Germans.
All German daily papers in the early 1850s were
Democratic. When Republicans called a mass meeting for
July 1854 in Madison to build a German strategy they
were thwarted because German papers refused to print
their notices. Not about to be silenced, Forty-
eighters started their own papers, three weeklies, in
the fall of 1854: the Wisconsin Demokrat at Manitowoc,
the Pionier at Sauk City, and the Korsar in Milwaukee,
which was edited by Bernhard Domschke, a Forty-eighter
destined to become not only a great German Republican
but also a great civic leader in Wisconsin (9). While
Germans in the Democratic party argued for a separate
antinativist stance in politics, Domschke articulated
his view with an article in the Wisconsin Demokrat on
August 17, 1854: "The idea of forming a union of
foreigners against nativism is wholly wrong, and
destroys the possibility of any influence on our part;
it would drive us into a union with the Irishmen, those
American Croats. In our struggle we are not concerned
with nationality, but with principles; we are for
liberty, and against union with Irishmen who stand
nearer barbarism and brutality than civilization and
humanity. The Irish are our natural enemies, not
because they are Irishmen, but because they are the
truest guards of Popery." In this blunt statement,
Domschke typifies an approach that repeatedly ruined
whatever chances Forty-eighters had for popular influence. They alienated the masses, first the Irish and
eventually their own countrymen, whom they occasionally
called Stimmvieh, stupid cattle blundering aimlessly in
the ballot box. Not slavery but temperance and Know-
Nothingism were the issues that haunted average Germans
in Wisconsin. Catholic and Lutheran clergymen were also
troubled by the Forty-eighters´ aversion to clerics,
whether their nationality happened to be German or
Irish (10). Some German papers struck back with excessive rhetoric as when the Seebote on November 6, 1858,
said the Republican party was composed of "Temperance
men, abolitionists, haters of foreigners, sacrilegious
despoilers of churches, Catholic-killers . . . a blood-
thirsty tiger ever panting for your gore." Forty-

eighter Republicans were not always what the rhetoric
made them appear. They admonished "not a word about
temperance in the party platform," and worked assiduously to rid their party of whatever smacked of the
Know-Nothings. In the 1857 platform we find the resolution, "we are utterly hostile to the proscription of
any man on account of birthplace, religion, or color."

By the end of the 1850s the Germans had grown to
such strength that both parties courted them by placing
Germans on the ticket. Francis Huebschmann of Milwaukee was a Free-thinker candidate for nomination as
governor by the Democrats but was defeated at the
convention. Carl Habich of Dane County was nominated
for state treasurer. German Republicans put forth men
such as Domschke and Carl Schurz. In 1857 Schurz was
nominated for lieutenant governor but was defeated by
the Democrat even though his running mate, Governor
Alexander W. Randall, was successful. Non-German
Republicans were not ready to cast their ballots for a
German Candidate (11). In Wisconsin Schurz's influence
became tangled with petty accusations, the most out-
rageous being that he was in Wisconsin as an agent of
the Prussian government to spy on fellow exiles from
Germany. The only evidence was that Schurz's property
had not been confiscated by the Prussian government.
When the wing of the Republican party that favored the
foreign-born and wanted to overcome the liability of
Know-Nothingism tried to nominate Schurz for governor
in 1859, only 48 convention votes were cast for Schurz
out of a total of 174. Having been defeated previously
for lieutenant governor, Schurz declined the second
nomination slot. Disaffected Germans denounced the
nominated candidate, Alexander W. Randall, but Schurz
retired from state politics and moved from Watertown to
Milwaukee, a better location to build a national antislavery base in the presidential campaign of 1860.

In May 1860 Carl Schurz headed the Wisconsin delegation to the Republican convention in Chicago, where he
seconded the nomination of Senator William H. Seward,
who noted the "irrepressible conflict" between the
North and South (12). When Seward's chances started
sinking after the third ballot, Schurz joined the new
bandwagon, seconded the motion to make Lincoln's nomination unanimous, and brought the Wisconsin delegation
with him. The platform that Schurz helped write contained his plank to increase the political rights of

the immigrant. Taking charge of the national Republican party's "foreign department," Schurz now fielded squads of speakers who fanned out across the North soliciting the votes of Germans, Scandinavians, and Hollanders. He stumped in the states of Pennsylvania, Illinois, Missouri, Indiana, and New York before returning to Wisconsin for a final effort.

Because of Carl Schurz and his efforts on behalf of Lincoln, the Germans of Wisconsin have been quick to take credit for the election of the Great Emancipator (13). This self-accreditation came long after Civil War wounds had healed. In the heat of the 1860 and 1864 campaigns, it appears, the Germans in Wisconsin voted with an eye toward their own interests, especially in matters of prohibition and nativism, rather than for the national ideal. No one can argue convincingly that there was a grand strategy on the part of the Germans to insure the election of Lincoln. German Catholics continued their long tradition of voting Democratic along with the Irish. German Lutherans, who were strong in eastern Wisconsin, apparently voted for Lincoln, although not in large numbers and not because he was the candidate who opposed slavery. To older Lutheran churchmen, slavery was not an immoral practice. The Forty-eighters, of whom Carl Schurz was indeed the most prominent, were vociferous in opposition to institutional slavery through their newspapers and in speeches, but their effectiveness was not clear. They were also articulate in opposition to an institutional clergy, which irritated Lutherans and Catholics. In Wisconsin it was native Americans and not the foreign-born who elected Lincoln (14).

During the Civil War the Germans readily took up arms in defense of the Union, but there is no evidence to suggest that they did so with any clarity that they were ridding the nation of the odious institution of slavery. Being the most numerous, they contributed the most units to the Union army, but the Norwegians also did their share, as did the Irish. As a matter of fact, when President Lincoln called for volunteers and Governor Randall reiterated it by requesting all existing military companies to enlist, a number of German units disbanded rather than serve (15). The Watertown Rifles and the Governor's Artillery, both made up of Germans (as well as some Irish outfits), suddenly discovered they had familial, financial, and other

Immigrants and Politics: The Civil War Period   33

obligations that kept them at home. Democrats of Irish
and German birth were especially reluctant to heed the
Republican Lincoln (16). Among the more vocal Germans
was attorney and school superintendent Frederick W.
Horn, who commanded the Cedarburg Rifles of Ozaukee
County. A Prussian by birth, and in 1854 Wisconsin's
commissioner of immigration, Horn resigned his command
and denounced the war as a scheme to strengthen the
Republican party and the business interests of the
Northeast. Horn decried the "plundering of the Midwest" for the benefit of "Pennsylvania's Iron Mongers
and New England Manufacturers" (17). The editor of the
German-language <u>Milwaukee Seebote</u> referred to the war
as an outbreak of the "irrepressible conflict between
east and west," and as a revival of Whiggery. Nevertheless, the required ten companies were available on
April 22, 1861, and Randall telegraphed Lincoln that
Wisconsin had done its part. By the end of 1861,
Wisconsin had fielded thirteen regiments of infantry,
several companies of sharpshooters and cavalry as well
as artillery batteries, making a total of 14,000 men.
Of these, 10,400 were American-born. The 3,600 foreign-
born made up only a quarter of the soldiers while they
comrpised one-third of Wisconsin's population. Moreover, immigrants were younger and consisted of a
greater number of males so that the eligible men of
foreign birth made up about half of the potential
military participants from Wisconsin. Thus natives
enlisted at about three times the rate of the foreign-
born (18).

Officially the foreigners were categorized as the
Germans (including Swiss and Dutch), the Irish, the
Norwegians and Swedes, and the British (including
Canadians, Scots, and Welsh). The 1860 census does not
break down men of military age into categories of
foreign and native birth but the 1870 census does. And
since there is but a 5 percent variation on all other
data between 1860 and 1870, it is fair to point out
that in 1870 Wisconsin had a total of 192,331 males of
draftable age, of whom only 86,593 were American-born,
leaving 105,738 foreign-born. In other words, only 45
percent were native while 55 percent were foreigners.
Since the Germans were consistently the largest among
the nationality groups, it may also be fair to say that
the Germans were the least willing to volunteer. This
is understandable if we but look at the political

affiliations of the majority of Germans. They were
Democrats! German Catholics and most of the less-
educated German Protestants belonged to the Democratic
party. German radicals, commonly known as Forty-
eighters, were Republicans and among the earliest to
volunteer. Several organizations such as the Milwaukee
Turners (19), led by German liberals, volunteered
collectively to form entirely German companies. Often
Republican Governor Randall succeeded in recruiting
Germans if a Forty-eighter took the lead, the Ninth, or
"German," Regiment being raised by one Milwaukee Forty-
eighter and commanded by his brother. Eventually the
Germans dominated the Eighteenth Regiment and formed
minorities in many others (20).

The Irish in the early period of war also chose to
leave the fighting to the Republicans. They lagged
behind other English-speaking immigrants in volunteer-
ing for service, although their proportion increased
after action was taken to recruit immigrants from
Ireland for the Seventeenth Regiment and call it the
"Irish Brigade" (21). When the draft was initiated,
the Germans were the strongest in opposition, but the
Irish, especially in rural areas, likewise opposed it.
As Democrats, both foreign groups resented the fact
that it was the Republicans who had taken up arms. But
the Germans, who never did feel an affinity for the
South, instinctively opposed secession, the fragmented
situation in which autonomous states splintered off to
pursue their own ends selfishly, as had been the case
for centuries in their native Germany. Likewise the
Irish, at their mass meetings in Milwaukee in 1862,
left no doubt concerning their loyalties. They criticized the Republican administration but they never
wavered in support of the Union. Was not the South in
part pinning its hopes on securing support from
England? "The rebellion is England, but it is not
England open armed, but England in her own masked,
assassin, slimy, serpentine character" (22). Certainly
the Irish had no compassion for a cause they felt was
at least partially instigated by the English.

Besides the Irish and the Germans, the Norwegians
were the only sizable foreign element in Wisconsin when
the Civil War broke out, having left Norway in large
numbers following disastrous crop failures in 1860.
From a mere 1,900 in 1860, annual arrivals reached
8,900 in 1861, a figure higher by 2,500 than the

previous annual peak in 1857 (23). Typical was the
comment of a Norwegian who arrived in 1861: "Many of
the young men who came on the <u>Flora</u> have already
enlisted in the war." Their wartime leader, Hans
Christian Heg, spoke for his countrymen: "To arms for
the defense of the old Union, established by Washington." Wisconsin contributed from 3,000 to 4,000 Norwegians to the Union cause, substantially more than
from any other state in the Union. Commanded by
Colonel Heg, the "Norwegian Regiment" (Fifteenth Wisconsin) has been regarded by Norwegian immigrants and
their descendants as a token of their patriotism to
their adopted country. Recruiting for the Regiment was
championed not only by Heg but also by the Norwegian
paper, the <u>Emigranten</u> (24). Heg lectured in many communities, declaring that never had there been a better
opportunity "to fight for a noble cause, to win an
honored name and proud memories for the future, and an
experience that could not be had elsewhere." By March
2, 1862, enough Norsemen had answered the call that the
unit could leave Camp Randall in Madison for duty in
the South. With such salty names as Wergeland Guards,
Odin's Rifles, Norway Bear Hunters, and St. Olaf
Rifles, the men—at last 128 of them bore the first
name of "Ole"—went into battle in Missouri, Kentucky,
Mississippi, Tennessee, Alabama, and Georgia. Following tight engagements and heavy losses, the regiment
was mustered out in early 1865 at Chattanooga, with
one-third of its men dead or in hospitals as a result
of battlefield casualties.

His career cut short at Chickamauga, Colonel Heg
became a hero who embodied the Norwegian contribution
to preserving the Union and freeing the slaves. Bronze
statues commemorate him on the capital grounds at Madison, in the Norwegian community of Muskego, and at Lier
in Norway, whence the Heg family had emigrated (25).
Apparently Heg and the other Norwegian heroes also
inspired the Norwegians on the homefront for, in the
re-election of Lincoln in 1864, they supported the
president. Calls by a few Norwegian newspapers that
Scandinavian voters turn their backs on Lincoln in 1864
landed on deaf ears. Unlike German immigration, which
declined substantially during the Civil War, the Norwegians continued to come mainly because Norwegian
immigration between 1854 and 1865 was reaching the
United States not through ports on the East Coast but

through Quebec, where nine-tenths of the 44,000 arriving between those dates docked (26). From there they
traveled via the Great Lakes to Wisconsin.

By no means as large as the German, the Norwegian-
language press in the 1850s and 1860s was nevertheless
a political force. The first Norwegian newspaper was
the Nordlyset ("Northern Light"), established at
Muskego in 1847. It was initially edited by James
Denoon Reymert, who was a member of Wisconsin's constitutional convention and the first Norwegian-American to
hold state office. Like subsequent Norwegian papers in
Wisconsin, however, the Nordlyset in its first issue
carried the opinion that "the editors will make every
effort to preserve the strictest possible neutrality in
matters of politics and religion" (27). The emerging
Norwegian Lutheran church in 1852 initiated the influential and long-lived Emigranten, which was headed by
Reverend C. L. Clausen. Claiming to be "independent
Democratic," the paper was against slavery and in favor
of a liberal land policy. After 1857 it sided with the
Republican party and reflected Norwegian voters'
enthusiasm for preservation of the Union, dismantling
of "slavery for black or white," and free land under a
Homestead Act, which came into being in 1862. In due
time the secular Norwegian press made politics one of
its major concerns.

Although Wisconsin attracted a lot of Finns, second
in numbers only to Michigan and Minnesota, they did not
come until much later in the nineteenth century and
therefore did not play any part in the politics of the
state until well after the Civil War. Nor were there
Italians of any statistical significance until the turn
of the century. The Poles likewise were not present in
significant strength during the Civil War and large
numbers of Swedes never found Wisconsin suitable for
permanent homes. Wisconsin's immigrants in the Civil
War, therefore, were the Irish, the Germans, and the
Norwegians plus a few Danes, Belgians, and Bohemians.

By coincidence, Wisconsin men on Civil War battle-
fields brought to the governor's seat in Madison the
only immigrant ever to hold that office until Julius
Heil won election in the 1930s. Connecticut-born Louis
Powell Harvey, who succeeded Governor Randall in January 1862, set out almost immediately with surgeons and
medical supplies on a Good Samaritan journey to visit
sick and wounded Wisconsin men in field hospitals. On

the rainy night of April 19, in stepping from one
riverboat to another, he slipped between the two
vessels and disappeared. Days later his body was found
sixty-five miles downstream. This brought lieutenant
governor Edward Salomon into office. Salomon was
Prussian by birth, a Lutheran in faith, and a Forty-
eighter who had studied at the University of Berlin.
When the 1848 Revolution failed in Germany, Salomon
left for the United States, lived for a time in Manitowoc, and subsequently ran a bar in Milwaukee. In
1861 the Republicans turned to him as one who could
elicit the German vote and recruit German volunteers.
One of his brothers organized and another commanded the
German Ninth Regiment. In the balloting, Edward Salomon ran well behind the rest of the Republican ticket,
so he may not have added many votes to the victory of
the Republicans in 1861.

Shortly after Salomon took office in April 1862,
President Lincoln, on July 2, issued a call for an
additional 300,000 men, 11,000 from Wisconsin. With
federal pay and bounties as well as county subsidies,
Salomon by September had enough men to fill fourteen
new regiments of three-year volunteers, considerably in
excess of what the state was required to contribute.
But on August 4 the War Department called on the
governors to supply nine-months militiamen, which meant
an additional 11,000 from Wisconsin. Salomon now
required a quota from each county and instructed the
sheriffs to compile lists of men from eighteen and
forty-five years of age. The governor had trouble
because many claimed exemption on the grounds of
alienage, but by the end of October, Salomon had filled
quotas for all but a few Lake Michigan counties where
Roman Catholic immigrants were numerous (28). Catholics were reluctant to volunteer because there was a
lack of Catholic chaplains, the Irish Seventeenth being
the only regiment with a Catholic priest. When the
predominantly German Twenty-fourth was formed, Father
Francis Fusseder was commissioned on September 3, 1862,
as its chaplain, but by then German Catholics were
already convinced that the army was insensitive to
their needs. One year after the war began there were
472 Union army chaplains, of whom only twenty-two were
Catholics whereas fully one-fifth (100,000) of the
Union army was Catholic. Always Democrats, these Catholics did not care much for Republicans, who had been

ith Nativism and by excessively liberal and godless Forty-eighters. Some German Catholics were of the opinion that the Republicans were ready to annihilate the Germans and the Irish to make room for the Negro. Others felt that they had left their homelands specifically to escape the draft. They reasoned that a draft must surely be unconstitutional in a democratic nation (29).

Unable to supply enough volunteers, Governor Salomon scheduled the draft to begin in the laggard counties on November 10, 1862. On the tenth and eleventh of November antidraft riots broke out among the Belgian farmers in Brown County. In Washington County some twenty Germans descended on the draft commissioner in West Bend and drove him out of town. German-speaking rioters also stormed the Ozaukee County commissioner, William Pors--a German and a Democrat, but a Protestant and a Free Mason as well--and threw him from the building, destroying the boxes from which names for the recruits were to be drawn. Half of the county's 15,000 residents were Roman Catholics from Luxembourg, or Protestant Germans. Both of these foreign-born groups resented Lincoln, abolitionists, the war, and the Republicans, not to mention each other. When the county's quota was set at 575 the citizenry complained that it exceeded the limit set for any other Wisconsin county of comparable population size. Explanations that the quota was so large as a result of earlier low enlistments found no sympathy. As a result the governor had to send eight companies of the Twenty-Eighth Regiment to occupy the Ozaukee county seat at Port Washington and support the provost marshal in making dozens of arrests (30). In Milwaukee, a mere twenty miles to the south, it was feared there would be riots of uncontrollable proportions, but with proper precautions, including soldiers along all roads leading into the city, the drawing of names took place without incident. Dispatching the men for training camps was another matter. Of the 4,537 drafted for military service over one-third (1,662) failed to report for duty, and only 1,739 were mustered in. The remainder, mostly Germans, found excuses or joined a regiment of nine-months conscripts in the Thirty-Fourth, thereby negatively affecting Wisconsin's long-term yield for the Union army. Wisconsin was the only western state (in addition to Indiana) that had to resort to the

draft in 1862 and the only to experience troublesc
riots. Wisconsin-German support of the Union was ____
than enthusiastic. The draft riots of 1862 were more
characteristic of the true German sentiment. Popular
historians have given too much credit to the Germans in
general, and those in Wisconsin in particular, for
their contribution to the Civil War effort and to the
election of Lincoln. Joseph Schafer was more accurate
when he concluded that "Lincoln would have won in
Wisconsin if all German votes had been given to
Douglas, as doubtless five sixths of them were."
German Catholics were almost unanimously in the Democratic camp. German Protestants, nowhere more numerous
than in Ozaukee County, where the draft riots were at
their worst, at no time gave a Republican presidential
candidate a majority until the 1916 election, when
Charles Evans Hughes won over Woodrow Wilson. The fact
is that not even Lincoln´s greatest Wisconsin support-
er, Carl Schurz, was able to swing the Wisconsin Germans in his favor, before or after the war was in
progress. One Watertown German wrote of Schurz, "His
head was too much in the clouds for him to fraternize
with the local politicians even of his own nationality"
(31). Other hometown Germans called Schurz "the damned
Republican whose few friends could easily be seated in
one bus" (32).

In the meantime, Governor Salomon of Wisconsin had
other worries (33). By the fall of 1862 the Sioux
Uprising had occurred in Minnesota and rumors of worse
things to come spread like wildfire into Wisconsin.
Roads filled with refugees and farmers who had left
their crops to rot in the fields. An army captain in
Hudson indicated that the whites and Indians were out-
doing each other in mutual fear--"While the Whites are
running in one direction, the Indians are running in
the other." In response, Salomon formed the home
guards and distributed available arms. He even peti-
tioned Secretary of War Stanton for permission to
divert his newly recruited soldiers from the Union army
to local defense, but without success. When the fear
gradually subsided, a lingering anxiety persisted that
the South was about to rekindle this Indian threat as a
fifth column in the North to divert large numbers of
soldiers from the front lines. Indian murders in the
New Lisbon area of Juneau County in the summer of 1863
did nothing to dispel the popular belief that a wide-

scale Indian massacre was about to erupt. On request
of Salomon, General Pope eventually did send to New
Lisbon a company of the Thirteenth Regiment, as much
for protection of Indians from whites as the other way
around.

During 1863 there were more draft riots, notably in
the town of Lebanon. In this German Protestant region
of Jefferson County, just north of Watertown, 300 armed
Germans demonstrated in front of the Lebanon school-
house but dispersed voluntarily when soldiers appeared.
When Lincoln called for still more soldiers in July
1863, Salomon persuaded the War Department to give him
time to fill the quota with enlistments rather than
draftees, which was done skillfully in the predominantly Republican districts. There was a marked deficit
in the German Democratic counties, especially Milwaukee, Ozaukee, Dodge, Washington, and Sheboygan. By
October 1863, the weary governor had another request
from Lincoln for a 10,281 quota of men to be filled by
January 5, 1864. Even though Salomon knew he would be
out of office by the critical delivery time, he worked
hard on filling the required number through volunteer-
ing, thus avoiding another draft. More and more of his
fellow immigrants were claiming alienage as an excuse
even though they had declared their intentions to
become citizens and had exercised the right to vote.
In 1863, therefore, Lincoln ruled that aliens were not
exempt from service and that, to assert a right to
alienage, the draftee had to present an affidavit
swearing that he had neither declared for citizenship
nor cast a ballot (34).

Beleaguered and abandoned in his home state, Governor Salomon decided not to seek renomination. The
Republicans believed he would not be useful in soliciting German votes and his compatriots in the Democratic
party held him responsible for the odious draft. After
returning to private life, Edward Salomon picked up his
law practice in Milwaukee and then returned to New York
City, where he served clients from the German element
in business there. He was also appointed counsel to
the German Consulate General of New York. Born at
Stroebeck near Halberstadt, Prussia, in 1830, Salomon
was educated in Berling. A Democrat when he arrived in
Wisconsin in 1849, Salomon switched to become a Republican, supported the Emancipation Proclamation, and
originated a law giving Wisconsin soldiers in the field

the right to vote. His brother Frederick rose to the rank of major general in 1865 after participating in many campaigns against the Confederacy. When Edward retired from his law practice in 1894, he returned to Germany, where he lived at Frankfurt am Main until his death in 1909 (35).

When the draft was implemented again on September 19, 1864, fully a third of those whose names were drawn—7,901 out of 20,804—failed to report. The final draft in 1865 called 2,656, of whom 1,144 refused to respond, bringing the figures of all draft dodgers in Wisconsin to 11,742 for the war (36). Reasons for the poor showing varied. The examining surgeon in Green Bay, for example, reported that enlistments were difficult to obtain because the Belgians there were "mostly Roman Catholics and as such were generally hostile to the conscription act." The Bohemians, he reported, were ingenious at failing the physical examination by pretending to be blind in one eye or by taking drugs to make the heart run erratically. Others resorted to more drastic efforts, such as an incision through which they inserted a blowpipe to fill the scrotum with air. More often, the unwilling able-bodied immigrants and Americans simply ran away, especially to the lumber camps of the north woods. An Austrian-born priest-professor at St. Francis Seminary called the draft the destroying angel of the Bible. The Rector of St. Francis, Michael Heiss, born and educated in Germany and subsequently Bishop of La Crosse and Archbishop of Milwaukee, wrote to Germany in 1863 that a dozen of his German-speaking seminarians had escaped to Canada for fear of being drafted. Heiss reported that no one cared to risk his life for such a "wretched cause." When the 1864 draft was scheduled, the rector wrote again that "within two days about sixty of our one hundred students had disappeared. The professors too, priests and laymen, took to flight" (37).

In the course of the war, Wisconsin contributed fifty-three regiments but clearly had done less than other states in the Midwest for the Union army. Minnesota, Ohio, Illinois, Indiana, Iowa, and Michigan all had furnished more troops in relation both to white male population of military age and to total population. About 80,000 soldiers from Wisconsin served. Of these, approximately 40 percent were foreign-born, a percentage that rose in the latter three years of the

war compared to the first year, when only 33 percent of
the foreign-born volunteered. Presumably bonuses lured
new arrivals to the camps where job security was
assured. Considering, however, that the foreign-born
made up well over half of the state's men of military
age, then surely it is fair to say that the 40 percent
foreign-born contribution by Wisconsin warrants the
conclusion that immigrants to Wisconsin were not in
favor of the war and not idealistic about its cause
(38). Since the Germans were the most numerous immigrant group, one may observe that they were quite
unwilling to serve. The Germans did not elect Lincoln,
they did not support him, and they did not follow Carl
Schurz and his liberal cohorts in fighting the war (39).

Chapter Four
The Post-Civil War Period

Wisconsin following the Civil War is often characterized as comfortable, with sometimes corrupt Republican
majorities lording it over the coalition of Democrats
who from time to time were able to oust the Republicans
by an issue that temporarily united the challengers.
Such issues could be categorized as ethnic, religious,
urban-rural, and progressive-conservative. After the
turn of the century politics took on a new atmosphere
when Robert M. La Follette entered upon the scene.
From the Civil War to 1900, native-born Americans continued to dominate state affairs. In 1850 some 36
percent of Wisconsin's population was foreign-born; by
1870 it was still 35 percent. At the turn of the
century 515,971 persons in Wisconsin had been born
abroad, over 25 percent of the total population. By
1930 the percentage dropped to 13 percent and down to
4.3 percent by 1960. The highest number of foreign-
born occurred in 1890, when they tallied 518,989 or 31
percent of white residents. There were at least thirty-
nine different nationalities represented in the state
in 1870, which figure reached forty-six in 1900. In
1870 over 15 percent of Wisconsinites had been born in
Germany, followed by Ireland and Norway with 4 percent
each, and England with 3 percent. By 1900 the German-
born amounted to 13 percent followed by the Norwegians
with 3 percent, the Polish and Swedish with 2 percent
each, and the Irish with only 1 percent (1).

Most of the state was Republican, but Milwaukee,
with its 50 percent foreign-born population in 1870,
usually returned Democratic majorities. As industrialization progressed, labor party candidates emerged
under Socialist leadership. Political leaders in all
parties knew and often feared ethnic communities
because religion was often a deciding factor and
religion was scarcely separable from ethnic affiliation. In 1896 Catholic churches in Wisconsin were

designated according to nationality as follows: 172
German, 113 Irish, 41 French, 29 Polish, 13 Bohemian, 7
Dutch, 4 Italian, 2 Belgian, and 1 Swiss. In the immigrant Protestant churches of Wisconsin in 1890, there
were about 170,000 communicants, of whom perhaps
161,000 were adherents of Lutheran synods, mostly
German or Norwegian (2).

Catholic Germans were especially active in founding
parochial schools. When Catholics attacked the practice of readings and prayers from the King James Bible
as "improper in the public schools" they were joined by
German Lutherans in an action during the spring of
1890, which resulted in a landmark judicial decision in
the Edgerton Bible Case, when the state supreme court
ruled that prayers and Bible readings in public schools
were unconstitutional. A coalition between German
Catholics and German Lutherans developed further
because both groups sought general tax revenues for
their parochial schools. Was this a question of ethnic
preservation or was it religious tolerance? Or was it
rather self-interest couched in religion? As Richard
Jensen has pointed out, "religion was the fundamental
source of political conflict in the Midwest" (3). The
most overt manifestation of religio-ethnic politics was
the Bennett Law controversy, which dominated Wisconsin
politics in the elections of 1890. In that year Wisconsin's democrats polled 51.8 percent of the vote, the
highest proportion the party had received since 1873.
This achievement had a three-fold cause: the defection
of German Lutheran voters from Republican ranks, retention of the German Catholics, and some defection from
the Republicans to the Prohibitionists on the part of
Norwegian and Swedish voters (4).

In 1889 Wisconsin lawmakers passed "An Act Concerning the Education and Employment of Children," which
bore the name of its chief sponsor, Assemblyman Michael
John Bennett of Iowa County. Wisconsin had a compulsory school law since 1879, but its inefficacy was
revealed in 1888 when state superintendent Jesse B.
Thayer called attention to a decrease in public school
attendance as compared to an increase of school-age
population. The superintendent was unable to provide
statistics about the numbers of children who attended
parochial schools (5). Between 40,000 and 50,000 children ages seven to fourteen attended no school at all.
An alarmed Governor William Dempster Hoard in his first

message to the state legislature in 1889 exclaimed, "I
would recommend such legislation . . . to require that
reading and writing in English be daily taught . . ."
(7). In the bill sent to the floor, one clause provided: "No school shall be regarded as a school under
this act unless there shall be taught therein, as part
of the elementary education of children, reading,
writing, arithmetic and United States history in the
English language." It passed without a dissenting vote
and Governor Hoard affixed his signature on April 18,
1889.

Christian Widule, a Milwaukee German-American member
of the Lutheran Church who chaired the senate committee
on education, found in the bill nothing objectionable
for his constituents. But the objection of other con-
stituencies was swift. As early as June 25, 1889,
Wisconsin Synod Lutherans passed a resolution labeling
the Bennett Law "oppressive and tyrannical," a threat
to the synod's schools and churches, and demanding its
repeal. Days later the Missouri Synod denounced the
law for its interference with the rights of parents and
with liberty of conscience. The following February,
nineteen Lutheran congregations in Milwaukee passed a
joint statement abhorring the law and announcing their
intentions to support only candidates who would work
for its repeal. In its 1890 municipal platform the
Milwaukee Democratic party condemned the law as "wholly
uncalled for, and uselessly harsh and unjust." The
city's Germania newspaper said it was the duty of every
citizen, "especially of the German citizen who is
willing to assert freedom of conscience and the rights
of the German parochial schools to enter his protest by
voting against the Republican Party."

German Catholics solidly united with their doctrinal
opponents on the matter of the Bennett Law. All three
bishops at the time spoke German as their mother tongue
and the parochial schools in their dioceses taught for
the most part in the German language. On March 12,
1890, therefore, Archibishop Michael Heiss of Milwaukee, Bishop Killian Flasch of La Crosse, and Bishop
Francis X. Katzer of Green Bay condemned the law as a
blatant interference with the rights of parents to
educate their children. Both Heiss and Flasch died
soon after the struggle commenced, but Katzer ably led
German Catholics in a campaign to have the law
repealed. A joint statement by the bishops saw in the

law the intention "to destroy the Parochial School
System altogether" (7). The bishops mentioned that
their dioceses had 264 parochial schools, 14 colleges,
several academies, select schools, and nine orphanages.
They claimed to lead 350,000 Catholics who would
consider the law an affront to their intelligence, for
in nearly all of their schools at least some English
was being taught. Wisconsin's only major seminary, St.
Francis in Milwaukee, was founded on the principle that
both German and English would be the basis of service
to the Catholics of Wisconsin (8).

> As long, however, as any other language--be it
> German, French, Polish, Dutch, Bohemian, or any
> other--is in many parts of our state the language of
> home and family, we consider it a great advantage
> for children to know, besides the English, the lan-
> guage of the home circle, and we cannot possibly see
> what disadvantage to State and society there could
> arise from the instruction of our children in more
> than one language. (9)

The Bennett Law meant to German Catholics in Wisconsin an attempt by Americanizing Yankees to extinguish
the German Language in the United States. Quite different was the viewpoint of the liberal heirs of German
Forty-eighters. Often members of the Turnvereins,
these Freethinkers were nearly unanimous in support of
the Bennett Law. The German press saw the rapid growth
of English as a built-in decrease in subscriptions and
advertising. Thus, even though Turners and Freethinkers supported the Bennett Law, the German press
attacked it as a curtailment of personal liberty (10).
The clergy also had a vested interest in preserving
German, Norwegian, Bohemian, Polish, etc., because they
recognized the non-English language as a device by
which the laity could be held in the embrace of the
faith. A pietistic trace ran through the Bennett Law
opposition. Interlaced with the pietism was also a
streak of German nationalism. After the founding of the
Empire in 1871, the achievements of Germany in domestic
and foreign affairs lent pride to Americans of German
ancestry, a pride that non-Germans perceived as arro-
gance (11). Arguments ran that in Wisconsin the German
language was no more a foreign language than English,
which had also been imported from a foreign land.
Charges of Nativism and Know-Nothingism resurfaced and

German Day celebrations in 1890 were used to laud
contribution of the state´s German population.
   Understandably, it was the language that identified
the immigrants as "foreign" in the eyes of the
Nativists. Children were "discovered" all along the
eastern side of the state who were unable to speak a
word of English, even though they had been born and
reared in Wisconsin. From Manitowoc came the statement
the not one in ten of the parochial schools in the
county taught a word of English. Reports appeared in
newspapers that even the public schools in the thickly
settled German districts were conducted wholly in
German. The <u>Manitowoc County Chronicle</u> commented,
"Strike the two words <u>in English</u> from the law and not a
churchman in the State could be found to raise his
voice against it (12). Anti-Bennett Law clubs were
formed throughout Milwaukee and editor George Koeppen
of the German-language <u>Germania</u> declined Governor
Hoard´s appointment as a regent of the state university
to protest the Bennett Law. Recognizing an opportunity, Democrats in the spring of 1890 put a plank in
their platform calling for repeal of the Bennett Law as
harsh, unjust, uncalled for, and offensive to the right
of conscience. A call went out on May 10 from the
Catholic and Lutheran centers of the state for a
special anti-Bennett Law convention to meet in Milwaukee on June 4, 1890. Bishop Katzer of Green Bay, about
to be appointed Archbishop of Milwaukee in January
1891, asserted that the Masonic Order had secretly
authored the law (13).
   After the sides were drawn, the Lutherans made the
difference because they had traditionally supported the
Republican party in Wisconsin. Bohemians, Poles, and
Catholic Germans were Democrats anyway and their position on the Bennett Law was not decisive. Parochial
schools were also maintained in some Norwegian communities, and therefore Scandinavians were affected by the
law to some degree, but they had always been traditionally Republican and eager for Americanization of their
children. Opponents of the Bennett Law successfully
recruited these Scandinavians by stressing a clause in
the law that required districting. This clause is best
illustrated by the comment years later of Father W.
Hackner:

   According to the law, I would have been obliged to
   build a second school in the second ward (of Fountain

City, Wisconsin which had two wards but only one
Catholic parish and school). Moreover, there were
many children attending the parochial school from
three country districts. Consequently, I would have
been compelled to construct three additional
schools. Such a "luxury" of schools neither I nor
the Lutherans could have enjoyed. (14)

Thus many Norwegians voted for the repeal of the
Bennett Law in spite of their instinctive support of
Republicans. A key figure in winning Norwegian support
was Rasmus Bjorn Anderson, whose emotional arguments
awakened the indifferent Norwegians. In 1876 Anderson
had written powerfully in defense of the common school
and in opposition to the parochial school for Norwegians (15). The common school, in his opinion, was
the cornerstone of the American constitution. But the
heat of politics in 1889-90 caused Anderson to switch
his position. According to Anderson, parochial schools
were no longer a threat to the common school; rather
the Bennet Law raised the specter of Know-Nothingism
(16).
      Throughout the campaign anti-Bennett Law songs and
slogans were on every Domocrat's lips. Democratic
organizers who deserve the most credit for turning the
Bennett Law into such an effective issue for victory
were Ellis B. Usher and Edward C. Wall (17). Wall
established smooth relations with Bishop Katzer and the
Catholic hierarchy, secured the German Lutheran vote,
and kept the influential Germania newspaper with its
Forty-eighter origins from backsliding to the Republican party. Importantly he held the Irish, Polish, and
Bohemians firmly in the Domocratic camp. Usher and
Wall had a heyday because the 1890 campaign had but one
issue, one that was blatantly ethnic and openly religious. What did it matter, said the stalwart William
F. Vilas, whether one said "two plus two make four" or
"zwei und zwei machen vier" (18). German-born Colonel
Conrad Krez, a veteran of the Civil War, wrote comic
poetry during the campaign and won a seat in the Wisconsin assembly. With others he demanded that German
be recognized as the second official language but the
Irish were not of similar mind. Intrareligious animosity therefore rose to unprecedented heights as
Archbishop Ireland of St. Paul gratuitously repeated
his approval of the Bennett Law and wrote his support

to Governor Hoard.

When the balloting was over, Democrat George W. Peck in 1890 defeated incumbent Governor William Dempster Hoard by 28,320 votes. The post of Lieutenant-Governor went to Bohemian-born Karl Jonas, editor and owner of the Racine-based Slavie, a liberal, Czech-language newspaper that carried much weight on behalf of the Democratic party both in Wisconsin and nationally. Born in 1840 and distinctly past his prime in 1890, Jonas was an avid liberal who had served the Democrats loyally. He was pleased to deliver his Bohemians to a cause he could support, if only half-heartedly, for he did think along with the German liberals that English was the wave of the future. Parenthetically, Jonas won re-election in 1892, but failed to carry either his home city or county of Racine. By 1894 he resigned to seek a consular post (he had been embroiled in a debacle over a consular seat in his native Prague from 1885 to 1887) and was stationed first in St. Petersburg, later in Krefeld, Germany, where he died in 1896 (19).

The cruelest blow to the Republicans in 1890 came in the congressional and legislative races (20). The only one of seven Republicans to survive was Nils P. Haugen, whose security lay not only in his heavily Scandinavian district but in the fact that the Norwegians were the least ardent of all ethnic voters against the Bennett Law. In all parts of the state Democrats won large pluralities, and Republicans knew why they lost resoundingly: John C. Spooner, a blue-blooded Republican, wrote of his defeat: "The school law did it--a silly, sentimental and damned useless abstraction, foisted upon us by a self-righteous demagogue" (21). Ex-congressman George Hazelton wrote similarly: "Hoard with his school question drove all the Lutherans away from our party, the German Lutherans especially, and the Norwegians stayed away from the polls" (22). A tabulation of the votes shows that the Democratic landslide of 1890 must be ascribed to the Germans. Ozaukee County had the highest percentage of Germans in the state and gave 83.5 percent of its votes to George W. Peck. Of the ten counties with the largest Democratic gains, nine were among the fifteen most German counties in Wisconsin. In sample German townships all across the state the Republican vote fell precipitously, in Berlin township in Marathon County, to a meager 3

percent. In both rural and urban settings, the Republicans lost wherever Germans resided.

In four heavily German Milwaukee wards, the Republican vote dropped by an average of 20 percent from the
1888 level while Democratic percentages climbed between
19 percent and 35 percent. In such predominantly Norwegian counties as Vernon, the only two townships to
switch from Republican to Democratic in 1890 were Hamburg, which had the highest percentage of German voters
in the county, and Hillsborough, whose population was
composed of Germans, Bohemians, and Irish. It is significant that those German areas that recorded the
heaviest Republican losses were exceptionally Protestant (23). In most of them, Lutherans predominated.
In Green and Buffalo counties, the Swiss returned large
Democratic gains. Traditionally the only Catholic
group in Wisconsin to vote Republican, the Belgians,
switched to the Democrats in 1890. English and Welsh
areas remained as Republican as ever. Two sample townships, White Oak Springs and New Diggings in Lafayette
County, gave Hoard a higher percentage in 1890 than in
1888, suggesting that the Bennett Law gained votes for
the Republicans among English-speaking immigrants. The
Polish were as Democratic in 1890 as in 1888. Dutch
Catholics were still Democratic while their Protestant
countrymen remained Republican (24). The Bennett Law
issue illustrates above all else that the Germans for
once seized the state's ballot boxes. Because of their
division into two major religious bodies, Catholic and
Lutheran, they never formed an ethnic monolith except
in the election of 1890. In many instances prior to
1890 there was an ethnic vote in Wisconsin, but in none
was it decisive. Periodically immigrant voters squared
off against natives and often religious overtones made
immigrants appear to have common interests. Frequently
there were coalitions but these only gave the impres-
sion that immigrants had organized into blocs.

Prior to the victory of Germany over France in 1871,
the Germans in Wisconsin were Bavarians, Hessians,
Swabians, Pomeranians, all more or less voicing antipathy toward the Prussian Eagle. After 1871 and the
growing prestige of Germany in international affairs,
they acquired a nationalistic view of their own importance. The reorganization and establishment of the
Turner groups and Turnlehrerseminar in 1875 in Milwaukee would not have been successful if the Germans had

not found a new nationalistic identity following the
1871 event. Likewise the German Teachers' Siminary,
which opened its doors in Milwaukee in 1876, would not
have met with success if the Germans had not suddenly
felt a new pride in their nationality (25). This is
not to say that they formed a homogeneous group in
Wisconsin. Herman Deutsch has observed that, among the
Germans, "religious issues did not only infest politics
as parasitic growths but politicians were not averse to
using them as a virus to poison the minds of the
electorate. . . . Personal prejudice not civic spirit
was the object of their appeal" (26).

Probably the worst such virus in Wisconsin ethnic
politics was the issue of temperance. Using temperance
as a fulcrum, related battles were waged: nativism,
nationalism, religion, morality, and others that set
German culture in opposition to Yankee traditions (27).
New Englanders with Puritan mores controlled Wisconsin
politics, exacting high license fees and strict pen-
alties for liquor-law violations. A year after achieving statehood, Wisconsin passed the toughest bill on
liquor control of any state in the Union, requiring a
$1,000 penal bond and the right of women to bring suits
for damages against vendors (28). In 1859 a law was
passed forbidding the sale of liquor on the first day
of each week and at places and times of town meetings.

The liquor question was intensified in 1872 when
Representative Alexander Graham sponsored a bill
calling for a $2,000 bond for anyone to sell liquor,
damage clauses, and a heavy penalty for drunkenness.
Counterresolutions were offered by the Germans, who
organized conventions to "campaign for freedom of
conscience, and religious and industrial liberty, and
against temperance laws and other oppressive measures .
. ." (29). Incidents of infractions led to the law's
being contested in several German centers, notably
Milwaukee, but also in Madison. German newspaper
editors were sarcastic, as were organized brewers and
malt dealers. Cries for repeal of Graham's law echoed
in the campaigns of 1873 and 1874 until the license
fees and surety bonds were mitigated by compromise. A
Yankee Republican called the result "a mixture of
German license and Democratic logic." A German Democrat remarked with bipartisan abandon: "It seems that
when temperance is in, brains are out, just as when
whiskey is in" (30). When Republicans decided that

"Cold Water" could not longer win elections, a Prohibition party formally got started in 1881. In the meantime the Germans tactfully ignored temperance by describing the German Sunday as a family day spent out of
doors, where alcoholic beverages created sociability.
They calmly ignored Yankee arguments that the Fatherland could tolerate liquor Sundays because it operated
as a police state, and spoofed the Yankee view that in
the United States liquor tolerance had become a license
for immorality.

Other issues took the limelight from liquor contenders. In 1878 came a proposal to limit the use of
scriptures in public and state normal schools. Yankee
churchmen supported such activities, especially the
Presbyterians and Methodists, while German Freethinkers
strongly opposed it. Bills were introduced to prohibit
compulsory attendance at religious exercises in state
institutions, but never passed. Gradually the controversy moved from the political stump to the pulpit
resulting in the rapid growth of parochial schools in
Wisconsin. The 1875 campaign foreshadowed the Bennett
Law controversy when Republicans accused the state's
Democrats of creating a loophole in school taxation.
Democrats wanted only those parents whose children
attended public schools to pay the school tax (31). In
these and other matters, the Norwegians worked with
Wisconsin's native elements and were rewarded with
seats in state government. The Germans were strikingly
unsuccessful in placing members of their ethnic group
in government jobs. The editor of the Milwaukee Daily
News pointed out in 1874 that, according to percentage
of the voters, the Germans ought to have had about
forty members in the legislature whereas they never had
more than a dozen. There had never been a German on
the supreme court of the state and although Germans
were prominent in world education, there was not one on
the board of regents of the state university, and not
one on the boards of the state hospitals, although many
of the patients spoke only German (32). The German-
language Seebote in 1876 bemoaned the dearth of Germans
in state positions, indicating that even the Negro
element in Wisconsin was much better represented. Because Wisconsin Germans were outraged to learn in 1872
that the United States was arming France, Germany's
traditional foe, renewed efforts were made to curry
German voters by running German-born candidates in

state elections. In the end, internal ethnic discord usually checkmated such efforts of party leaders (33).

Many reasons could be cited for the unwillingness or inability of the German element to dominate state politics in the post-Civil War Period. The Germans were split on religious grounds between Lutheran and Catholic, they were not well informed because they did not read the English papers, and they maintained their own societies, their own churches, and their own schools. The German Lutherans varied in their support of the Democratic party in relation to the German province of their origin. The strongest Democrats among German Lutherans were the Pomeranians, followed in descending order by the Hanoverians, the Mecklenburgers, the Oldenburgers, the Palatines, and the Württembergers. When German Lutherans came into contact with German Catholics, however, the pattern was reversed. Rather than producing a "German melting pot," exclusiveness increased: Lutherans and Catholics took each other as negative referents. For example, Pepin County's Lima Township was peopled by German-Austrian Catholics and always returned large Democratic majorities even though the county was a Scandinavian stronghold that always voted Republican. In Manitowoc County, Mishicott Township was Wisconsin Synod German Lutheran, but Democratic. Meeme Township was German Catholic, also Democratic. But in Manitowoc Township where there was direct social contact between German Catholics and German Wisconsin Synod Lutherans, the latter voted Republican in opposition to the "Catholic party," i.e., the Democrats (34). Similar patterns prevailed in German Catholic and Lutheran wards of Milwaukee. Geographic propinquity was a determinant in ethnic politics. To the extent that they were near Catholics, German Reformed, German Methodists, and Germans of the Evangelical Association voted less and less Democratic. Data illustrates this for Lebanon in Dodge County, Barton and Wayne Townships in Washington County, as well as New Glarus, Sylvester, and Washington Townships in Green County (35).

Wisconsin's Norwegians were Republican. Wherever found, regardless of economic prosperity or lack of it, Norwegians seldom supported the Democratic party. In 1880, Norwegian townships such as New Hope and Scandinavia in Portage and Waupaca counties in the heart of the state, Martel in Pierce County on the western edge,

as well as York in Green County in the South, all
failed to deliver even 10 percent of their votes to the
Democrats. Norwegian Franklin Township in Jackson
County in 1880 gave no votes at all to the Democrats.
The cleavages that existed from time to time among the
Norwegians are traceable to religious differences, for
a serious disparity existed between the Norwegians who
were affiliated with the Norwegian Synod and those who
were more pietistic and affiliated with the Hauge movement. The antiliturgical Haugeans were more determined
anti-Democrats than their Norwegian brothers. In northern counties the Swedish Lutherans also proved to be
staunchly anti-Democratic.

Irish Catholics were persistently Democratic with no
reference to place, be it urban or rural, northern,
southern, or western. But, Irish Protestants were
strongly Republican. It is difficult to pinpoint an
area with a sufficiently solid concentration of Irish
Protestants to determine exactly how great was their
percentage in support of the Republicans, but wherever
there were Irish Protestants, for instance in Medina
Township in Dane County, the Democratic percentages
were low (36). Similarly, Dutch Catholics in Van den
Broek Township in Outagamie County were consistently
Democratic while their Dutch Reformed countrymen in
Holland Township in Sheboygan County and in Alto Township in Fond du Lac County always handed a majority of
their votes to the Republicans. Nearly always, religious motivation was much more significant in the de-
termination of political loyalty than ethnic back-
ground. By the same token, Poles in Milwaukee and in
the Polish townships of Stockton, Hull, and Sharon in
Portage County, in southern Trempealeau County, and in
Eaton Township of Brown County always returned banner
pollings for the Democrats. Bohemians, too, were often
Catholic and thus Democratic, whether in Kewaunee
County, in Castle Rock Township in Grant, or in Oak
Grove and Trimbelle in Pierce County, whereas the non-
Catholic Bohemians of Union Township in Vernon County
tended to vote Republican.

There is ample evidence of conflict among the Catholic ethnic groups in Wisconsin. The Irish resisted
control by German bishops (37) and the Poles complained
of both Irish and German domination of the church. But
all Catholics always seemed to come together in the old
adage that if a man is a Republican he is not a Catho-

lic. Out of this Paul Kleppner has distilled his
thesis that "the more ritualistic the religious orien-
tations of the group, the more likely it was to support
the Democratic Party; conversely, the more pietistic
the group's outlook the more intensely Republican its
partisan affiliation." This insight leads to an understanding of the Bennett Law controversy. During the
latter half of the century, the public school gained
ever greater support from those who agreed that
children should be "Americanized." America meant
various things to different individuals. To the more
pietistic, whether a Puritan Yankee or a member of the
Methodist Church, whether a fundamentalist Baptist or
an immigrant Norwegian of Haugean persuasion, the word
America meant a theocentric, highly moral society where
the practice of religion was individualistic. The
successful efforts of Catholics, particularly the
German Catholics of Wisconsin, to establish and maintain their own schools struck at the very heart of this
pietistic view of America. It meant to Protestant
Pietists that the young would never be taught the
"American" value system through the agency of the
public school, which would homogenize the generations
of the future into a moralistic social unit.

Although Lutherans were negative referents for Wisconsin's Catholics, there was one societal unit they
held jointly, and that was the parochial school. Both
German groups sought to perpetuate their values through
their schools, a key strategy of which was preservation
of the language (38). It is interesting to note that
those Lutheran Germans from provinces in Germany that
were more pietistic than doctrinal in orientation
tended to be less supportive of parochial schools. For
example, the Lutheran Württembergers were less committed to doctrine, more pietistic in outlook, not as
supportive of parochial schools, and more likely to
vote Republican. The staunchly doctrinal "Old Lutherans" who had come to Wisconsin from Saxony and Pomerania were less pietistic but were the most solidly
Democratic of Wisconsin's Lutherans. Mingled among
them in dozens of German communities were the ration-
alists who demanded that religion be in harmony with
scientific knowledge (39). The ordinary German knew
immediately if the liturgy was being conducted in
German or in English. He did not always know what was
going on in the classroom. But he understood that if

the language was shifted from German to English, the
children would be Americanized and abandon their
values. The new values had come to be associated with
preachers of temperance, holiness of the Sabbath, and
social norms of the Yankee establishment. To the
Pietist, be he an Irish Protestant or a Norwegian
Haugean, there was always the view that the word "immigrant" meant hordes of papal foreigners invading the
citadel of "good" America, an influx of "corrupt"
Catholics into a land that had been constituted according to the gospel as read by undogmatic but "true"
Americans. Religion, much more than ethnic background,
was the determining element in Wisconsin politics (40).

Ethnic politics after 1892 was the politics of
prejudice. Anti-Catholicism spread and the American
Protective Association joined forces with the Republican party to exploit latent biases (41). Under a veil
of secrecy the APA advocated that no Catholic be
allowed to hold office. Data on membership in the APA
is skimpy but suggests that this ultra-American organization actually drew a significant membership from
immigrant groups, especially from Great Britain,
Canada, and the Scandinavian countries. There is suf-
ficient evidence to suggest that Protestant Irishmen
were prominent in the leadership (42). As such, the
APA was an extension into the United State of the
problem besetting Northern Ireland. Swedish papers
were sympathetic to the APA and became APA organs.
Quick to Americanize, the Scandinavians as a rule were
just as quick in setting up patriotic protection
against the ancient foe, Romanism. Among the most
credulous APA members were the Swedish Baptists (43).
There were Germans in the APA, too, heirs of the Freethinkers and Turner groups. Once the Republicans were
back in power after the 1894 elections, the influence
of the APA in Wisconsin faded rapidly (44).

Before concluding we need to consider briefly
Governor, and later, Senator, Robert M. La Follette
(45). Of French Huguenot and Scots-Irish stock,
Robert's family came to Primrose Township in
southeastern Dane County in 1850, where the boy was
born in a log cabin in 1855. An infant when his father
died, Robert worked hard to help his family. In 1873
he determined to get a university education, moved to
Madison, and graduated from law school. One of the key
elements in his rise to power was the Norwegian vote,

the second largest in the state after the Germans. La
Follette spoke some Norwegian and courted his friend
Nils Haugen, the Norwegian Civil War general and
congressman who was the only Republican to survive the
Bennett Law election of 1890. With the aid of ex-
governor and dairyman Hoard, La Follette even persuaded
the reluctant Nils Haugen to run for governor in 1894.
Although he lost, Haugen did follow a progressive
career, specializing in taxation and railroad legislation (46). His most lasting contribution to the movement was his suggestion in 1894 that Wisconsin initiate
the direct primary for party nominations, which La
Follette eventually enacted. From its beginnings, the
Progressive Era owned much to the solid support of the
Norwegians and eventually also of the Swedes in the
more lately settled northern counties. A case is made
by Stuart Brandes that Wisconsin's Norwegian-Americans
were the true source of the Progressive Movement, for
both La Follette and Haugen grew up among Norwegians,
who were underrepresented in politics. In 1895, the
Norwegians comprised one-eighth of Wisconsin's population but held only one-tenth of the county offices.
Only five of Wisconsin's legislators had Norwegian
blood, Norwegians never had a United States senator,
and only Nils Haugen in 1887 made it into the House of
Representatives. Thus, the Progressive Movement may
well have been conceived by Haugen and other Norwegians
in Wisconsin as a means to achieve social and political
equality for the Norwegian-Americans (47).

Efforts of the Democrats to defeat La Follette with
the help of Germans resulted in the nomination for
governor of German-born Louis G. Bomrich of Kenosha in
1900, but La Follette won, becoming the first Wisconsin
governor to post a plurality of over 100,000 votes. As
he moved ahead first through one term, then another, he
sought the support of dissident Democrats, giving his
Republican ticket ever more the look of a non-Republi-
can. When 1904 came into view, old Republican stalwarts fielded the prominent German-American judge Emil
Baensch of Manitowoc as a gubernatorial candidate, with
a platform of anti-third term governors (48). During
the campaign, fighting Bob developed his roll-call
campaign technique, reciting stalwart Republican legislators' votes on important bills and demanding of the
audience that they retire those who backed the
"interests" rather than the people. The final bal-

loting put La Follette Republicans in control of the
executive and of both legislative branches of the
state. The ideological framework of "the people versus
the interests" had triumphed.

At the pinnacle of his power in the state in 1905,
La Follette resigned to take a vacant seat in the
Senate in January 1906, leaving the governorship to a
Norwegian ex-storekeeper, James O. "Yim" Davidson.
Almost immediately he abandoned this first Norwegian to
hold a governorship, committing the worst blunder of
his political career. In Davidson's place, La Follette
advanced a Swede, Irvine L. Lenroot, for the 1906
gubernatorial election (49). Feelings between the two
nationalities were running high because Norway in 1905
had just dissolved its union with Sweden, almost
sucking both nations into a bloody war. In Wisconsin,
where the Norwegians outnumbered the Swedes by more
than three to one (in 1900 there were 155,122 versus
only 48,812 of Swedish birth or parentage), the Republican stalwarts backed Davidson. Germans (709,969 by
birth or parentage in 1900) alleged that Lenroot was a
prohibitionist and papers such as Milwaukee's Germania
attacked him mercilessly. In the primary, therefore,
Lenroot was inundated, securing only three heavily
Swedish northern counties: Douglas, Price, and
Burnett. Milwaukee German Democrats joined the state's
Norwegians by voting in droves for the victorious
Davidson.

Ironically, this was the first direct primary election, a cause for which La Follette had fought hard,
and it delivered him his first stunning defeat. Progressivism lived on, but when Francis E. McGovern took
the governor's chair, he gave it an urban mark of
socialism. By the time La Follette bid for the presidency in 1912, McGovern decided to endorse Roosevelt
for the presidency, causing La Follette forces to
harass him by rejecting his appointees and thwarting
any legislation that might benefit him (50). The elections of November 1914 therefore marked the end of an
era even if the Progressive Movement lingered on as a
smoldering torch carried by "Fighting Bob." On the
horizon loomed the trauma of World War I and the effect
it would have on Wisconsin.

Chapter Five
The Wisconsin Idea
in Progressive Politics

In 1914, when Republican Emanuel Philipp became governor with only 43 percent of the total vote, there were
five candidates, his chief competitor being Democrat
John C. Karel, a Nebraska-born Bohemian (1). Assimilation continued after the Bennett Law controversy and
accelerated during the first decade of the 20th century, but the pace was sometimes glatial and the private
schools impeded its advance. Founded for religious
protection in the 1880s, the Catholic schools of Wisconsin allegedly imparted more ethnicity than theology.
J. A. Burns reported that in 1906 German Catholic
parishes in the United States served 1,519,978 pupils
above the age of nine:

> Schools had to be established for [German immigrant]
> children in which German should be, at least for a
> time, either the only or, at any rate, the chief
> medium of instruction. . . . It was natural that
> their mother-tongue should be the language of the
> school as it was of the home and church and that if
> English were to be taught at all, it should be
> taught much as French and German are taught today in
> the high school, and for much the same reason. (2)

Burns argued that if German immigrants were allowed to
preserve their cherished language, habits, and institutions subject only to social and civic forces, they
would soon go over to English in the curriculum and
become assimilated. During the same period (1906-
1912), according to Burns, Polish leaders in Wisconsin
also recognized the need for increasing the use of
English in the schools.

> Even now, more time is given to English in Polish
> schools than was given ten years ago. . . . At the
> present time the schools are filled mostly by the

children of the immigrants, and from one-fourth to
one-half of their time . . . is given to the study
of Polish or to study in Polish. . . . Children of
the Polish immigrants, even though living in closely
crowded and self-sufficient communities, appear to
take to English as readily as did the children of
the German immigrants. (3)

Assimilation was progressing quietly although ethnicity
persisted. Higher education in Wisconsin also bore the
marks of ethnicity both in origin and implementation.
Achieving national status during the 1890s the university crusaded under the leadership of President Charles
R. Van Hise and Governor La Follette to solve the
problems of society, industry, and agriculture. Most
of the intellectual tenets of Progressivism were generated at the university and vigorously promoted
through the extension and vocational education systems.
The extension budget alone ballooned from $20,000 in
1907 to $125,000 in 1912 as stations expanded through-
out the state (4). In Wisconsin an idea was born of a
European, more specifically a German, genesis that
pervaded the educational and legislative halls of the
state.
    The idea took shape in 1912 when two books were
published that brought national attention to the
progressive idea in Wisconsin. One was by Charles
McCarthy, The Wisconsin Idea, the other by Frederic C.
Howe, Wisconsin, An Experiment in Democracy (5). Both
emphasized the marriage between higher learning and
service to the public. Both authors gave credit for
the Wisconsin idea to Germany and its Prussian-based
educational system. McCarthy said flatly that Wisconsin was a German state and Howe echoed him, stressing
that Germany had identified politics with service more
than any other nation. According to Howe Wisconsin had
made the German idea her own. Neither McCarthy nor
Howe was a native of Wisconsin.
    Called by some the embodiment of the ideal public
progressive administrator, Charles McCarthy was born in
North Bridgewater, Massachusetts, in 1873, studied at
Brown, and took his Ph.D. at the University of Wisconsin. He was chief of the Legislative Reference Library, which he turned into a bill-drafting department.
McCarthy also conducted seminars at the university and
organized conferences on marketing, farm credits,

cooperatives, and industrial relations. Later he
helped set up the state Council of Defense and the
Selective Service, which detracted from the good name
he had won with ethnics of Wisconsin. Consequently, in
1918 he was unsuccessful in his bid for the Democratic
nomination as a United States senator. Although closely identified with Robert La Follette, he was maligned
by many, including Governor Philipp, who attacked him--
and through him, the university--for operating a "bill
factory." Frequently McCarthy pointed to Germany as
the prime example of what could be done through intelligence mobilized by the state. In the McCarthy scheme
of things, the University of Wisconsin generated the
ideas, the state bureaucracy carried them out.

Frederick C. Howe was even more explicit in credit-
ing Germany for Wisconsin's progressive ideas and the
university for training civil servants to implement
them. He called the university the fourth branch of
government, the nerve center of the commonwealth. Of
American stock from the North of Ireland, Frederick
Howe was born in 1867 in Pennsylvania, where he graduated from Allegheny College. In 1892 he took his
Ph.D. at Johns Hopkins, which had been set up in 1876
on the precise model of a German graduate university
(6). But Howe's Germanophilia was not necessarily
generated at Johns Hopkins. He had spent time investi-
gating inner-city conditions in several European countries and had studied in Germany at the University of
Halle. In 1905 he also reported officially to the
United States government on the municipal ownership of
public utilities in Great Britain, and in 1909 delivered a series of political lectures at the University
of Wisconsin, which led to his book. So explicit was
Howe in the first paragraph of his preface that he
would have been arrested if he had written in 1917 what
he stated five years earlier.

> Wisconsin is doing for America what Germany is doing
> for the world. It is an experiment station in poli-
> tics, in social and industrial legislation, in the
> democratization of science and higher education. It
> is a state-wide laboratory in which popular govern-
> ment is being tested in its reaction on people, on
> the distribution of wealth, on social well-being. (7)

In select places throughout the book Howe quickened his

admiration for the German system. "The American city
waits on freedom. . . . The German city has such
freedom. It can do almost anything an individual can
do. . . . With this freedom, Germany has produced the
greatest cities in the modern world, great in ideals,
in experiments, in achievement . . ." (8). Nowhere did
Howe wax more eloquent than when describing Germany's
happy marriage of learning and politics.

Germany has identified science with politics more
closely than any other nation. The state universities, technical and commercial colleges are con-
sciously used for the advancement of the fatherland.
. . . Higher civil service is recruited from the
universities, as is that of the cities. . . . The
achievements of Germany during the past forty years
in industry, commerce, and transportation, in her
army, navy and merchant marine, in the perfection of
her cities are largely the result of the close
identification of science with politics. In no other
country is the expert the alter ego of the statesman
and the administrator as he is in that country. The
public service attracts the most distinguished talent of Germany. . . . Wisconsin is making the German
idea her own. The university is the fourth department of the state, along with the judicial, executive, and legislative branches. . . . It has adjust-
ed its teaching to state problems. (9)

Even as Howe's popular book was being read, office
holders in Wisconsin were bickering about progressivism
and the ethnic pride it generated. Governor Philipp
sniped at Howe, McCarthy, and the university, especially because its president, Charles R. Van Hise, of Dutch
ancestry, epitomized the Wisconsin Idea. Van Hise was
a classmate of La Follette who long nursed the idea of
making him president, which he accomplished as governor
in 1903. But after La Follette tried to defeat Davidson in the 1906 primary, the latter actiely thwarted
Van Hise. Quarreling distracted attention from the
ethnic blocs in Wisconsin politics, but ethnic politics
remained operative nevertheless. On the surface the
debate was issue-oriented but practical politicians
knew they had to stick to the time-tested techniques of
ethnic catering if they were to win votes. The parties
continued to print literature in a variety of lan-

guages, a technique that the Social-Democrats of Milwaukee exploited. Fully conscious of their reliance on the votes of foreign-tongued workers, they established both English and German newspapers, which for a time appeared daily. In 1909 they also started a Polish newspaper. These organs were in addition to the usual campaign material which was distributed in dual language editions, German-English, or Polish-English (10). Platform orators in foreign languages were in demand for bilingual rallies. Bohemian, Norwegian, German, and Polish were common on the stump. In Sheboygan in 1910, campaigners at a gathering of the Personal Liberty League spoke in a total of four languages (11). Some papers, including the German Lutheran _Germania_ and the Norwegian _Skadinaven_, merited more attention from campaign managers than did English papers with far greater circulation because non-English papers were so influential with their readership. Democrats in Milwaukee always had to "mind their p's and ski's" in political appointments or face the consequences in the next election (12). Sometimes simpler rewards were doled out to keep the immigrant vote in tow. Offering instruction in German, Polish, and Italian in both the public as well as in the parochial schools always won popularity. So did the use of German as a second official language in municipal publications or the use of interpreters in local courts. The absence of temperance legislation or even the lack of attacks on the immigrants' parochial schools always curried favor. When it suited their purposes, politicians were never above exploiting ethnic in-fighting and prejudice. The astute chairman of the Wisconsin Democratic Committee in the 1890s used prejudice with great skill, calling it a "far more potent factor than argument" (13). Stock phrases in the various tongues always electrified the audience if they did not exactly enlighten anyone. La Follette's shaky Norwegian, learned when he was a youth in southern Wisconsin, was a great drawing power. Attendance at German summer picnics and Norwegian _Syttende Mai_ celebrations (May 17, Norwegian Independence Day) always lured voters in November.

In the business of ethnic politics, party leaders had to be especially astute in dealing with the clergy, for ethnic politics was scarcely separable from religious politics. Republicans always solicited the Catholic clergy but seldom got the Catholic vote. Thomas

Kearney of Racine once rented a pew in a Catholic
parish although he attended the Presbyterian church
(14). The mayor of Milwaukee, David S. Rose, did him
one better by contributing sums of money to the Milwaukee Catholic congregations. Always nervous about
creeping socialism, especially as expounded by the
German-speaking Victor Berger, five Polish churches in
1900 announced Rose's contributions on Sunday morning
preceding the elections and at two of them distributed
sample ballots duly marked for the Democratic nominees.
A few Catholic churches opened their pulpits for Rose
to denounce the Socialists (15).

If Milwaukee was a polyglot ethnic hotbed, the opposite corner of the state was no less so. In 1908 in
Wisconsin's Eleventh Congressional District, composed
of the thirteen northernmost counties, youthful Irving
Luther Lenroot, born of Swedish immigrants and a
protégé of Robert La Follette, played ethnic politics
in the Republican primary. A member of the state
assembly, Lenroot in 1906 lost the Republican nomination for governor against Norwegian James O. Davidson,
whose ethnic group widely outnumbered the Swedes in
Wisconsin. In 1907 Lenroot had been a contender for
the United States Senate but lost. The 1908 primary
pitted him against Republican John J. Jenkins, who had
been in Congress since 1894. Not only did Lenroot
defeat him in the primary by capturing 61 percent of
the vote but in November he went on to overwhelm his
Democratic opponent, J. S. Konkel, by a three-to-one
margin. Lenroot demonstrated his talent for ethnic
politics. Until 1905 Norway had been under the Swedish
monarchy. Lenroot had alienated the Norwegians when he
campaigned against Davidson in 1906. In 1908, therefore, he sent his Norwegian friend Nils P. Haugen to
Chicago to try to elicit an endorsement from the Norwegian Skandinaven, but the paper "proved itself a
traitor" because of "Swedophobia" (16). Nevertheless,
Lenroot enjoyed the support of the major Norwegian
political leaders in Wisconsin, Haugen, Herman L.
Ekern, John M. Nelson, and, after some wooing, Governor
Davidson. Lenroot's base, however, was his polyglot
home district. In Douglas County the Swedes were on
top with 3,557 followed by the Norwegians (2,341),
the Finns (500), and the Danes (252). There were also
nearly 3,000 British-Canadians, over 1,000 Germans, 632
French Canadians, 685 Irish, 300 Poles, and 300

Russians. Churches included the Polish Catholic St.
Stanislaus Congregation, the Swedish Methodist, and
many others. Comparable mixes were present in
Bayfield, Ashland, Iron, and Price counties. In both
1910 and 1920 these counties, along with Racine and
Kenosha in the Southeast, were havens for the largest
percentages of ethnic stock populations in the state (17).
 Since the early days of statehood, when the immigrants gained numerical importance in Wisconsin, the
"balanced ticket" had always been a campaign manager's
delight. It was easy at caucuses and conventions to
hand one office to the Germans, another to the Poles,
etc. Republican tickets always included at least one
German and one Norwegian. The direct primary frus-
trated this process, however. Whenever no Polish
candidates emerged victorious in Democratic primaries
in Milwaukee, the Poles simply abstained from voting.
This spelled disaster for the Democrats because in
1910, 70,000 or 22 percent of Milwaukee's 313,000
people were Polish (18). With only the totals of
primary votes doing the nominating, no mastermind
campaign manager could rebalance the ethnic fringes of
any ticket. The Progressives tried repeatedly but
failed to put a German on their tickets between 1906
and 1914. The direct primary for which the Progressives had worked so hard, therefore, turned out to be a
major cause of their decline.
 In the ethnic atmosphere that held sway during the
first decade of the twentieth century, Wisconsin's
immigrant press flourished. There were seventy-nine
German-language papers published in forty-one cities,
towns, or villages. Of the seventy-nine, thirty-six
were issued in five places: Milwaukee had twenty,
Appleton and La Crosse each had five, Manitowoc and
Sheboygan three a piece. Each year the editors and
publishers met to discuss problems and plot strategy
(19). Understandably, they stressed continued use of
the German language. They fought prohibition and
women's suffrage, opposed all attempts to restrict
immigration, and attacked anyone tainted with Know-
Nothingism. In the early twentieth century, they
sympathized with the problems of industrial workers and
echoed Howe and McCarthy by taking pride in Germany's
social legislation. With total ethnic commitment and
candor, the German-language papers favored balancing
tickets; those that were Democratic urged Charles

Weiss, on the basis of his German extraction, for the 1910 gubernatorial nomination. The German Republican papers in the same year pushed Gustav Kuestermann for re-election to Congress. More than anything else, the Germans fought prohibition. In 1909, when temperance legislation was threatened, the Wisconsin State Journal maintained that the Germania had killed the measure and speculated as to how many Germans placed the saloon above loyalty to party, home, and church. In rebuttal the Germania not only denied such allegations but propounded with glossy terms: "The Germans of Wisconsin at all times place the defense of personal liberty and the preservation of the good name of the state above the party" (20). The Germans also opposed women's suffrage, warning of pollution of home, family, and motherhood if women entered the dirty arena of politics. "We hold women high in our esteem and refuse to see them degrade themselves by participating in the struggle for political power" (21).

When Woodrow Wilson received the Democratic presidential nomination in 1912, the German Democratic papers in Wisconsin supported him because he was "right on prohibition and immigration." But Republican and Socialist papers such as the Germania and the Vorwäts dug into Wilson's History of the American People to illustrate by his own remarks that he was not a friend of the immigrant. Republicans were also able to show that Wilson was in sympathy with prohibition. If the papers could not tolerate Wilson, neither could they bring themselves to support La Follette. Although La Follette was "right" on most matters in Wisconsin, he had come to espouse women's suffrage and judicial recall, which were anathema to Germans. Wisconsin's Germans, however, did support him in his call for economic and labor reforms and for greater participation of the working man in the industrial life of the nation. Some acquiesced to citizen initiative and referendum because these views sprang from McCarthy and Howe. In the elections of 1910, 1912, and 1914, the statistics show that the counties returning the largest Democratic percentages had the largest numbers of Germans. Republican strength in Wisconsin during the 1910-1914 period illustrates a close connection to Scandinavian counties. The ten most Scandinavian counties consistently returned Republican majorities of at least 60 percent. Polk County passed the 75 percent

Republican mark six times in gubernatorial elections
between 1896 and 1914. In 1902 and 1904 the Scandinavians gave strong support to La Follette and only once
between 1896 and 1914 did one of the ten Scandinavian
counties return a Democratic plurality (22).

During the pre-world War I era, Republican support
came from the Norwegians, Swedes, Danes, Belgians,
Canadians, Finns, English, Welsh, and Scots, along with
the older stock Americans. Geographically, this means
the counties along the southern border of the state,
and those comprising the northwestern third of Wisconsin. Democratic support, by contrast, came from the
Germans in General and the Catholic Germans in particular. The Irish remained Democratic as did the Poles
and Bohemians. Russians--a category that includes a
lot of Poles, Austrians, many Bohemians, and numerous
South Slavs--were also Democratic. In precisely those
twelve counties (23) that most consistently delivered
Democratic majorities, the Germans were the most
numerous ethnic group, except in Kewaunee, where the
Bohemians outnumbered them. All are concentrated in
eastern and north central Wisconsin. The Dutch and
Swiss in these areas split readily along religious
lines, the Protestants voting Republican and the Catholics Democratic. As a rule, ethnicity and religion
were inseparable. A Norwegian was Lutheran. A Pole or
an Irishman, although he had rejected the Roman Catholic Church, was still a Democrat. A few counties such
as Buffalo and Trempealeau, near the Mississippi,
reveal ethnoreligiously heterogeneous situations.
Between 1894 and 1914 the Protestant German and Swiss
townships joined the Norwegians in returning Republican
majorities over the Catholic Germans and Poles. Careful analysis reveals that the results were consistently
along ethnoreligious lines (24). The most ethnically
diverse county in Wisconsin was Brown, with Green Bay
in its center, a veritable melting pot of Germans,
Dutch, Belgians, Danish, Canadians, Polish, Irish,
Norwegians, and old stock Americans, none of whom made
up even 20 percent of the county's voters in 1905. Of
the eleven precincts that persistently voted Republican, two had a majority of Belgians, two were strongly
Danish and Norwegian, and only one had a majority of
Germans, but they were Protestant.

In Milwaukee the consistently Democratic wards
were the Third, which was Irish and Italian; the 14th,

which was largely Polish; the 18th, which had mostly
Poles and some Irish; and the Fourth, which had "new"
immigrants--Hungarians, Greeks, and some Irish. Milwaukee's German wards voted Democratic if they were
Catholic, Republican if they were not. If they had
groups of Freethinkers, they voted for the Socialists.
The German Forty-eighters by the 1890s, however, had
little influence on politics in Wisconsin (25). For
all of Wisconsin's seventy-one counties the political
pattern of ethnicity holds true: the Democratic areas
consisted of family heads from Germany, Poland, Bohemia, Austria, Ireland, Holland, Switzerland, Russia,
Hungary, Italy, and French Canada. Not one single
voting unit of Wisconsin that was regularly Democratic
had a clear majority of Scandinavian, British, Belgian,
or older stock American voters.

But, if any party is to be characterized as having
a totally ethnic cast, it would be the Social-Democrats. Largely a movement of German intellectuals and
German union leaders, this party was conceived in the
1880s. By 1900 it had found its guiding spirit in the
person of Victor Berger, who joined with Eugene V. Debs
to form the "Social Democracy of America" and sponsor
candidates in Milwaukee elections. They dominated the
Federated Trades Council, sought remedies to contagious
diseases, initiated food inspection, sponsored school
medical examinations, and fought for the reduction of
industrial accidents. In line with what Howe and
McCarthy had been saying, they disseminated information
about European methods of social legislation and the
plight of injured workers (26). There was frequent if
unspoken admiration for Bismarck's social programs in
Germany, and as late as 1954 veteran Progressives
claimed success for these reform ideas not just in
Wisconsin but throughout the world. Often the Milwaukee Socialists conducted their meetings in German. By
1904 they reached out to other ethnic groups by establishing the English-language Social Democratic Herald,
which yielded positive results at the polls, where they
secured four wards and nine aldermanic seats. Their
real strength, however, lay with the German working
classes. Later the Italians and some Poles came along,
but opposition of the Catholic Church to socialism
proved almost insurmountable. Only when some Poles
broke with their mother church to form the Polish
National Catholic Church could the Milwaukee Socialists

win Polish converts. The 14th Ward, with it 76 percent
Polish population, delivered a solid Social-Democratic
victory in the Milwaukee municipal elections of 1910 (27).
Outside Milwaukee there were substantial Socialist
vote totals in the German wards of Racine, Sheboygan,
Manitowoc, and in heavily German rural settlements such
as Kiel and Two Rivers, but no victories. Isolated
rural towns went Socialist only when they had large
percentages of Swedes or Finns. The Finns were especially noted for their "red" leanings in the Townships of Knox in Price County, Lynn in Oneida, and Oulu
in Bayfield County. The lumber villages usually had
mixed ethnic groups, but were strongly German and
Swedish, and sometimes returned large Socialist votes.
Elsewhere in Wisconsin, especially in the staunchly
German or Norwegian counties, socialism never had much
appeal. The party attracted the ethnic vote all right,
but not without the presence of an additional dimen-
sion--the suppressed working class to which recent
immigrants tended to belong.
In concluding about Progressive Wisconsin before
World War I, we should return briefly to La Follette
and chart how he fared between the years 1904 and 1912.
Protestant Germans and Dutch proved to be stalwart
Republicans and withheld support from La Follette.
Norwegians and Swedes were won over by the charming
campaigner. Belgians gave them their votes. In Green
Bay, for example, La Follette ran well ahead of the
state ticket in the Belgian wards. La Follette was
also popular with the German Catholics. By 1912, however, La Follette's abortive presidential candidacy,
his denunciation of both Taft and Roosevelt, and a host
of other developments created a chaos that is difficult
to analyze. The Rough Rider ran well among Swedish
voters, Taft carried the Norwegians, and the Danes
split. Central European nationalities, including German Catholics, Poles, and Bohemians, were ambivalent
about La Follette. They rejected some of his favorite
ideas, such as women's suffrage, the income tax, and
other schemes the bushy-haired senator had devised,
including the direct primary, initiative, and referendum. La Follette engineered the "open" primary. The
problem with the direct primary was that it allowed
members of the opposing party to exercise their choice
in the selection of their opponents for the general
election. Sometimes primary returns were ridiculously

lopsided. In the 1906 primary, Milwaukee voters cast
ten Republican votes to every Democratic one even
though the city was roughly equal in registered Republicans, Democrats, and Socialists. That year the
solidly Democratic Irish ward turned in 565 Republican
and only 39 Democratic ballots. The Democratic Polish
14th, however, refused to play the cross-over game,
coming through with only 102 Republican and 1,614 Democratic tallies (28).

As a general rule, the Scandinavians in the northwestern part of the Badger State supported Progressive
nominees. The northern lumbering areas with their
hodgepodge of ethnic voters, however, tended to vote
with the southern Yankees for the stalwart Republicans.
The Bohemian gubernatorial candidate, John C. Karel, in
1912 and 1914 drew well among his fellow countrymen but
not especially well with his next-door neighbors, the
Germans. The Norwegian Andrew H. Dahl was a favorite
among the Scandinavians in 1914 but unfortunately split
the Progressive vote with William Hatton and thus
handed both the nomination and the election to Emanuel
Philipp (29). During the period of Progressive politics, the nationality groups in Wisconsin rested on
well-established traditions, only some of which
harkened back to the Old World. In the New World they
had formed new political allegiances that had special
meaning for would-be political candidates. They had
also formed new churches and realigned themselves on a
host of issues, such as temperance, women's suffrage,
and the referendum, which could not possibly have been
matters of concern back home. If, as we shall see
later, the World War drove ethnicity in Wisconsin
underground, it might be useful in the following
chapter to summarize and survey the status of each
ethnic group in Wisconsin as it appeared in 1910.

Chapter Six
Immigrant Wisconsin: The 1910 Status

The immigrant in Wisconsin in 1910 had achieved his
American dream, having acquired not only a new land but
a fair share of its riches. In 1910 the foreign-born
and foreign-stock populations of Wisconsin enjoyed
sweeping equality and satisfactory coexistence with the
native stock in the state. Occasionally disagreements
surfaced, but politicians, church leaders, ethnic
chieftains, and labor organizers easily settled them.
Assimilation was underway but many social institutions
still existed along parallel lines--parochial as well
as public schools, Catholic as well as Lutheran (and
other) churches, rural as well as urban centers, and in
almost every Wisconsin county, at least one strong
foreign-stock element alongside some other foreign
element or perhaps a native-born group. A certain
harmony prevailed, which masked the differences that
punctuated all of life. The allotment of wealth was
almost utopic although the foreign-born did lag behind
the native-born by about thirty years (1). Not surprisingly, the English fared best next to the Yankees,
followed by the Irish. Next in line to accumulate the
available riches were the Germans, followed in descending order by the Scots, the Dutch, and the Norwegians.
The distribution of wealth in Milwaukee, for instance,
was far more equitable in 1910 than in the cities of
Oslo or Berlin, whence numerous immigrants had arrived.

The pace setter among Wisconsin industrial centers
between 1880 and 1910 was Milwaukee. In 1880 its
population was 40 percent foreign-born, of whom over
two-thirds were from Germany. Ireland was second with
8 percent, Poland third with 4 percent. The Poles had
not yet arrived in mass numbers. By 1910 the most
dramatic shift was the decline of the foreign-born
percentage for the Germans, being replaced by the
Poles, who in 1910 constituted 20 percent of the city's
foreign-born. The Germans were found in every ward of

the city. In 1910 they still held the west and northwest parts, Wards 2, 6, 9, 10, 13, 15, 19, 20, 21, and
22, the same areas they settled beginning in the 1840s
(2). Milwaukee in 1910 was unusual among cities its
size: it had only two major ethnic groups, each of
which dominated whole sections of the city. Relatively
few Irish, Italians, Jews, Serbians, Greeks, Latvians,
or Bohemians settled in Milwaukee and even the black
community was very small until after 1940 (3). The
Poles gathered in the south-side Wards 11, 12, and 14
(which contained 53 percent of all the German national
Poles in Milwaukee), in Wards 2 and 15 on the near west
side, and in Wards 13 and 18 on the northeast side.
Small colonies of eastern and southern Europeans--
Italians, Slovenians, Russians, Hungarians, Greeks, and
Slovaks--clustered around the central business district. Italians also formed a settlement in Ward 3
along Lake Michigan on the south side, where they
succeeded the departing Irish. Tiny east and south
European groups were in Wards 2, 6, 9, and 13 on the
west side. The English and Irish by 1910 preferred to
live near the Menomonee River and along the eastern
lakeshore in Wards 1, 7, and 18.

The years between 1900 and 1914 were complacent ones
for the foreign-stock peoples of Wisconsin. In the new
homeland as well as in the old ones a smug contentment
prevailed. Take the Norwegians. The year 1914 marked
the centenary of a Norwegian constitution whose ratifi-
cation at Eidsvold transformed Norway from a Danish
province into an autonomous, although not entirely
independent, nation. All over Wisconsin celebrations
of the event were organized in the Norwegian communities for May 17, 1914. In Milwaukee Norwegians were
impressed by Governor Francis E. McGovern, who addressed his audience with considerable insight into the
nuances of Norse history. In La Crosse a program
featured 500 singing Norwegian children plus an address
by their pro-La Follette politician, James Thompson.
Thousands of Wisconsin Norwegians who had achieved the
good life booked passage on steamship lines that summer
to visit the homeland. As it turned out, most went to
the regional, agricultural districts whence they or
their parents had come, but a respectable number did
convene in Kristiania (Oslo) for national festivities.
The enormous citizens' parade included a Norwegian-
American section of perhaps 3,000 led by the Luther

College band. Weeks later, on July 4, the cousins from
America turned over to officials in Norway their cen-
tennial fund donation, on which occasion the speaker
used the phrase "Love of wife should never extinguish
love of old mother." The Norwegian press characterized
the events with a cartoon aptly stereotyping emigrants
to America. Queried how he might evaluate the Exhibi-
tion in Norway the Norwegian-American replied, "Well,
as for being in Norway it is not so bad, you know" (4).

Inasmuch as the years 1910-1914 can be characterized as the high-water mark of ethnicity in Wisconsin,
it would be valuable to survey the major groups as of
that time in order to comprehend their statistical
size, religious affiliation, political loyalty, and
geographic location.

Taking first the Scandinavians (defined here according to Guy-Harold Smith and others to mean Norwegians,
Swedes, and Danes only) we note that in 1910 there were
over 128,000 Norwegians either born in Norway (57,000
Norwegian-born) or having both parents born there,
compared with 48,000 Swedes (25,700 Swedish-born) and
only 32,000 Danes (16,400 Danish-born) (5). The Norwegians were the earliest Scandinavians and the most
numerous. By the time the Swedes and Danes began
arriving, much land for settlement had been taken. For
all three, the Scandinavian Lutheran churches were
instrumental in clustering the settlements, which in
turn perpetuated the Scandinavian culture and language
(6). By 1910 colonies of 100 or more Norwegians could
be found in almost every county of Wisconsin. Eight
had more than 5,000 residents of Norwegian parentage:
Dane had 13,694, Trempealeau 7,795, both Vernon and La
Crosse over 6,000 each, followed by Barron, Douglas,
Dunn, Eau Claire, Jackson, Waupaca, Pierce, Polk, and
St. Croix. On a percentage basis, Trempealeau was the
most concentrated with 34 percent, followed by Jackson
with 25 percent, Vernon with 23 percent, and Barron
with 20 percent. The people in unassimilated Norwegian
settlements in Wisconsin continued to live quite as
they had in Norway. English remained a foreign
language. But, sooner than most ethnic groups in Wisconsin, the Norwegians recognized the advice of Ole
Running in his guidebook: "Before having learned the
language fairly well, one must not expect to receive so
large a daily or yearly wage as the native-born American." Most Norwegians were peasants back in their

homeland and in Wisconsin many worked for Yankee
farmers to learn agricultural methods, and English (7).
The Norwegians in Wisconsin were badly divided along
religious lines. Most were Haugeans, Lutherans who
abandoned the state high church in favor of Hans N.
Hauge, a peasant lay preacher who stressed individual
piety and deemphasized the role of the ministry. Until
they merged into the Norwegian Lutheran Church in
America in 1917, the Norwegians were organized into at
least five separate Norwegian Lutheran synods (8).

Wisconsin Norwegians were usually rural and content
with small farms where they raised wheat before the
days when all Wisconsin farmers were wiped out by the
chinch bug and switched to dairying. There is one
exception: the unexplainable preference of the Norwegians for tobacco raising, although they had never
known it in the Old World (9). Usually these were
lucrative endeavors. Nevertheless, the average value
of farms owned by Norwegian family heads was well below
the state average, suggesting that they arrived later
than necessary for the best choice of land values or
lacked the vision to acquire more when it was available. But this did not bother them for they had little
intention of selling anyway. If one considers the
average income per farm according to the 1905 Wisconsin
state census, then most Norwegian townships appear
prosperous, especially in tobacco-rich Dane and Vernon
counties and in the dairy regions of Trempealeau,
Pepin, and Pierce counties. Familiar with the movement
in Scandinavia from the 1860s onward, the Norwegians
were in the forefront in developing rural cooperatives
in the United States (10). They were virulently anti-
Catholic and despised the politically active Irish. In
the Bennett Law election of 1890 many expressed their
displeasure by not voting at all. As Democratic campaign manager Edward C. Wall remarked, a dollar spent
appealing to the Norwegians is like throwing it into
the fire.

It was difficult for the Norwegians to grasp the
folk-hero style of rugged individualism that characterized American society. They were suspicious of middle-
men, corporate business, and the practice of buying
land for speculation. They were rural folks, often
related to each other, who had come from the same
community in Norway. Many set sail on the same ship
and settled in America as a unit. Norwegians from the

same valley, the Bygd ("community") of Gulbrandsdal,
established Coon Prairie; those from Numedal founded
Jefferson Prairie, and those from Sogn settled Sogn in
Goodhue County, Minnesota (11). Social stratification
was lacking. Because Norwegians shied away from aggressive capitalism, they were slow to become involved
in big business. All of this made it easy for them to
support reform measures, to side with La Follette, and
later to gain a toehold in the Nonpartisan League in
North Dakota and Minnesota. For this their stalwart
Republican leaders occasionally accused them of rank
socialism and even communism (12). The Norwegians
before World War I were numerically large enough in
Wisconsin communities to perpetuate their Old World
culture. In other respects they developed traditions
perceived as distinctly Norwegian, which had nothing to
do with the Old World. For example, the "Sons of
Norway" lodges are secret societies like their American
models and the raising of tobacco certainly has no link
to the mother country. So, too, eating lutefisk and
lefse in America takes on an importance that would be
out of place in Norway. On the other hand, attention
to the Bygd, the localized region or valley from which
a Norwegian had emigrated, created subunits among
members of the Norwegian settlements and neutralized
nationality feelings of the group (13).

Studies of the rural community of Coon Prairie and
Folsom-West Prairie (the Utica Settlement) in Vernon
County near Viroqua illustrate patterns of evolution,
depending on the valley whence the members hailed. In
the Vernon County situation, the Norwegians built up an
independent, socially self-sufficient cultural heritage, enabling them to withdraw from the Yankee-domin-
ated city of Viroqua. From 1878 to 1930 they displaced
Yankees who gave up farming. The Utica settlement
expanded while the Coon Prairie one consolidated and
gave way on the fringes to other ethnic groups, especially the Germans. By contrast the Blue Mounds communities in Dane County were more homogeneous, being
settled only by Telemarkings. The groups in Vernon
County were Sognings separated by Flekkefjordings. In
the Blue Mounds case, ironically, the settlements grew
more expansive and less self-contained; in the Vernon
County case they grew more concentrated and more able
to maintain their social, economic, and cultural heritage. Church attendance, club association, and even

interhouse visitation occurred almost exclusively along
ethnic lines (14).

No other ethnics, neither the Swedes nor the Danes,
were as faithful to the Republican party as the Norwegians. The Swedes, of course, were far less numerous
and Johnny-come-latelies. There were only 673 in the
whole state in 1860. By 1900, however, eight counties
had more than 1,000 born in Sweden, and Douglas County,
near Lake Superior, tallied 3,557. By 1910 there were
48,000 of Swedish parentage in Wisconsin, 25,739 of
them Swedish-born. The largest settlements were in
western Wisconsin from the Chippewa River basin northward through Pepin, Polk, Burnett, Bayfield, and
Douglas counties to Superior. Swedes also settled in
the cutover forest counties of Price in north central
Wisconsin and especially Florence and Marinette in the
Northeast. Because the land still available when the
Swedes arrived was poor and the climate where they
settled unfavorable, their average annual income compared badly with other ethnic household heads in 1905.
Like the Norwegians, however, they staunchly supported
the Lutheran Church, namely the Augustana Synod. Soon
after their arrival the Swedes abandoned their native
tongue and punctuated this decision by abandoning all
calls for parochial schools on the ground that such
would retard Americanization and that these institutions smacked of Catholicism (15). Public schooling
was a key factor in the rapid assimilation of the
Wisconsin Swedes. The church did assist in preserving
the Swedish language until World War I, but never with
the intensity common among the Germans, who fought
fiercely for their parochial schools and their language.

As deeply anti-Catholic as their Norwegian confreres, the Swedes in the 1890s swallowed the bitterly
phrased propaganda of the American Protective Association, which feared that the pope would land in New York
any day and take over Washington, D.C. (16). Because
of their small numbers the Swedes were never effective
in Wisconsin politics. The most successful was Irvine
L. Lenroot, who served first as speaker of the state
assembly, unsuccessfully challenged the Norwegian
Davidson for governor in 1906, and won a seat in the
United States Congress in 1908. In that year he
unseated a stalwart Republican and in 1918 joined La
Follette in the United States Senate. After serving

with distinction he was defeated in his bid for re-
election in 1926 by John J. Blaine, whose strength came
from the concentrated German counties (17). By the
time of his death on January 26, 1949, Lenroot was
almost completely forgotten. Few remembered that this
Wisconsinite born of Swedish parents might have been
president in place of Coolidge, for in 1920 the Republican vice-presidential nomination was his for the
taking; if he had accepted he would have succeeded
Harding to the top office in the land. During the
Progressive Era, Sweidsh voters always returned overwhelming majorities to the Republicans, rarely falling
below 75 percent in the townships with the heaviest
Swedish populations. La Follette always did well with
the Swedes, even when Lenroot split with him. When
Roosevelt ran in 1912 on the Progressive ticket,
Swedish voting was unique in support of Teddy. In 1912
and 1914, a few Swedish precincts returned pluralities
for the Social-Democratic ticket, unlike their confreres, the Norwegians and the Danes.

By 1910 there were 32,000 Wisconsinites of Danish
birth or parentage, by far the largest number of whom,
over 7,000, lived in Racine County (18). Unlike the
Norwegians and Swedes, many lived in urban areas.
Racine is to this day the center of the Danish element
in Wisconsin, although there are significant colonies
in Milwaukee, Oshkosh, and Neenah. In 1910, Brown,
Dane, Polk, Waupaca, and Winnebago counties all had
Danish-born populations of over 500, while Polk had
over 1,000 (19). In 1893 a Danish settlement was estab-
lished near Withee in Clark County, where they lived
adjacent to, and in part acculturated with, their
Polish neighbors (20). Others developed in Waushara,
St. Croix, and Adams counties, and near Rosholt in
Portage. Some lived with the Icelanders on Washington
Island in Door County.

The Danes were in the main Lutheran. The earlier
arrivals mostly belonged to pietistic sects within that
group and came to America to escape the Danish state
church. Among them were believers who owe their origin
to the Danish poet, preacher, and patriot Bishop N. F.
S. Grundtvig, whose youngest son, Frederick Lange
Grundtvig, in 1881 came to Wisconsin to live in Outagamie County. The Grundtvigians represented the more
orthodox faction of the Danish Lutherans in Wisconsin
while the more pietistic elements seceded to form the

United Danish Evangelical Church. There were also
others including the Norwegian-Danish Methodists, the
Adventists, and a Free Mission Danish sect. From time
to time the Danes tried to found schools but with
little success. Even their Luther High School and
College, founded in Racine in 1902, flourished only
temporarily. In 1870 Wisconsin had the highest number
of Danish in the nation but was superseded by Iowa in
1890 and by California in 1920.

In 1910 the Danes were most heavily represented in
Racine in the Southeast and in Polk County in the
Northwest in a community named, appropriately, West
Denmark. (Subsequently both the township and the
village names were changed to Luck.) Marinette temporarily flourished as a center of Danish culture in the
Northeast. In the center of the state, Danes were in
Clark and (southwest) Waupaca counties and at Denmark
in Brown County. But wherever they settled they were
too sparse to control their local destiny and thus even
in Racine, where they boasted having the most Danish
city in the Unites States, other ethnic groups outnumbered them by a large margin. Danish culture and
the Danish language had little chance for survival.
During World War I, preaching in Danish disappeared
from the churches and by the depression of the 1930s
even the Dania Society of Racine abandoned the native
tongue (21). The Progressive La Follette received
handsome majorities in Danish areas. In 1906 the
Norwegian Davidson and the Swedish Lenroot each won
three of the Danish political territories. Racine
wards, although they always returned Republican pluralities, did not vote as overwhelmingly Republican as the
percentages of the Danes living in them would warrant.
Wherever there was a large working class, the Social-
Democrats significantly detracted from the Republican
pluralities. The Germans in these wards could not have
accounted for all Socialist ballots; some had to come
from the Danish workers. Thus urban Danes were less
Republican than their rural landsmen (22).

The Finns in Wisconsin, sometimes classified with
the Scandinavians, concentrated in the northwest
counties of Douglas, Bayfield, Ashland, Iron, Vilas,
Price, Oneida, and Lincoln. A few settled in Marinette, Milwaukee, and Kenosha. The largest numbers of
Finnish-born in the year 1920 were in Douglas (1,062)
and Iron (1,181), which persisted in 1940, however,

with declines in the totals respectively to 1,123 for
Douglas and 724 for Iron (23). Fully two-thirds of the
Wisconsin Finnish-born ultimately settled on the land.
They began in the mines and quarries, in the logging
camps and the sawmills, as dock and railroad workers,
as helpers in factories and on fishing fleets. In
these jobs they became active in the labor movement as
Socialists, Communists, and as members of the Indus-
trial Workers of the World--the notorious IWW of the
World War I period.

On the land the Finns clung to a meager existence on
the cutover, the only place where these latecomers
found any remaining opportunities. Dazzling newspaper
advertisements and savvy land agents played on the Finnish desire for land and the independence it promised.
In 1909 the G. F. Sanborn Company of Chicago offered to
build a cabin for every purchaser of eighty acres of
its land near Eagle River. Some of their native styles
of construction, notably the log sauna, still pepper
the far northern Wisconsin rural horizon (24). Eventually Finns developed a "Clover Belt" in northern
Clark County near the communities of Owen and Withee.
Those who still cling to the land in the counties
farther north maintain farms but find supplementary
income off the land. The Finns were primarily Lutheran. In 1936 there were twenty-five Finnish congregations in the state, all Lutheran, but affiliated with
three separate synods. As a rule the Finns supported
temperance societies and the usual fraternal, cultural,
and social organizations. Their newspapers, notably
the **Tyomies** of Superior, were an influential mainstay
of their lives. Like the Norwegians, the Finns were
supportive of the cooperative movement in purchasing
and selling farm goods. What attracted the greatest
attention, especially during World War I, was their
passionate belief in socialism.

A few statistically inconsequential Icelanders
settled in Milwaukee, on Washington Island off Door
County, and in Shawano County, but their impact has
been far larger on the imaginations of journalists than
on the state as a whole (25).

Dutch, Bohemians, and Belgians took up residence in
Brown, Door, and Kewaunee counties. Most Bohemians,
Belgians, and about half of the Dutch settlers, notably
those in the Fox River Valley, were Catholic (26).
They had priests who spoke their respective languages

and thus were able to perpetuate separate cultures even
though their religion should have pulled them together.
For reasons that are unclear, the Belgians gradually
became Republicans; the Bohemians were firm Democrats.
The Dutch emulated the Germans in splitting along religious lines, the Protestants becoming Republican and
the Catholics Democratic. The Dutch Protestants were
divided by schisms in the Dutch Reformed Church, from
which the rigid Calvinists broke away and headed for
America. Catholic Dutchmen seem to have migrated less
for religious than for economic reasons, even in the
earliest days of Wisconsin statehood. The first wave
of Dutch came between 1850 and 1860. From a total of
about 5,000 Dutch in Wisconsin at the outbreak of the
Civil War, Dutch immigration declined steadly until
1880, when an agricultural depression in the homeland
revitalized it. By 1910 there were 7,379 Dutch-born
Wisconsinites and 16,554 of Dutch parentage. Protestants outnumbered Catholics. Mostly the Dutch settled in the Fox River Valley although Sheboygan County
had the largest single concentration of Dutchmen, 3,362
in 1910, 1,445 of them Dutch-born (27).

Religion was a powerful force among Dutch settlers
in Wisconsin. Hollanders gave up opportunities for
social, economic, and political involvement just to
maintain compact Dutch settlements where their piety
could be perpetuated. Parochial education was the rule
for their children and ministers saw to it that Dutch
Protestants lived completely isolated from their Catholic landsmen. In Sheboygan and Fond du Lac Counties
the Dutch were highly successful in economic ventures,
particularly in growing barley and other grains. Both
here and in the Catholic Dutch township of Outagamie
County, incomes were high, at or above the state average, especially after Wisconsin switched to dairying.
Among the Dutch Catholics in the Fox River Valley,
however, there was an ever-increasing tendency toward
amalgamation of all Catholics--Germans, Irish, French,
Belgian, as well as Dutch--into common parochial
schools, which rendered these Hollanders less "Dutch"
in their daily lives. Because they were considered
"disreputable people" by pietistic Dutch reformers,
Dutch Catholics were totally ignored by Dutch Protestants. When a Wisconsin Dutch Reformed pastor in 1897
wrote a purported history of the Dutch in Wisconsin, he
never even mentioned the thriving Dutch Catholic colony

in the Fox River Valley. This is surprising because he
provided a list of Hollanders who had held public
office, most of whom were Catholics from Brown and
Outagamie counties in the Fox Valley (28).

All Hollanders at first supported the Democrats but
beginning with the Civil War Protestants switched and
remained in the Republican camp. The Catholics remained loyal to the Democratic party along with their
Irish, German, and Belgian co-religionists. A man with
the Dutch name of Roosevelt was unable to lure Dutch
Catholics away from the Democrats, not even in 1912,
when the Bull Moose candidate was no longer on the
Republican ticket. Although conservative in most matters, the Protestant Dutch were attracted to the Rough
Rider, more for his Dutch Protestant ancestry than his
ideas. Wisconsin's Progressives drew little support
from Dutchmen of either religion. Within the Republican
party, Dutch Protestants supported Republican stalwarts
against the Progressives. Neither La Follette nor his
candidates ever received much help from the Dutch. On
one political issue, however, Protestant and Catholic
Dutch united, namely in opposition to women's suffrage.

The Belgians settled near, and interspersed with,
the Dutch in the greater Green Bay area of Wisconsin.
They also paralleled them in numbers, with 4,600
Belgian-born in the state in 1860 (29). At work on
farms and in the nearby forests Wisconsin's Belgians
prospered and were fed by increments of newcomers
almost all of whom settled in the original Brown, Door,
and Kewaunee colonies. By 1910 there were 14,000
Wisconsinites of Belgian parentage, 4,020 of them born
in Belgium. Most still resided in the same counties,
although smaller settlements sprang up in Superior and
in urban settings such as Milwaukee. Most concentrated
on agriculture and many Belgian farms in 1905 exceeded
county averages for value and income, but fell below
state averages. Predominantly Catholic, the Belgians
avoided the intragroup animosity that beset the Hollanders. Where Protestant and Catholic Belgians lived
side by side, they sometimes helped each other construct and finance their respective churches (30).
Belgian influence in polling places came early when in
1858 their priest, Xavier Martin, marched 230 of them
to the voting booths, double file, with ballots already
marked. For years thereafter Martin served as their
elected justice of the peace, town clerk, school super-

intendent, and registrar of deeds. Ironically, the
Belgians veered from the pattern of their fellow Catholics by voting Republican except for the Bennett Law
election. In the seven most Belgian townships, all in
Brown, Kewaunee, and Door counties, the Republicans
consistently averaged in excess of 70 percent of the
vote. La Follette was not popular in the Belgian
counties, probably because he alienated a congressman
from that area, while Roosevelt secured impressive
pluralities.

Bohemians differed from the Dutch and the Belgians
by settling in scattered areas throughout the state
(31). The first arrivals acquired farms adjacent to
the Belgians and the Dutch in Kewaunee and northern
Manitowoc counties. By 1870 colonies of Bohemians were
in Racine, Crawford, Grant, and Richland counties.
Later-arriving Bohemians and settlers from the established areas moved into Wood, Barron, Shawano, Marathon, Langlade, St. Croix, Oconto, and Pierce counties
(32). By 1900 there were 36,000 descendants of Bohemian parentage in Wisconsin, of whom 14,145 were foreign-
born. By 1910 it would appear that they had increased,
although by that time the census categorized them among
the Austrians, leaving us to guess their numerical
strength.

The Wisconsin Czechs came primarily from southern
Bohemia (the provinces of Plzen (Pilsen) and Ceske
Budejovice (Budweis), the most Slavic, least Germanized
portion of the old kingdom. Although many left to
escape Habsburg oppression and Germanizing influences
in their homeland, the fact is that in Wisconsin the
Bohemian settlements were associated with or contiguous
to German communities. Their settlement, like that of
the Germans, began by 1860 and thrived in two widely
disparate sections, the one along the eastern lakeshore
in Racine, Milwaukee, Manitowoc, and Kewaunee counties,
the other on the western side of the state in La
Crosse, Vernon, Grant, Crawford, Richland, and Pierce
counties. Most Czechs were initially farmers although
some drifted into the larger cities, and after the
1860s migrated from Wisconsin to western states, especially Saline County, Nebraska. Thus while Czech immigration to the United States exceeded 75,000 between
1870 and 1890, Wisconsin experienced a net decrease.

Bohemians came to Wisconsin, not in search of
religious freedom but for economic betterment. Al-

though they arrived slightly too late for the best
farmland, they proved themselves tenacious, had low
tenancy ratios on farms, and enjoyed a high percentage
of debt-free ownership. Their farms in 1905 in Manitowoc and Kewaunee counties were valued in excess of
the state average, although on a statewide basis their
income per farm fell considerably below the average
(33). Most Bohemians were Catholic although a sizeable
number were Freethinkers, anticlerical, and abrasive to
the Catholics. Freethought was a continuous and divi-
sive problem. Expatriated revolutionaries from the
Prague uprising of 1848 succeeded in de-Catholicizing
urban Bohemians in Wisconsin but in the rural areas
they remained the most Catholic of Czech groups in
America. A major difficulty was procuring Czech-speak-
ing clergymen. When such did arrive, they often found
churches that had been built by laymen who were reluctant to surrender them to diocesan ownership. Wisconsin's Czechs were aggressive not only in founding
fraternal societies but also Czech-language newspapers,
particularly in the case of Karel Jonas's _Slavie_ in
Racine and Antonin Novak's _Damacnost_ in Milwaukee.
Politically the Bohemians preferred the Democrats
although there is ample evidence that the minority
Protestant element voted for the Republicans. Leaders
from among them, like Karel Jonas, nominated in 1890
for lieutenant governor, and John Karel, at the head of
the Democratic ticket in 1912, helped stablize the
Bohemians for the Democratic party (34). When Karel
ran again in 1914, the Republican Philipp failed to win
even 30 percent of the ballots in eight of the eleven
Bohemian townships. Nor did the Social-Democrats pick
up many Bohemian votes. The two most Bohemian townships in the state cast their ballots faithfully with
the Democrats, and economic status had little to do
with this determination. Where there was switching, it
was caused apparently by the Germans and other nationalities who were interspersed among them. Rural Bohemians tended to vote alike, no matter what part of
Wisconsin they lived in or what was their income.
    Polish people did not arrive in Wisconsin in numeri-
cal strength until after 1880, when the Polish-born
numbered 5,263. They tripled in strength to 17,660 in
the decade between 1880 and 1890 and doubled again to
31,789 by 1900, at which time there were 74,657 of
Polish parentage in the state. Milwaukee represented

by far the largest settlement in 1900 but some of the
outstate colonies, notably in Portage County, were
large and tenacious. Recruited by the Wisconsin
Central Railway in the 1870s, the settlement in Portage
County was the largest rural Polish community in the
whole United States (35). Many from Prussian Poland
also settled in Trempealeau County around Independence
and subsequently in Marathon, Clark, Brown, Oconto, and
Shawano counties. In addition to Milwaukee, urban
centers developed in Manitowoc, La Crosse, Beaver Dam,
Menasha, Superior, Ashland, and Berlin. Some were
employed in the lumber camps of northern Wisconsin
where a few settled permanently, for example in
Marinette (36). The relatively late arrival of the
Poles left them only poor soils and the cutover areas
(37). Consequently, in 1905 Polish farm values
averaged less than half that for the state and only the
land in one township in Portage County and another in
Trempealeau County came up to the state average. Their
incomes reveal a dismal story in comparison to state
averages. Poles in urban settings were equally rele-
gated to the lower ranks on the income scale. But they
worked hard and sometimes industries such as Patrick
Cudahy Packing recognized their capacities to the
extent that they would hire them ahead of all other
groups. Some, including E. P. Allis (later Allis-
Chalmers), hired them readily but did not try to master
their Polish names, referring to them simply as "Mike
1," "Mike 2," "Mike 3," etc. Polish girls were especially sought after for the knitting industry because
they "appeared to have peculiar aptitude to the work" (38).

Always the Catholic Church was the key ingredient for
successful establishment and maintenance of a Polish
community. Although first and foremost Catholic, the
Poles were also highly conscious of their ethnicity.
Their clergy found it easy to perpetuate the Polish
language, to insist on endogamy, and to build and
operate parochial schools separate from the parishes of
other Catholic nationality groups. For decades into
the twentieth century, Polish priests also resisted
Americanization, including the shortening of Polish
surnames. By the opulence and the excellence of their
churches, the Polish have left their endurable mark on
the Wisconsin landscape. The St. Josaphat Basilica in
Milwaukee is the largest Polish Catholic church in the
United States, and the ones in the tiny hamlet of

Polonia in Portage County and at Independence in
Trempealeau County bear the marks of greatness (39).
Milwaukee incorporated unto itself a Polish city
numbering more than 100,000 by 1910, with seventeen
Polish Catholic parishes and one Polish National Catholic parish, five Polish newspapers, one Polish Catholic
orphanage, three free Polish libraries, a Polish
theater, and over a hundred fraternal societies to
answer its needs (40). By local estimates the Milwaukee Poles in 1890 numbered 30,000. By 1900 the figure
had reached 58,000 and an estimated 90,000 Polish-
Americans by 1920, with perhaps 10,000 more in the
suburbs (41). Nearly 90 percent had come from sections
of their mother country that had been incorporated into
the German Empire, and thus were escaping Bismarck's
Kulturkampf. By comparison, Chicago's Poles were only
36 percent from Germany, 39 percent from Russia, and 25
percent from Austria.
    The Poles in Milwaukee contributed heavily to the
Polish Catholic churches and even mortgaged their homes
to construct the enormous St. Josaphat Basilica, which
nevertheless was forced into receivership in 1910.
Many operated groceries, bakeries, butcher shops, and
saloons. They were not well represented in the professions of lawyers, doctors, architects, etc. Beginning
in 1878, they did well in electing representatives from
the Polish wards, particularly the Fourteenth, to city
and county offices. The Socialist Leo Krzycki was
elected to the city council several times and Republican John C. Kleczk was elected congressman by the
Fourth Congressional District in 1918. Their own
Kosciuszko Guard, formed in 1874, became Company K of
the Wisconsin National Guard. At its armory, built in
1886, the Poles gathered for ethnic celebrations and
rallies. In January 1896 the Poles organized the
Polish Educational Society, which was dedicated to
improving opportunities for children of Polish descent.
Their goal was to secure for Polish children the same
concessions that the Germans had wrung from the School
Board: native-language instruction in the public
schools. But this proposal foundered when the drive
was perceived as an attempt by the more prominent
secular leaders of the Polish community to deal a death
blow to the parochial schools. Next the schools-in-
Polish campaign became entangled with the drive of
Milwaukee Poles to have their own Polish-speaking

bishop. It was years before they got the needed 250
pupils in one school to justify Polish-language public
education. Since Bishops Katzer and Messmer succeeded
each other as German archbishops, the appointment of a
Polish bishop was likewise slow in coming. When Czech-
born Joseph M. Koudelka of Cleveland came to the arch-
diocese in 1911 as auxiliary bishop, the Poles took
little comfort. When Koudelka was transferred to Superior, Edward Kozlowski was finally installed as the
first Wisconsin Polish bishop in January 1914, although
he died shortly thereafter. Paul Rhode, born in Prussian Poland, in 1908 became the first Polish bishop in
the United States. Having studied at St. Francis Seminary in Milwaukee, he was consecrated and first assigned in Chicago in 1908 before being transferred in
1915 to Green Bay. The same year Father Francis
Conczak established in Milwaukee the first three units
of the schismatic Polish National Catholic Church,
begun in the East a good decade earlier by Anton Kos-
lowski (42).

In politics the Poles exhibited a willingness to
fight for what they could achieve. Led by their concerned clergy, they learned the rules in struggles with
their German-speaking bishops of Milwaukee. Politics
sometimes was but an extension of religious in-fighting. Almost universally they supported the Democratic
party, returning 90 percent majorities for the ticket
in Portage County and in the Polish wards of Milwaukee.
By threatening to run third-party candidates, which
they did since the municipal elections of 1886, the
Poles repeatedly reminded the Democrats that they held
the balance of power in Milwaukee. Priests drove home
the point, on occaison threatening that parishioners
could not be considered Catholics if they did not
support the Democratic ticket. Priests also opened
parish halls to Democratic campaigners, preached Democratic "virtues" from the pulpit, and if necessary
turned over the chancel to a candidate. Because of
heated internal church fighting, priestly control began
to wane around 1910, with the result that the Social-
Democrats among the Poles grew in direct proportion as
the Democratic party lost ground. Out in the Polish
rural areas, only Presidents Roosevelt and Taft won
more than 20 percent of the total vote in 1912. Most
of the voters displayed a tough and durable aversion to
the Republican party, even when completely surrounded

by Republicans, such as by the Scandinavians in Trempealeau County. The one characteristic about the Polish vote was that it could be mobilized as a bloc only for the Democrats.

The Irish were in Wisconsin from territorial days. Unlike some settlers from continental Europe, they were not strongly attached to the land. But like their confreres from the British Isles, they knew the English language and could move both geographically and politically, bettering their chances along the way. Compact Irish communities were the exception rather than the rule and, by 1910, the few that had existed were rapidly dispersing. Only the township of Erin Prairie in St. Croix County had a majority of Irish heads of families in the year 1905. In this township, both land value and personal income were substantially ahead of the state average. Likewise, in urban Milwaukee, Irish ward dwellers had moved up into middle-class status (43). The Irish were Catholic and Democratic. They understood how to rise to the top in the Catholic hierarchy and in a political party. In both spheres of power, they exercised influence well beyond their numerical strength. Milwaukee's Third Ward was largely Irish until a fire in 1892 dispersed them. By 1905 the Italians had taken over that territory. Since Wisconsinites were permitted to cross over in the primaries, the Irish voted Republican, especially in the 1906 and 1910 primaries. When they voted Republican, they supported Progressive candidates as a rule, but neither La Follette nor his supporters were ever able to convince the Irish to come over to the Republican side in a general election. When the stakes were final, the Irish remained staunchly Catholic and Democratic.

The Swiss were strong in the villages of New Glarus and Monroe in Green County, and especially in the Fountain City area of Buffalo County. In both counties the election returns favored the Republicans, especially the stalwarts, illustrating a conservative streak in Swiss voting behavior. Most attended the German Reformed Church and were prosperous. It is hard to detect whether they ever voted as an ethnic bloc, because they moved easily among the Protestant Germans and were often close neighbors to Norwegians and other Republican voters. Representing the New Glarus area, John Luchsinger served long and well in the Wisconsin state legislature but claimed that his countrymen were

reticent in political matters. In the heaviest Swiss
townships, farms were valued in 1905 at nearly double
state averages and per farm income for New Glarus was
the highest of any rural area, far in excess of the
state average. Other Wisconsin Swiss settlements included agricultural concentrations in Sauk, Dane, Iowa,
Dodge, Rock, and Lafayette counties, and a large urban
gathering in Milwaukee (44). The real home of the
Swiss in Wisconsin remains Green County, where the
Wilhelm Tell festival occurs annually in New Glarus
over the Labor Day weekend.

The Austrians in Wisconsin were numerous, with
15,000 in the first and second generations in 1900 (by
1910 the census included Bohemians and others in
Austrian totals), but were scattered and all too easily
identified with the Germans. The township of Lima in
Pepin County had a majority of Austrians. There they
formed a Catholic--and a musically talented--island in
a Scandinavian sea, but nowhere else in the state did
they comrpise the largest ethnic group in an identifiable civic area. The island charcter at Lima extended
to their Democratic voting patterns in a solidly Republican seascape. The highest vote ever elicited by a
Republican in Lima was by La Follette in 1902, with 25
percent of the total.

Germans easily made up the largest element in Wisconsin. In 1890 there were 259,819 German born in
Wisconsin, a figure that explodes to 551,834 when we
include those of German parentage. This figure ballooned to just under 710,000 in 1900, surpassing by
100,000 the entire population of old stock Americans in
Wisconsin. The figures for 1910 are 233,284 German
born and 396,640 of German parentage--630,000 total.
There were more than four and a half times as many
Germans as Norwegians, the second most numerous foreign
stock in the state. At the beginning of the twentieth
century, the Germans accounted for 34.8 percent of the
total population and nearly 50 percent of those with
foreign parentage (45). Although more than three-
quarters of a million Germans immigrated to Wisconsin
the group was from the outset heterogeneous. Not even
rural communities were able to preserve for long the
uniformity of religion and dialect. In the solidly
German counties of Ozaukee, Dodge, Calumet, Washington, and Jefferson, as well as in the German sections
of others, there usually stood three different German

churches: one Lutheran, one Catholic, and at least one
other German Protestant denomination, sometimes an
Evangelical, sometimes a Reformed, sometimes a German
Methodist or Baptist. While the religious splits were
often bitter, the dialect variations, too, markedly
soured North and South Germans from each other. Language differences usually had religious ties.
Religious differences were the reasons for early
German immigration to Wisconsin. The Lutherans came to
protest their disagreement with the Prussian Union of the
Reformed and Lutheran churches into a State Church.
The Forty-eighters came because they had attempted
unsuccessfully to initiate a democratic government in
the Revolutions of 1848. These were not in sympathy
with the conservative Lutherans, who resisted the
Union, or with their mundane countrymen, the Catholics.
During Bismarck's running battle (Kulturkampf) with the
Catholic Church in Germany between the years 1871 and
1878, many Catholics arrived in Wisconsin. While these
three groups came for reasons of protest, thousands
more came for economic improvement, perhaps to avoid
military service, or to join satisfied family members
or acquaintances already in Wisconsin. The latter
swelled Wisconsin's German element, particularly from
1880 to 1910. The anti-Prussian Alt-Lutheraner, as
they called themselves, arrived first and settled especially in Ozaukee County near Milwaukee. After the
achievement of statehood, Wisconsin got a German-speaking bishop, John Martin Henni, who attracted many German Catholics from the Prussian Rhine provinces. Soon
the counties of Dane, Sauk, Washington. Sheboygan,
Calumet, and central Manitowoc, in additin to Milwaukee, were populated heavily by German Catholics, largely southern Germans. The Protestants, usually northern
Germans, were in the majority in southern Ozaukee,
Dodge, Jefferson, and in much of Urban Milwaukee. Mainly Protestant settlements developed in Marquette, Marathon, and Shawano counties, although there were Catholics interspersed in most of these. La Crosse and
Buffalo also had mixed Protestant and Catholic German
settlements, as did the counties of Wood, Waushara, and
Green Lake. Germans seemed to have a good eye for fine
soil and for good access to markets by waterways.
Later they settled along railroads, notably the
Wisconsin Central.
As a rule Germans, whatever the religious affilia-

tion, exhibited good farming skills, paid careful
attention to livestock breeding, and stayed permanently
on the land (46). German diligence, willingness to
accept change, and readiness to experiment with new
methods paid off handsomely, for German farms in the
southeastern counties of Wisconsin had both the highest
land values and the best annual incomes in the state.
Only a few Swiss townships had equally high farm
incomes. In county after county, those areas with the
largest percentages of Germans were the most prosperous
(47). Germans in the urban areas also prospered, dominating the enormous brewing industry and participating
in many industrial activities. In addition, the German
laboring force possessed skills acquired before leaving
their native land that gave them an economic edge in
urban Wisconsin. Much has been said about the German
Forty-eighters, intellectuals who came to Wisconsin in
the early 1850s (48). Actually the number of these
individuals is extremely slight in comparison to the
hundreds of thousands of simple folk who were less
interested in government at home or in the Fatherland
than in securing for themselves a better life. German
observance of the Sabbath incited Republican Yankee
reactions, which nudged the masses of simple Germans
into the Democratic party, where they remained despite
efforts of the Republican Forty-eighters during the
Civil War and thereafter. Positive effects of the
Forty-eighters were felt primarily in Milwaukee, which
bloomed with German theater, music, poetry, the arts,
debating clubs, and free libraries. Likewise, the
Turner societies (gymnastics) and secular private
schools were organized wherever German men of letters
settled. Milwaukee in the 1870s housed national German-
American institutions including the Gymnastic College
and the German-American Teachers' Seminary (49).

In many respects the Forty-eights were a religious
group in their own right, for they were vitriolic in
their attacks on both Lutheran and Catholic clerics,
supercilious in their attitudes toward their uneducated
countrymen, and impertinent toward newcomers who wanted
to retain the conservatism of the Old Country in
Wisconsin (50). In the long run, some but not many
Germans were converted to their style of life. Consequently the effective leadership that the Forty-
eighters could have provided in politics was severely
handicapped. In response to their brash affront, Ger-

man Lutherans as well as Catholics became more conservative than might otherwise have been the case (51). To this day, the Wisconsin Lutheran Synod is doctrinally among the most conservative of Lutheran bodies in America. Conservatism and the success of Germany after the Franco-Prussian War of 1870-71 served to instill in Wisconsin's Germans a sense of pride in the Fatherland. In the 1870-1890 period this development boosted <u>Klein Deutschland</u> and retarded the process of Americanization. Perhaps animosity toward the German element during World War I would have been less pronounced if the Germans had not been so self-satisfied with their ethnic heritage from 1875 to 1915 (52). For these complicated reasons, the Germans made no great contributions to the political life of Wisconsin. Not until 1939, when Julius F. Heil took office, was a German-born governor elected, although Lieutenant Governor Edward Salomon served capably during the Civil War after Harvey died in 1862. The only German-speaking senator to be elected from Wisconsin prior to World War I was Paul O. Husting of Dodge County and he was never pro-German in his political views. Only a few Germans served in the House, none before 1878. The most prominent ethnic German (he was Austrian) in Congress was Victor L. Berger, the Social-Democrat, who scarcely commanded the respect of Wisconsin's German Catholics and Lutherans. Still, Berger did sweep into office again and again from his base in Milwaukee and the surrounding area, which kept him in the House of Representatives for years, even when that august body threw him out. No other politician of German stock in Wisconsin ever came near achieving the board support accorded to Berger. In spite of the Berger success, the fact remains that except for the Bennett Law issue in 1890, the Germans in Wisconsin never voted as an ethnic bloc. Besides that law, only liquor-limitation laws from time to time succeeded in uniting the Germans of Wisconsin.

Germans were divided along religious lines. The Freethinkers and many Protestants supported the Republicans; German Catholics, the Democrats. Prohibitionist tendencies of Republicans alienated most Germans. The Republicans more or less counted on the Freethinkers to articulate their ideas among the Germans. During the 1890 elections these liberals were either too old, and therefore incapable, or on the wrong side of

the issue, and therefore discredited, and were replaced
as political spokesmen by Catholic of Lutheran clergymen. The 1890 election illustrated that not only could
they swing an election if they had to, but that they
would do it for the sake of their culture if forced
into a corner. In the short run they won a tremendous
victory. In the long run, the victory proved their
undoing because it made non-German Wisconsinities wary
of German behavior, setting the stage for the World War
I debacle. Perhaps the fears were unwarranted. In
Milwaukee in 1898 and 1900 the Republicans ran Germans
for mayor, men who spoke English so haltingly that
younger German voters withheld their votes and the
candidates were defeated. Internecine strife crippled
German electoral effectiveness. In 1890 Democrats
tried to capitalize on German support by running German-
born, Protestant Louis Bomrich, formerly City Attorney
of Kenosha, for governor. Their strategy failed. Bomrich was a lackluster campaigner who left himself open
to charges of both anti-Semitism and strong anti-German
feelings, charges he stridently denied (53). German
Democrats were disastrously unsuccessful between 1900
and 1914. Adolph C. Schmitz tried repeatedly in vain
for the gubernatorial nomination as a progressive Democrat.

Above all, the Germans in Wisconsin disapproved of
the direct democracy that La Follette advocated. They
also resisted women's suffrage, fearing that women
would quickly implement prohibition. Led now by their
clergymen, the Germans were under the influence of
instinctively conservative men, made so in part by
overly liberal and anticlerical Forty-eighters. Clergymen's fears were revived in the early twentieth century
by Social-Democrats of the Victor Berger ilk. Only
gradually did German Catholics espouse social reform,
not by supporting Socialists but by working from within
their own "social-justice" organization orchestrated by
German-speaking Archbishop Sebastian G. Messmer of
Milwaukee (54). In 1910 the Republicans lost heavily
in German areas. In Sheboygan County, where the liquor
question was raised by the Democrats, the loss for the
Republicans ranged up to 24 percent. Marathon County
reported a coalition of Democrats with stalwart Republicans to defeat the Progressives and the village of
Kiel in Manitowoc was the first out-state unit to go
Social-Democrat. In 1912 German defection from the
Republicans continued and even Theodore Roosevelt's

1904 popular success in the German areas of Wisconsin declined dramatically. Emanuel Philipp, although of German-Swiss extraction, did little to recapture the German vote in the election of 1914 (55).

A difference between rural Germans and urban German laborers is evident from studying the German wards in Milwaukee, Sheboygan, and Manitowoc. Here the Social-Democratic vote moved up on the plus column but none of these wards was ever as unanimous as obtained in German rural areas, where a strong correlation existed between Protestant-Republican as compared to Catholic-Democratic townships. Voting was not dependent upon family income. Wealthy German Catholics in Dane County voted exactly as Democratic as the much less prosperous German farmers in the Marshfield area. Two highly prosperous townships, Lake Mills in Jefferson County and Herman in Dodge County, both with incomes per farm double that of the state average, split respectively between Republican-Protestant in the one and Democratic-Catholic in the other. Ozaukee County illustrates a similar religious bias in German voting (56). Throughout Wisconsin's political history the German vote was always affiliated with religion. Switching parties occurred only within the non-Catholic element. Such prominent Americans as La Follette did not have substantive German support before 1916, nor was it courted more than occasionally. Unwittingly, however, La Follette Progressivism may have opened up politics to the common man so that the Germans were drawn to take stands as individuals rather than as block voters, which may have helped them abandon their _Deutschtum_ in favor of Americanization after World War I. In that sense, the Progressive Era conditioned the Germans for the World War I experience, which hastened this largest of all ethnic groups in Wisconsin along the road toward assimilation.

Chapter Seven
Wisconsin's Hyphens and World War I

When the opening shots were fired during August 1914 in
Europe, President Woodrow Wilson admonished Americans
to be "impartial in thought as well as in action" (1).
A United States declaration of war would not be enacted
for two and a half years, but the war against "hyphen-
ism" at home began in thought and action by 1915.
Newspapers blasted off verbal salvos supported by car-
toonists' artillery (2). The United States in 1915 had
just completed half a century of unprecedented immigration. Between 1890 and 1914 immigration had been
especially large from the "alien" areas of Europe,
notably Italy and the Austro-Hungarian Empire as well
as from Germany. Poland had contributed an estimated 1
million immigrants from 1889 to 1910, Italy 2.7 million, and the Germans were still coming at a rate of
more than 30,000 each year from 1900 to 1914 (3). Many
of the nationality groups by 1914 were gradually assim-
ilating into American society, but there had not been
enough time for the nation to absorb its immigrants.
Sympathies with mother countries were fostered in
ethnic enclaves by the foreign-language press, ethnic
churches, and parochial schools, which were maintained
partly to teach dogma, partly to preserve ethnic cultures. During World War I campaigns were mounted to
suppress usage of any but the English language, which
proponents called the "American Language," although
outright proscriptions on non-English languages were
enacted only after the United States entered the war in
1917. Generally such action was taken by state coun-
cils of defense, but often school boards bowed on their
own to public sentiment. Irish-Americans were also
antagonized by the pro-British stance of the Wilson
administration (4).

Fearful of the vast numbers of first- and second-
generation immigrants in the United States, pro-British
forces stirred up a tempest of intolerance and a demand

for conformity that was unheard of before or since in American history. Violent words and violent laws created violent individuals—outbursts of hysteria that in today's calmer atmosphere, are difficult to comprehend. Wisconsin's experience during this time was not entirely different from that of the rest of the states, but the presence of certain leaders, notably Robert M. La Follette and Victor L. Berger, intensified feelings and attracted the unfavorable attention of the nation. Senator La Follette as well as nine of Wisconsin's eleven congressmen voted against the Declaration of War on April 6, 1917, in the belief that they were voting the wishes of their constituents. This near-unanimous opposition to the war on the part of Wisconsin's legislators gave credence to the national view that Wisconsin was pro-German. The Milwaukee Journal therefore launched a crusade to rid Wisconsin of its disloyalty image, pleading on December 7, 1917:

> We want no more German-American banks, or Polish-American restaurants, or Italian-American bond companies, or Deutscher Clubs. . . . This is America. America it must be, wholly and unitedly, for all time to come. And, any club, society, company, or organization that retards or conflicts with that spirit should change its purpose, close up, or be put out of existence. Appeal to racial or alien ties must be forever banished from American soil.

For waging a successful campaign to turn back the opinion that Milwaukee was "the disloyal city," the Pulitzer Prize Committee in 1919 awarded a gold medal for meritorious service to Milwaukee Journal editor Lucius W. Nieman (5).

The "disloyal" charge was inextricably linked to La Follette, the colorful politician who was unswervingly opposed to the war. Unlike his colleagues, he found it politically unsafe to join his onetime cohorts for neutrality who now supported American participation. In the nation's press he was virulently attacked. From the outbreak of the war to its conclusion, he fought a lonely battle for strict neutrality, contending that nothing in the conflict was of enough concern to the American people to warrant a single American soldier's death (6). Believing in the Wisconsin model as articulated by McCarthy, Howe, and himself, La Follette con-

sidered military preparedness the height of foolishness
not only because it could lead to commitment but because it detracted the public from its agenda of reform
politics. In Congress, he introduced a resolution
calling for the nationalization of the armaments industry. Although unsuccessful, he did get the 1916 Rev-
enue Act, which provided America its first excess-
profits tax on munitions. He also opposed loans made
to belligerents through American banks and supported
the Gore-McLemore Resolution, which warned Americans
against traveling on vessels of belligerent nations
(7). La Follette's behavior secured for him the loyalty of Wisconsin hyphenates, but it cost him the support
of prominent state leaders. Irvine L. Lenroot, Nils P.
Haugen, and the editor of the Wisconsin State Journal
denounced the senator for his opposition to the war.
The state legislature passed a resolution condemning
him. Even the University of Wisconsin, which had been
the key component in his drive for Progressivism, ob-
jected. Its president, Charles R. Van Hise, and 418
faculty members signed a petition to

> protest against those utterances and actions of
> Senator Robert M. La Follette which have given aid
> and comfort to Germany and her allies in the present
> war; we deplore his failure to support the govern-
> ment in the prosecution of the war. (8)

Believing that the United States would remain "impartial in thought as well as action," the Wisconsin
Germans in 1914 emotionally sided with the Fatherland,
not necessarily with its war objectives. German Red
Cross drives were especially successful in the state.
German war bonds were bought readily in the German
areas and German newspapers tried vigorously to bend
public opinion by alleging British perfidy and the
dangers of a Yellow peril (9). Letters arriving in
Wisconsin from relatives in Germany illustrate the
ideological commitment of the German people to the
righteousness of their cause: the war had been forced
upon them by their jealous enemies, France, Russia, and
England, who feared their industrial capacity and their
rapid emergence as a world power. Base greed on the
part of the English drove the French and Belgians into
preparations for an attack on Germany. Should Germany
have permitted French air surveillance and motorized

access through Belgium to continue? No, the German
relatives of Wisconsin citizens argued, they should
immediately outstrip contemptible and brutal England.
The German cousins further explained to their Wisconsin
readers,

> Under our constitutional monarchy in Germany we have
> a government more absolutely honorable, reliable,
> intelligent, uncorrupted, and honest than has ever
> been found in the world. . . . In whatever pertains
> to civil freedom, we feel that we, by our system of
> order, honesty, and exactness, are just as fortunate
> as the freest Americans. (10)

Wisconsin had an active chapter of the National
German-American Alliance (11). State membership was
37,000 while the national total was over 2 million. In
1914 Wisconsin's chapter president was German-born Leo
Stern, who served as assistant superintendent of
Milwaukee public schools. On August 28, 1914, Stern
addressed a crowd of more than 11,000 gathered at the
Milwaukee Auditorium, where he called for support of
Wilson's declaration of neutrality. The following
November 13, 1914, at least 7,000 Milwaukeeans gathered
in the name of the Alliance to hear Dr. Eugene
Kühnemann of Breslau University address them for two
hours concerning the chances of German victory. At
this meeting $1,000 was collected for the German Relief
Fund (12). When in May 1915, off the Irish coast, a U-
boat sank the Cunard liner *Lusitania*, and 128 Americans
lost their lives, the United States public was
outraged. In hopes of forcing Wilson to adhere to his
promise of neutrality, Leo Stern in June sent the
president a telegram declaring that "40,000 members and
an overwhelming majority of the citizens of our state
are opposed to drastic action against Germany."
In June 1915, veterans of the German and Austro-
Hungarian armies numbering 10,000 gathered in the
Milwaukee Pabst Park for a picnic and to hear speeches
in defense of Germany and the German-Americans (13).
In July 1916 the state chapter of the German National
Alliance held its annual meeting in Marshfield, where
they protested the United States drift from neutrality.
In October Leo Stern addressed an audience assembled to
hear the German Sea Battalion Band, which, returning
home from China, was interned in the United States for

the duration of the war. Having turned the Milwaukee
Auditorium into a beer garden, waitresses served beer
and wine in costume, Gemütlichkeit prevailed, and
German songs wafted to the rafters, the only non-German
number being the Star-Spangled Banner. When Stern
proclaimed that German armies would soon march into
Paris, crowds cheered wildly. Nor did anyone object
that the band's appearance was to raise money for
German and Austrian war victims (14). The greatest
spectacle of this nature occurred in March 1916, when
the Charity War Bazaar was also held in the Milwaukee
Auditorium. Some 25,000 people attended each day and
one day 5,000 had to be turned away. In all, 173,474
passed through its gates, providing receipts of over
$150,000. The best money-making item at the bazaar was
a cross with the letter "W" for Kaiser Wilhelm on which
was embossed the date "1914" in gold lettering. Even
Archbishop Sebastian G. Messmer is supposed to have
contributed. Sales of the crosses alone brought in
$4,115.26.

During the years 1914-1917, the National German-
American Alliance sent a total of $866,481.24 to the
German and Austrian ambassadors for transfer to Europe
for relief purposes, although a goal of $2 million had
been set by its president, Dr. Charles John Hexamer, an
American-born civil engineer of Philadelphia (16). The
Milwaukee Sonntagspost saw no reason why a target of
$10 million could not be met if wealthy German-
Americans would set aside 1 percent of their incomes
for this purpose. Although the amounts received were
much smaller, the Wisconsin chapter employed many
devices to secure contributions. Selling pictures of
Kaiser Wilhelm II and of Emperor Franz Josef was quite
lucrative. Leo Stern brought in a tidy sum when he
auctioned off a greeting card he had received from
Captain Paul König of the Deutschland, a merchant
submarine that had paid a visit to the United States in
July 1916. German-Americans could also sign their
names in a Goldenes Buch honoring the Fatherland at so
much per page (17). Perhaps nothing irritated the
American-on-the-street more than the haughty attitude
assumed by the German-American Alliance. On November
22, 1915, its president addressed an audience in
Milwaukee with bristling criticism of the lowly status
of Yankee American culture: "No one will find us
prepared to step down to a lesser Kultur; no, we have

made it our aim to draw the other up to us . . . to
transmit to the American people the depth of German
feeling, that seeking after all that is good, beauti-
ful, and true." His colleague, the eminent historian
and assistant registrar of copyrights for the Library
of Congress, Ernst Bruncken, appealed to Americans of
German dissent: "It is in the end a blessing rather
than a calamity for any nation . . . to put forward its
whole power and to sacrifice everything for an idea" (18).

Even more infuriating to the American public in
Wisconsin was that a sizable number of Germans were
Socialists and that Milwaukee industry was a hotbed of
Socialist activity (19). The Socialist movement gained
attention in 1888 when prominent labor leaders of the
city met to nominate Herman Kroeger for mayor from
their Union Labor party. A more demanding element
among them was led by Paul Grottkau, who edited the
Arbeiter Zeitung. Renaming it from Union to Socialist
Labor party, Grottkau advocated municipal reforms,
abolition of child labor, stricter factory inspection,
better disposal of industrial waste, the sale of wood
and coal to citizens at cost, and the right to recall
city officials (20). In 1892 a newcomer to the Milwaukee scene took over Grottkau´s Arbeiter Zeitung, re-
titling it the Wisconsin Vorwärts. He was Victor L.
Berger, born in Austria in 1860, who attended universities in Vienna and Budapest before coming to America
in 1878. Active as a teacher of German in the public
schools and in the southside Milwaukee Turnverein
(athletic society), Berger in 1897 married his former
student Meta Schlichting, who not only assisted him in
his editorial and political affairs but held minor
Socialist positions herself. Berger was a short,
stocky, studious, and somber European radical whose
image was enhanced by his mustache, steel-rimmed glas-
ses, and accent (21).

Victor Berger and his Socialists were international
in their outlook. In Wisconsin, however, it was
assumed that socialism and Germanism were synonymous,
because both coalesced in the personaltiy of Mr.
Berger. In 1910 the Socialists swept into municipal
power in Milwaukee and sent Berger to represent the
Fifth District in the House of Representatives, the
first Socialist ever to occupy a seat in that body. In
1916 Socialist Daniel W. Hoan achieved the mayor´s
chair, a victory that had implications not so much as a

Socialist triumph but as an antiwar statement by the
Milwaukee Germans (22). On August 16, 1914, a mere two
weeks after the eruption of war in Europe, the Socialists had organized the International Anti-War and Peace
Demonstration, which perennially ran Eugene Victor Debs
for the United States Presidency. Two days following
the American declaration of war in April 1917 they
published their militant antiwar position, pledging
"continuous action and public opposition to the war
through demonstrations, mass petitions and all other
means within our power." Written at the St. Louis
convention this remained the official Socialist
platform throughout the war. Berger voted for it,
routinely defended it, and only half-heartedly rejected
support of it from pro-German elements in Wisconsin.

In Milwaukee the Socialists gained at the polls in
proportion as the Germans became disillusioned with
Woodrow Wilson. The president in 1916 lost Wisconsin
to Republican Charles E. Hughes, 191,000 to 220,000,
while disenchanted Milwaukeeans gave new victories to
both Mayor Hoan and Representative Berger (23). Although the Socialists opposed Wilson's conscription
bill of May 18, 1917, Berger advised Mayor Hoan to
cooperate and Milwaukee became the first city in the
nation to finish registration. Exceeding Berger's
advice, Hoan arranged Milwaukee Preparedness Day
parades, worked with the Council of Defense, and in all
measures acted in opposition to the St. Louis platform.
Such all-out cooperation with the war effort earned for
Hoan from Socialist party members the despicable title
of "Sewer Socialist." Berger urged greater platform
consistency: "The American people did not want and do
not want this war. They were plagued into this abyss
by the treachery of the ruling class of the country."
Because Hoan worked so hard in support of the war
effort, he faced a bitter battle for re-election in
April 1918, but won comfortably. Immediately the local
Council of Defense tried to remove him from office,
accusing him of winning the "pro-German protest vote"
and "the vote against the war," which it decreed to be
"a most unfortunate thing for Milwaukee" (24). Hoan
retained the mayor's gavel but was ousted from his
chairmanship of a Milwaukee County Council of Defense
Committee.

Victor Berger did not fare as well. Before the
declaration of war he was greatly encouraged by an

unofficial referendum held in Milwaukee under the
auspices of the German-American Alliance, in which
Milwaukeeans voted 300 to 1 against intervention in the
European war. In nearby Monroe, in Green County, which
was almost exclusively Swiss-American, an official
referendum held on the question of intervention pitted
the Monroe Swiss against United States involvement 954
to 95, which the Socialists gladly publicized (25). In
a Sheboygan referendum ballots in both English and
German ("Shall the United States enter the European
War?") were distributed in the churches, yielding 4,112
nays and only 17 ayes (26). Berger mistakenly took
such opposition to the war as a mandate to oppose it
publicly. For those who wanted to take aim at the
hapless Berger, there were plenty of laws on the books.
The Espionage Act of June 15, 1917, made it a crime to
report inexact news, to cause military insubordination,
and to obstruct conscription. Offenses brought fines
and twenty years' imprisonment. The Trading-with-the-
Enemy Act of October 6, 1917, stiffened the former act.
The Sedition Act of May 16, 1918, specified additional
offenses: attempts to obstruct the draft, publication
of disloyal matter, interference with the sale of government bonds, etc. (27).

Victor Berger became a prime target for the government's wrath. In September 1917, his paper, the
Milwaukee Leader, was denied second-class rates, in
effect a fine of $150 a day. Curiously, his German-
language Vorwärts was not denied use of the mails. In
March 1918 the government announced in the middle of
Berger's campaign for the senate seat vacated by the
death of Senator Paul O. Husting that Berger and four
other Socialist leaders had been indicted under the
Espionage Act for conspiracy. His offense stemmed from
editorial articles in the Leader in which he had denounced the draft law. Although he therefore lost the
election to the Republican candidate, Irvine L. Lenroot, Berger made a remarkably strong showing, receiving 110,000 out of a total of 424,000 votes. One-third
came from Milwaukee. He carried eleven of the outstate counties and got over 1,000 votes each in twenty-
eight of them (28). Berger outpolled his rivals by two
to one in the solidly German areas, claiming that his
supporters were converts to socialism. The vote probably meant only that one-fourth of Wisconsin's citizens
disapproved of Wilson's involvement in the war. That

fall Berger ran for re-election to the House of Representatives from the Wisconsin Fifth District and won
with a plurality of 5,470 votes, the largest of his six
victories, even though one week before the election on
November 6, 1918, he was again indicted for conspiracy.
This vote was interpreted as a protest against the war-
induced hysteria that was sweeping Wisconsin. The
following January 1919, Berger was convicted but freed
on bail pending on appeal. When he presented himself
before the House Speaker's desk on May 9, 1919, to be
sworn in, he was challenged. A resolution opposing his
seating was hastily offered and passed without dissent.
Berger was denied all rights as a member of the House
of Representatives.

Once the war ended, Wisconsin supported Berger vigorously. In a special election held in 1919 to fill
his vacant seat, Berger again ran a campaign of pro-
Germanism and opposition to prohibition, the war, and
high prices. On December 19, 1919, when the votes for
the special election were counted, Berger handily won
by 24,350 to 19,566, receiving 40 percent more votes
than he had the previous year. But once again the
House excluded Berger by a vote of 330 to 6, eliciting
from Berger the comment: "Twelve men . . . convicted
me of disloyalty, but 25,000 voters vindicated me, and
it was the duty of the House to seat me" (24). In yet
another election to fill his seat in 1920, Berger lost
in a Harding landslide but, in the non-presidential
year of 1922, was once more elected by the Wisconsin
Fifth District, by which time the Supreme Court had
thrown out his earlier conviction. When Berger now
appeared to take his oath in December 1923, he was
warmly welcomed. In subsequent re-elections he was
successful until 1928, when a Hoover landslide walloped
him. The next year Berger sustained injuries in a
streetcar accident and died on August 7, 1929 (30).

The years 1914-1918 were an age of propaganda, some
of it quite skillfully perpetrated, but much of it
coarsely ground by unperfected mills (31). Suffering
from a double-edged sword of suspicion, Wisconsin sur-
passed other states in implementing the war effort in
order to blunt the adverse propaganda that was hurled
in its face. Called the "50%" American state, Wisconsin was the first to organize a State Council of Defense. Ray Stannard Baker, after inspecting state war
organizations, proclaimed Wisconsin's "the best organ-

ized, the most efficient, the most constructive and the most far-seeing" (32). Less than 2 percent of Wisconsin men of induction age failed to respond to the draft, compared to 8.2 percent for the nation. At state expense Wisconsin equipped its own 20,000-man National Guard and sent it to camp. Under the leadership of Socialist Mayor Hoan, Milwaukee as well as other cities of Wisconsin provided an example for the nation by originating meatless and wheatless days to bolster the war footing. War bonds sold well and conributions by labor and volunteer organizations were laudable.

Not that such face-saving measures were accomplished without difficulty. Wisconsin author Charles D. Stewart in September 1918 wrote a troubled letter to the Atlantic Monthly describing what had taken place in Wisconsin, noting that "the district that has returned Berger has always gone `over the top´ in all wardrives" (33). Behind the propaganda and the negative national image of Wisconsin, Stewart identified enigmatic facts. The Wisconsin legislature had seventeen Socialists in the Assembly and four in the Senate. Washington County, Stewart´s home, which had always been solidly Democratic, during the war years voted Republican first, Socialist second, and sent Wilson "limping along at the rear." While the eastern papers were flailing Wisconsin for pro-Germanism and socialism, Stewart saw something more subtle happening. Much of the voting manifested disapproval of the status quo but could not in any sense be labeled anti-American. Stewart pointed out how behavior had been modified. Because of Wisconsin´s bad press, dealers nationally were refusing to buy goods made in Wisconsin. To protect and reassure itself of markets, Milwaukee had no choice but to "go over the top" in bond drives; this triumph was printed on all of its outgoing letters.

Workmen were persuaded to comply. If one did not, he lost his job or was declared "inessential" and therefore subject to draft. Bond salesmen offered to withhold money from paychecks. Companies readily complied or suffered a loss of business and boycotts. Farmers were tougher to deal with but a group of rough volunteers could usually bring them to sign up. In some instances bond squads brought along a banker to lend the farmer the money to make his liberty loan subscription. If he still refused, they posted yellow

signs on his premises telling passers-by of his failure
to contribute. Anyone who refused to buy was called a
slacker, a Hun, a baby-killer, a Kaiser-lover, an
enemy alien. A lady in Evansville who refused to
purchase bonds was taken from her home, placed in a
lion cage salvaged from a junk dealer, and hauled
around the city square. Eventually Governor Emanuel L.
Philipp felt called upon to protest such incidents.
Philipp's parents had immigrated from the German-speaking canton of Graubünden in Switzerland in 1848 and
settled among Swiss farmers in Sauk County. During
World War I, Philipp's Germanic background was ample
cause for embarrassment and he sometimes bent over
backwards to demonstrate his loyalty (34). Not one
newspaper in or outside Wisconsin issued a word of
opposition to the clearly illegal harassment that
grossly violated civil rights. Given such violations,
the pro-Republican and pro-Socialist votes in Wisconsin
between 1916 and 1921, in the view of Charles D.
Stewart, were not pro-German at all but pro-American in
the best meaning of the word.

Support for Robert M. La Follette during the war
years begs a similar interpretation. In 1916 he was
re-elected over his Democratic opponent by 116,000
votes, a record plurality achieved through the endorse-
ments of Scandinavians, who always liked him, and of
the Germans who originally were not fond of him. The
switch to La Follette of German Catholic voters from
their traditional home in the Democratic party was
noticeable in large cities and was dramatic in the
rural areas. In rural Wisconsin ethnicity was still
operational, causing a defection of the Germans from
Wilson averaging about 15 percent in 1916 as compared
to 1912 (35). The switch of German voters from the
Democrats in the rural areas probably means that the
leaders of large ethnic organizations and the editors
of German-language publications had lost their influence, for they did not shift allegiance until after
America's entry into the war.

The most notable for repudiating their traditional
stance in 1916 were the normally Republican Belgians.
In rural Belgian areas of Wisconsin, the vote resulted
in an astonishing 53 percent majority for Wilson, a
clear protest by Wisconsin Belgians of the invasion of
their homeland by the Germans. The Polish in Milwaukee
and in Portage County seemed satisfied with Wilson's

anti-German posture and held to the Democratic party in
1916. The Irish reflected the fact that the British in
1916 had crushed their Easter Rebellion and executed
its leaders. Astute political campaigners played on
this event when they organized the American Independence Conference on behalf of the American Irish and
Germans. At a meeting in Milwaukee in 1916 they sought
to unite religious and lay leaders behind the Republican candidate, Charles Evans Hughes (36). But religious leaders were reluctant to become involved. At
the outset of the war Swiss-born Archbishop Sebastian
G. Messmer had stood solidly behind the German cause.
Returning from his native Switzerland in 1914, he told
a Milwaukee crowd that he foresaw a German victory:
"The spirit with which the Germans entered into this
war is one that will win, and I can see nothing else
but that the German causes for the war were just" (37).
More cautious of political pitfalls by 1916, Messmer
forbade his priests to take part in the campaign and
leaders of the Wisconsin Central-Verein followed suit (38).

When the 1916 voting in Wisconsin was concluded, the
Irish proved strong in their traditional support of the
Democratic party and could not be swayed toward the
Republican Charles Evans Hughes. In the most Irish
townships of the state, the Democratic vote actually
increased from 66 percent in 1912 to 70 percent in
1916. Nevertheless, Wilson lost Wisconsin by 30,000
votes (49 to 42 percent). The Social Democrats polled
27,000 (6 percent). Wilson suffered declines of percentages in twenty-five counties, of which nineteen were
strongly German. In Marathon County, for example,
Wilson lost votes in all but five of the thirty voting
precincts that had a German population of over 50
percent (39). Dodge County had always been Democratic
and in 1912 Wilson carried the county by 60 percent.
In 1916 Hughes collected well over 50 percent of the
vote and his Republican colleague, Swiss-American
Emanuel L. Philipp, also carried the county. In neighboring Washington County, the Catholic German precinct
of Barton dropped from 72 percent Democratic in 1914 to
only 51 percent Democratic in 1916. This contrasts
with the returns from sample Norwegian precincts, such
as Christiania in Dane County, where party shifts from
1912 to 1916 were nonexistent. Similarly, the Polish
Catholic township of Dodge in Trempealeau County turned
in a 90 percent Democratic vote in 1914 and remained 87

percent Democratic in 1916 (40). Wisconsin over the
next two years became known as the "Kaiser's state."
   The year 1918 gave the national press yet another
chance to focus on the perceived national threat from
the Germans and Socialists in Wisconsin. Senator Paul
O. Husting, a Democrat who had engaged in a vigorous
campaign to curb the influence of the German-American
press, died of a hunting mishap in October 1917. To
any constituent with whom he corresponded, Husting
argued passionately but cogently in favor of Wilson.
Born in Fond du Lac in 1866, the senator's father had
immigrated from Luxembourg in 1855. In 1876 the family
moved to heavily German Mayville, which the young man
left to attend the University of Wisconsin Law School.
In 1902 he was back in strongly German Dodge County
where he served as district attorney until his election
to the Senate in 1906 (41). Following Husting's death,
Governor Philipp called for a special primary on March
19 and an election on April 2, 1918. Many contenders
waged the primary campaign for the senate seat. Victor
Berger ran on the Socialist ticket and the Republican
slate included three: James Thompson, a Norwegian-
American lawyer from La Crosse who was backed by La
Follette; ex-Governor Francis McGovern, who was despised by La Follette since their fallout of 1912, and
the Swedish-American Congressman Irvine L. Lenroot.
The Democratic choice was Joseph E. Davies.
   Because of La Follette's antiwar image, supporters
of Lenroot were able to smear Thompson as a disloyal
Republican. McGovern withdrew and the Norwegian Thompson narrowly lost to the Swedish Lenroot by 2,400
votes. Thompson, however, secured a majority of the
vote in almost every county with a large percentage of
Germans, including the very Democratic counties of
Jefferson, Dodge, and Washington, obviously because of
La Follette's antiwar stance. The primary election
results were complicated by the support Berger was able
to bleed away from the two major parties in the metro-
politan German centers. In the Davies versus Lenroot
heat for the general election, Davies argued that a
vote for him was a vote for Wilson. The president,
therefore, warmly endorsed Davies as did most of the
nation's political pundits. Before an audience of
5,000 in Madison shortly before the balloting, Wilson's
vice president, Thomas R. Marshall, spoke for Wilson on
behalf of Davies and against Lenroot: "Your state of

Wisconsin is under suspicion. . . . If the vote at the
primary is based upon the charges and countercharges you
have made each against the other, you are about half
for America, half for the Kaiser, and all against
Wilson. . . . Lenroot is now bidding for the vote of
the German sympathizer, the traitor, the seditionist,
the pacifist (42).

After Marshall's inflammatory speech, the Republican
Lenroot cleverly switched his campaign to portray himself as the true American patriot. He openly criticized the national administration for interfering in
Wisconsin's affairs and for smearing his loyalty. As a
result, Lenroot won handily with a plurality of 15,000
votes. Nevertheless, he collected the lowest percentage of the total vote of any Republican candidate
during the decade. The real "referendum" in this 1918
special senate seat election was expressed in the votes
split between Berger and Davies. Berger got four times
as many votes as the Socialists normally attracted, and
the national press quickly attributed Berger's success
to the "traitor vote." The Milwaukee Journal, Wilson's
most loyal mouthpiece in Wisconsin, sourly observed
that now the state had two La Follettes in the Senate
(43). Senator Irvine Lenroot was not loved by the
Germans. Then Representative Lenroot and only one
other Wisconsin legislator had joined Senator Husting in
voting for Declaration the previous April. While he
spoke ambivalently about women's rights, he was in tune
with his Swedish element in favoring both prohibition
and suffrage (44). When Lenroot was sworn in on April
17, 1918, by Vice President Marshall, both men were
noticeably embarrassed. Immediately after the cere-
mony, Marshall summoned the first Swedish-American
United States Senator over to his desk, where he apolo-
gized for his verbal drubbing in Madison, explaining
that his speech had come from "higher up" (45).

Meanwhile in the classrooms and churches of Wisconsin a battle was raging over the use of non-English
languages. The word "English," in fact, was supplanted
by the "American language" as the controversy over the
allowable use of the "enemy language" escalated. In
Milwaukee, 53 percent of the people were of German
background and 20 percent spoke German exclusively.
German was required in the schools unless special permission had been obtained for exemption, and the city
school system had hired a special assistant superin-

tendent to supervise and promote German instruction. He was none other than Leo Stern, who served simultaneously as state chapter president of the German-American Alliance. The Milwaukee Journal contended that in language, customs, literature, and attitude toward the law, the citizens of Wisconsin bore more similarity to Germany than to Britain or France (46). In most of Wisconsin's parochial schools German was not only taught but was the language of discourse and instruction. Churches conducted services in German. Theater in Milwaukee and musical organizations throughout the state functioned predominantly in the German language. Hundreds of Wisconsin newspapers were being published in German and read widely. Assistant superintendent Stern had the poor taste of acclaiming as late as 1918, "I confess Germanism intellectually and morally, and Americanism only politically (47). The Milwaukee Journal responded that the school board should not be using tax money to pay teachers to teach the enemy language. When a man wrote from Kiel, Wisconsin in defense of German, the Journal asserted that young children were leaving school without mastering either language, and that it was not the German language that was being taught in these classes but German ideas. Wisconsin soldiers encamped at Camp MacArthur in Waco, Texas, had to be taught English because they did not know how to respond to military commands in English (48).

In the face of an artillery barrage by "American Language" proponents, the Turnverein, Liederkranz, Männerchor, and Musikverein all adopted resolutions calling for retention of foreign-language instruction in the schools. The English press countered by urging parents to elect to their school boards members who would promise to discontinue German (49). In Madison, Theodore M. Hammond, President of the University Board of Regents, called for a ban on German-language instruction except at the university level and urged the elimination of all foreign-language newspapers. He gratuitously asked that no one do business with any firm in the state that contained the name of any foreign nation in its title (50). In various school districts committees were established to recommend changes in the German curriculum. In Wausau the board split 6-4 in favor of retaining German and one of the members publicly attacked those citizens who "through

race pride and prejudice, find some difficulty in
realizing that they are Americans fighting Germany."
Using the terminology of a later World War, he scathed
his colleagues for having "a racial question settled on
racial lines" (51). The Milwaukee committee on German
texts voted to exclude from courses in German all books
containing references to German history and German
songs. The Deutscher Club changed its name to the
Wisconsin Club. In Baraboo, pranksters gathered for a
bookburning of high-school German-language texts, after
which they wrote in the ashes for the photographer,
"Here lie the remains of German in B. H. S." (52).
Americanizers argued that the German language was being
promoted in Wisconsin at public expense, as a required
course in many districts, including the Milwaukee
public schools. They claimed that in certain schools
the children sang "Die Wacht am Rhein" and "Deutschland
über Alles," but that not a single one could name the
American national anthem, let alone sing by heart a
stanza of "The Star-Spangled Banner."

Milwaukee's superintendent of schools ordered that
no German be spoken on school playgrounds by students
or teachers. He followed with an order that teachers
tear out of all books the pages that had the poem "Die
Wacht am Rhein" printed on them (53). The association
of directors of fifteen Milwaukee church choirs forbade
the singing of German Christmas carols in 1918, including even "Silent Night" (54). When the war ended with
the armistice of November 1918, only one school in the
entire Milwaukee system was still offering German (55).
Americanizers argued that to make Wisconsinites think
German the conspirators of Teutonism had forced them
to speak German. Allegedly this was accomplished
through a secret conspiracy at the University of Wisconsin, where a spokesman for the German teachers'
association had said, "Above and before all, we must
firmly establish the German tongue in our grade
schools" (56). Resentful alumni also charged that the
evidence incriminated the University of Wisconsin,
where twenty-seven instructors were employed in the
German department while all other languages were represented by only twenty-six instructors. German was
required for graduation. Critics claimed that the
Board of Regents' lopsided German program constituted
"obvious propaganda."

The Wisconsin Council of Defense was an official

organization proclaimed by Governor Philipp and modeled
on the national one. The Loyalty Legion was a private
but popular movement established in the fall of 1917 as
the result of a petition by 150,000 signers who sought
to "repudiate, in the name of Wisconsin, every disloyal
word and deed calculated to misrepresent her and her
people" (57). The Loyalty Legion offered patriotic
education to lift Wisconsin's name from the list of
disloyal states, and to promote teamwork in spreading
loyalty. It enjoyed full franking privileges and operated a speakers' bureau. Some of its founders wanted
the Loyalty Legion to evolve into a political body that
would rid the state of "such men as La Follette and
Berger" and force the dissolution of the "Philipp-
Berger-La Follette pro-German alliance" (58). With
only 70,000 members at its peak, the Legion was not
politically powerful, but it exerted influence well
beyond the scope of its membership.

Incidents of seditious behavior were recorded in
Wisconsin, but few were attributed to a single ethnic
group. Cases were reported where Hollanders were unwilling to sign petitions touting the state's loyalty;
for instance, in one town of three hundred Hollanders
only three signers came forward. In agricultural
areas, the Swedes were "duly indifferent to the war;
not actively disloyal so much as stolidly and selfishly
unloyal." Some said Wisconsin had not failed in the
war effort so much as in her assimilation efforts.

It has not secreted enough digestive juice to
dissolve its foreign elements. Scattered around its
surface are little communities which retain each its
own nationality. Not German alone, but Polish,
Bohemian, Dutch, Swedish, Norwegian, Belgian. A
traveler among these people finds himself in an
alien land. . . . Here and now is Uncle Sam's opportunity to make this nephew state truly one of the
family. (59)

By war's end, a number of Wisconsin citizens had
been hauled into court on charges of violating one of
five laws: threats against the president, selective
service, espionage, trading with the enemy, and sabo-
tage (60). Under the Threats Act, seventy persons were
indicted and seven penalized. There were German-Americans among this group but ethnicity was not the decid-

ing factor. Under the Selective Service Act of 1917,
hundreds of men were indicted for draft or registration
violations but conflict of conscience more than ethnic
loyalty was at issue. A celebrated case of draft
dodging involved Congressman John M. Nelson of Madison
and his son, Byron. In Congress since 1906, Nelson
supported La Follette (managing his campaign for the
presidency in 1924) and voted against declaring war.
Byron, a student at the university, was dispatched
during the summers to Alberta, Canada, to run a family
farm. Both father and son were indicted, the former
for conspiracy, the latter for draft evasion, but both
indictments were quashed by a federal judge in January
1918 (61).

Under the Espionage act there were 2,000 actions
nationwide and 1,000 convictions with up to twenty-year
prison terms. In Wisconsin there were only ninety-two
indictments. Of these thirty-six were for remarks
supporting Germany, the Kaiser, or the hope that
Germany would win the war. Both Germans and Polish
expressed this view on occasion. Socialists often
condemned the war without reference to who should win.
Surprisingly thirty-two cases involved statements that
this was a "rich man's war." Criticism of bond drives
involved nineteen, recruiting seventeen, and war charities fifteen indictments. The most celebrated case of
"espionage" was that against Circuit Judge John M.
Becker of Swiss-American Monroe (where the vote was 954
to 95 against entering the war). The judge not only
threatened to run for governor on an antiwar ticket,
but criticized the guidelines for fuel and food allot-
ments, charging that this was a rich man's war. Tried
at Eau Claire in August 1917, Becker was sentenced to
one year in the federal penitentiary and removed from
office. Criticism of war agencies also was the downfall of Louis B. Nagler of Madison, a prominent sup-
porter and apologist for La Follette. Although convicted in a lower court as well as in the Circuit Court
of Appeals in 1917, the United States Supreme Court in
July 1921 ordered a new trial, at which time the case
was dropped. Convictions touched all nationalities:
Germans, Polish, Armenians, Lithuanians, and others.

Under the Trading Act, the most celebrated case
concerned Jacob A. Auer, publisher of the German-language weekly the <u>Eau Claire Herold</u>, who had editorialized that smallpox vaccinations would destroy the

United States Army. He failed to file a translation
with the postmaster for advance clearance as the
Trading Act required of all non-English articles that
pertained to the war. Later he cautioned his readers
not to believe that the Allies were sinking all that
many German ships and praised the German-Russian peace
treaty. Indicted in June 1918, he was found guilty
and, although his attorney asked for mercy by reason of
senility, the judge gave him a year at Leavenworth. A
similar fate befell Jacob Mueller, editor of the German
Dodge County Pionier at Mayville. His chief offense
was in reporting the Auer case and in supporting Victor
Berger. Since his trial came in March 1919, Mueller
got away with a $50 fine. Under the Sabotage Act, only
a few were arrested, eleven for flimsy reasons.

In June 1918, Senator Irvine L. Lenroot wrote a plea
for tolerance of his state (62). He confessed that
there were patches of disloyalty among the 240,000
German-born citizens of Wisconsin. The bad spots were
either German or Socialist, most likely both. Lenroot
listed twelve counties that were pro-German: Brown,
Buffalo, Calumet, Chippewa, Clark, Dodge, Jefferson,
Manitowoc, Milwaukee, Sheboygan, Ozaukee, and Washington. But, the senator insisted, Wisconsin had more
than adequately demonstrated its loyalty: the first
state to file its complete report of registration; a
state draft registration of 104.6 percent of the estimated number to be enrolled based on population, compared to Washington State's 50.9 percent; less than 2
percent failed to respond to the draft compared to 8.2
percent for the nation as a whole; the highest volunteer percentage, 54.2 percent, compared to Oklahoma's
22 percent, Minnesota's 31.5 percent; Wisconsin had
more men actually in battle than any other state;
Wisconsin subscribed Liberty Loans better than any
other state.

Others pointed out that Wisconsin's compliance with
the war effort was truly remarkable considering that it
had the nation's heaviest German population (63). In
sixty-nine of the seventy-one counties, 10 percent or
more of the population had been born abroad, and in
fourteen it exceeded twenty-five percent. Of the
foreign-born, 45.5 percent were Germans, far outdis-
tancing the second-place Norwegians, who held 11.1
percent. Of Wisconsin's white residents, 51 percent
had parents born in Germany, 10.1 percent in Norway

(64). During World War I, the United States compelled
noncitizens from the Central Powers to register as
enemy aliens. Most did without objections, while many
did not realize they were not citizens, believing that
first papers were in fact citizenship papers. Of the
enemy aliens who registered nationally, some 6,300 were
arrested but only 2,300 were interned. No one knows
how many were from Wisconsin. Arrests occurred for
pro-German activities in Rhinelander, Neillsville,
Janesville, Hayward, Superior, Wausau, Kenosha, Milwaukee, Ashland, Clintonville, Eau Claire, and undoubtedly
in other communities (65). Occasionally county branches of the Council of Defense were overly enthusiastic,
for example in forcing Marathon County citizens to buy
bonds through issuance of a summons to all rural residents. In Rusk County the Council forced a seventy-
year-old German to buy bonds and then burned his Franco-
Prussian war uniform in which the old man wanted to be
buried. The State Council wad disturbed when a report
arrived that the Baraboo library had ordered pro-German
books for its shelves. Some county organizations, such
as Winnebago, used strong-arm squads to silence disloyal speakers. Others prodded local editors to support
the war more vigorously. Many worried about German
textbooks in the schools and about the International
Workers of the World (66).

As the war progressed, German-American banks became
American or Security banks. The university revoked the
honorary degree it had granted in 1910 to Count von
Bernstorff, Germany's ambassador to the United States.
German societies disbanded, and in 1918 Congress revoked the charter of the German-American Alliance (67).
German-language papers switched to English or suspended
operations. The Loyalty Legion got Milwaukee to remove
from city guidebooks references to the "German Athens
of America" and to veil the statues of Goethe and
Schiller. They urged businesses to rework their architecture so that buildings would look less Germanic and
praised firms that offered English classes to employees
with non-Yankee backgrounds (68). In Rhinelander a
returned soldier led a raid on a pro-German farmer to
seize a picture of the Kaiser, which was burned in the
town square with festivities conducted by the local
judge. Individuals with German names were tarred and
feathered in Superior and Ashland. The Knights of
Liberty ran an ad in the Ashland paper offering $100

"for any information of pro-Germanism that we cannot handle and guarantee satisfaction." In October 1918, an Appleton farmer was aroused by a mob and partially hanged until he agreed to subscribe to $500 worth of bonds. Yellow paint and flag kissing were standard remedies. A Janesville banker was stripped to the waist and decorated with a yellow German cross. The meat market at Medford was painted yellow, then sold to a new owner, who repainted it red, white, and blue. A sixteen-year-old honor-roll girl at Wauwatosa High was forced to apologize to a student assembly for writing under a bulletin board poster of Wilson, "The Living English Jackass."

Extralegal activities seem to have broken out indiscriminately across the state. Yet four of the six most German counties (over 40 percent of the population having German parents) in the state had no extralegal incidents. Seemingly where the Germans predominated, there were no problems. Where the Germans in fifteen counties constituted from 15 to 19 percent of the population there were twenty-seven incidents. In none of the counties was there any correlation between violence and the strength of the Socialists (69). Wisconsin during World War I represented a special case in that two factors coalesced at an inauspicious moment: its disproportionately large German and Austrian population lived side by side with the Socialist party. Both elements came to a focus in Milwaukee, the most German and, during the war, the most Socialist city in the nation. Heightening the focus was the fact that Victor Berger epitomized to the indiscriminating national press the hated triumph of German-Austrian Kultur. In Wisconsin the Americanizers responded passionately to the very same flag-waving, martial music, and emotional appeals of the politicians ("a war to end war") that they decried in Berlin and Vienna (70).

Perhaps there was a third component--the maverick Senator Robert M. La Follette and his Progressive Movement. La Follette led the fight against a war declaration on the senate floor, whereas Senator Paul O. Husting, the Democrat from German Dodge County, voted for declaration. Nine of the eleven Wisconsin members of the House voted against declaration: Henry Allen Cooper of Racine; the Bremen-born Edward Voight from Sheboygan; John M. Nelson of Madison; William Joseph Cary and William H. Stafford of Milwaukee; James H.

Davidson of Oshkosh; John J. Esch of La Crosse; Edward E. Browne of Waupaca and James A. Frear of Hudson. Only David G. Classon of Oconto and Irvine L. Lenroot of Superior voted for it. Thus, one of the six senate votes and nine of the fifty House votes against declaration came from Wisconsin, approaching 20 percent of the national legislative opposition to declaration. The evidence suggests that these men did not vote their consciences but the will of their constituents (71).

Undoubtedly it is correct to say that Wisconsinites held the Wilson administration responsible for their trials and tribulations during the war. Oblivious to the facts, the national press simplistically associated political conservatism with patriotism and radical reform with pro-Germanism. Wisconsin was unduly condemned. Once the war was over, much had changed but there was no turning back. The rabid Americanizers kept up the pace! Radicalism shifted from fearing pro-German to dreading pro-Red. Confused, if not entirely "Americanized," Wisconsin's ethnic groups sought shelter both in anonymity and in political isolationism, which is the story of our next two chapters.

Chapter Eight
The Age of Americanization, 1918–1932

As the armistice wore into the 1920s, the marks of Wisconsin ethnicity gradually faded. Assimilation had already come far before the war and after it the maintenance of foreign cultures proved "unhealthy." Secular organizations—ethnic clubs and non-English-language newspapers—were the first to surrender. Persons whose religious values were connected to their ethnicity found the decision whether to support Americanization or to adhere to traditional values far more severe. Nationality groups controlled a maze of churches, schools, seminaries, hospitals, colleges, orphanages, homes for the aged, and insurance companies, all of which were identifiable as to ethnicity and as to religious affiliation. The German-speaking denominations, moreover, had suborganizations—Lutheran, Catholic, and Methodist—that were further divided into subgroups of Lutherans (Wisconsin Synod, Missouri Synod, etc.) and of Catholics (Rhinelanders, Bavarians, etc.). The church Germans considered themselves religiously loyal, not ethnically loyal, and refused to fade away.

At the core of Americanization, in the minds of educators, lay the "American" language. Spearheaded by the National Education Association, Congress passed the Smith-Towner Act in October 1918, which provided that no state could share in federal funds if it did not require that English be the primary language of instruction. At least fifteen states in 1919 took special measures to comply with the act and some, including Colorado, Indiana, Iowa, Nebraska, Ohio, Oklahoma, and South Dakota, went beyond the law by prohibiting any instruction in German through the eighth grade (1). The most celebrated postwar case outlawing German was played out by Robert T. Meyer, a teacher in a Missouri Synod Lutheran school in Hampton, Nebraska, who deliberately taught a class in German, thereby violating the state law, and voluntarily paid a fine. The Nebraska Supreme Court upheld its law, arguing that "the legislature had seen the baneful effects of permitting foreigners, who had taken residence in this country, to rear and educate their children in the language of their native land. The result of that conditon was found to be inimical to our own safety (2). In 1923, the Supreme Court of the United States overturned the Nebraska law in favor of Meyer on the basis of the Fourteenth Amendment, and on the same day threw out similar cases from a number of other states.

Wisconsin did not find the need to purge its schools of foreign languages. As early as 1898 the legislature had stipulated:

> No person shall receive any certificate who does not write and speak the English language with facility and correctness. Acquaintance with another language may aid in the instruction of children of foreign birth, or parentage, and this section allows one hour a day to be given to instruction in a foreign language, but the purpose of the provision is to limit, not to encourage the study of a foreign language in a common public school. (3)

The limit of one hour per day of instruction in a foreign language continued in the Wisconsin statues throughout the period of Americanization. The 1929 Wisconsin Statutes still provided that "all instruction shall be in the English language, except that the board may cause any foreign language to be taught to such pupils as desire it, not to exceed one hour each day." It was the 1919 bill that drew the most vociferous arguments. Speaking loudly in opposition was Ernest von Briesen of Milwaukee, who represented the Wisconsin and Missouri Lutheran Synod. He did not speak in favor of continuing German instruction, but emphasized the lack of any need for the measures called for in the bill. What the country needed was "union and cooperation" (4). Representing the Catholic Church in opposition to the bills was Father James J. Oberlie of Milwaukee, who contended that Wisconsin citizens would have their religion interfered with if the proposed legislation were enacted. He declared that the problem was taking care of itself and stressed the policy of

the bishops of Wisconsin that English be used in the
parochial schools. Speaking for the Polish Catholics
was A. J. Kukaszewski of Milwaukee, who declared, "We
have got enough Bolshevism in this country without
passing a bill of this kind, which only increases it."
Others said that the antilanguage bill interfered
with a mother in bringing up her child. Secular Polish
leaders pointed out that the bill would forbid the use
of Polish while its proponents kept mentioning their
opposition only to the German language. Senator Axel
Johnson spoke in defense of his bill:

> No educator of any note in the country is in favor
> of the teaching of the foreign language. A common
> language is the cement that builds up a nation.
> That is why Germany was strong. The teaching of
> several foreign languages only makes us a polyglot
> nation. Who is on the other side of this question?
> Those who wish to keep alive the foreign spirit in
> this country. You may defeat this bill today but
> the issue will arise again and again. It is too big
> a question. Like former President Roosevelt I
> believe there can be no divided allegiance to this
> country.

Mr. Cerwinski called the bill "a slap at the Poles of
this state. The real objection that I have to this
bill is that it is an opening wedge to unite church and
state." Mr. Metcalfe pointed out that "the socialist
party of the state and the federation of labor are on
record against the bill." When the bill was tabled,
Axel Johnson promised, "I'll introduce it in some form
or other every day from now to the end of the session."
The bill came back all right, but with different
names when Senators Louis A. Fons and Schultz sponsored
versions in February and March. Again opponents resisted with no new arguments. Reverend John Brenner
speaking for the joint Evangelical Lutheran Synod of
Wisconsin opposed the bill because the Lutheran Church
was German in origin and its literature and hymns were
in German. "I know the value of English but I do not
want to lose the spiritual value of that hymn." Senator Jennings argued, "I am personally of the opinion
that you ought to be stopped. This is not a Lutheran
question. . . . It is a German question." To which
Brenner replied, "It's just the other way. . . . It is

a Lutheran question and not a German question." With a
minimum of logic, senator Fons argued that the law was
needed because people preferred a picture of the Kaiser
to that of the president. He claimed to know teachers
whose hearts were not with English because they insisted that their children learn German. He claimed he
knew clergymen who insisted that the national language
of America be German. Fons had even greater worries:

> We are still at war with Germany. The terms of
> peace have not been signed, and yet a few weeks ago
> an attempt was made to revive German theatrical
> productions in Milwaukee. . . . Schools have been
> the breeding place of propaganda that proved detri-
> mental to the cause of Americanization. . . . (5)

When a similar bill was proposed in 1923 by Matt
Koenigs of Fond du Lac the intent was to ban classical
as well as modern languages from all grade, high and
normal schools of the state. Only the University of
Wisconsin could continue foreign languages. Xenophobia
by this date had been defused as the chief argument
against languages, but, Koenigs theorized, languages
were an all too expensive luxury. "If the teaching of
foreign language is abandoned, the state could save
between a quarter and a half million dollars every
year" (6). Koenigs argued, "I fail to see wherein the
study of foreign languages helps the student in the
acquisition of knowledge. He would do better to spend
that time studying the dictionary and so obtain a
better working knowledge of English (7). Like similar
legislation in 1919, the proposed 1923 language ban in
the Wisconsin schools was indefinitely postponed.
    The fuss about foreign-language education subsided
but programs on Americanization were ardently fostered
(8). The Wisconsin Americanization program managed to
build a system that circulated statewide, propelled by
the vocational schools. Reaching nearly all cities, it
offered classes in English and

> extended help to the foreigner in many ways besides
> teaching him to read, write and speak the English
> language. An earnest effort has been made in many
> cities . . . to give these people a realization of
> what America really means to a good citizen. . . .
> Realizing that the home is the real place which must

be Americanized, much work has been done with the
women through cooking, sewing, home nursing, home
management and like classes. (9)

Where vocational systems could not reach, the state
board of education did the chore. Factories also threw
financial power behind Americanization, when, prior to
the war, the Milwaukee giants of industry (Allis-Chalmers, International Harvester, and the others) had
begun programs for the "human side" of manufacturing.
After the conclusion of hostilities, crusaders bent
these programs into instruments to Americanize. They
taught the workers English and civics under the heading
of "safety," subjects that would enhance the security
of the nation, if not exactly safety on the worksite.
Classes in English became synonymous with classes in
citizenship. Milwaukee plant superintendents urged in
the same breath the purchase of liberty bonds and the
attendance at English classes, advising that any em-
ployee who did not participate should head "out on the
prairie away from the gaze of civilization and drain
the yellow blood out of his heart" (10).

The large numbers of foreign-born in the work force
did arouse fears for national security. According to
the 1920 Census Wisconsin had a total population of
2,632,670. Of these, half a million (460,123) had been
born abroad: one-third (150,548) in Germany and one-
ninth (50,58) in Poland, now in second place among
Wisconsin's foreign-born. Norway, for the first time,
stood in third place with 45,390 foreign-born, followed by Sweden (22,996) and Russia (21,452)--most of
the Russians being Germans and Jews from Russia. Other
nationalities with more than 15,000 were Czechoslovakia, Austria, and Denmark; with more than 10,000 were
Italy, England, and Hungary; above 5,000, Yugoslavia,
Ireland, Switzerland, the Netherlands, and Finland;
between 5,000 and 1,000 were Greece, Scotland, Belgium,
France, Lithuania, Luxembourg, and Wales (11). On a
percentage basis, the foreign-born were concentrated in
the two southeastern counties of Racine and Kenosha
(highly industrialized areas) and in the diagonally
located counties of the northwest: Douglas, Bayfield,
Ashland, Iron, Pierce, as well as Florence County in
the Northeast. Immediately preceding the war, incoming
Poles no longer went to Portage and other outstate
counties, but remained in Milwaukee, creating the most

concentrated foreign-born group anywhere in Wisconsin.
Led by their journalists and churchmen, they mimicked
the Germans in preserving their culture and their language, and inevitablty struggles broke out between the
two nationality groups, especially as they groped for
representation within the Catholic hierarchy (12). The
Swiss-born, pro-German Archbishop Sebastian Messmer
held the numerically powerful support of the Germans
and was not inclined to side with Polish interests as
articulated by Wenceslaus Kruszka, Michael Kruszka, and
Boleslaus Goral in their publications, the <u>Kuryer</u> and
the <u>Nowiny</u>. But, taking each other as antagonists, the
Germans and Poles in the Milwaukee church war actually
hastened Americanization. Instead of erecting common
defenses against American culture, the two sides lost
opportunities by fighting one another and crippled each
other's chances for preserving cultural autonomy.

A powerful thrust for Americanization came from
secular leaders, for instance Mary Wood Simons, who
became chairman of the Milwaukee County Council of
Defense Americanization Committee in October 1917.
Ironically she and her husband, Algie M. Simons, were
once prominent Socialists who had translated German and
French Socialist literature into English before giving
up on Victor Berger and the Germans in favor of the
wartime allies. Mrs. Simons now tried to enlist factories as crusaders for Americanzation. Companies,
such as International Harvester, Cutler-Hammer, Briggs
and Stratton, Pfister and Vogel, Cudahy, and Weinbren-
ner Shoes, followed her lead by establishing chapters
of the Wisconsin Loyalty Legion. A Pfister and Vogel
spokesman decried the shortage of labor brought on by
the lack of new immigrants and the draft: "Speaking
English will have a tendency to stabilize labor and
therefore reduce turnover. . . . Every manufacturer
should be interested in this Americanization proposi-
tion" (13). By making foreigners learn English and
become citizens, manufacturers would also be removing
workers from the influence of agitators, all of which
would increase safety and efficiency. Similar persuasion came from the Wisconsin Industrial Commission:
English is as important as a first-aid station; English
is the best means to reduce radicalism. At the urging
of Mrs. Simons, therefore, the Milwaukee School Board
assigned extension department teachers to offer English
classes in the factories. But neither the school board

nor the University Extension Division could supply the
needed personnel. In June 1919, YMCA-sponsored English-language programs were tried, but likewise unsuccessfully. In the fall of 1919 the Association of
Commerce became the chief sponsor of Americanization
but it ran afoul of Mrs. Simons, who called the leaders
of the association "a group of extreme reactionaries"
(14). By 1921 programs for Americanization became ever
more entwined with industrial opposition to the trade
unions with the result that workers were looked upon as
"the new enemy" rather than as poor Europeans who
needed the factory's help to meet the norm of good
citizenship. Americanization ventures into the "factory as classroom" had failed.

Mrs. Simons then sought to dramatize her objectives
by other means, such as organizing Americanization
conferences, which had proved successful in neighboring
states. Published proceedings of the Minnesota Council
of Americanization furnish insight into the mentality
of the Americanization efforts (15). Catholics saw in
Americanization an attack on the Church itself, as when
groups calling themselves "Guardians of Liberty" and
"The American Protective Association" had glorified
pseudo-Americanization schemes. "We look upon the
teaching of English as an instrument by which the
ideals of American citizenship may be acquired, but we
do not overlook the native tongue as a vehicle of
expression of democracy and Americanism" (16). Catholic
leaders believed Americanization would be best accomplished within the confines of the parish. Admit-
ting that many non-English-speaking Americans were
Catholics, bishops urged pastors to initiate citizenship programs and published materials for a "Civic
Education Program" (17). Citizenship courses were
offered also through the University of Wisconsin's
extension, in vocational schools, and in public high
schools, where a three-year program was mandated. A
standing professorship of Americanization was established at the university (18). Soon, however, the
topic of Americanization was replaced by other prob-
lems--the Socialist party, which frightened people with
threats of Reds, and the Nonpartisan League, strong in
North Dakota and Minnesota, but a distant drumroll also
in Wisconsin (19). Wisconsin's ethnic groups did not
need the League because they could always send their
protest signals to Madison or Washington by means of

the Socialist vote (20).
From the voting booth Wisconsin's ethnic groups
protested by rejecting Wilson Democrats. The Wisconsin
presidential vote in 1920 gave Republican Warren G.
Harding 71 percent (998,576) of the total compared to
only 16 percent (113,422) for Democrat James Cox and 11
percent (80,365) for Socialist Eugene Debs. Harding
thus became the first and the last presidential candidate in Wisconsin to carry every single county. The
Democrats gave up all but two seats in the hundred-man
Wisconsin Assembly and never secured more than six for
the remainder of the decade, which put them in third
place behind the Socialists. Residual loyalty to the
Democratic party came in descending order of percentages from Dutch Catholic villages, Polish rural
voters, Polish urban wards, Dutch Catholic rural
voters, Irish rural voters, German Catholics in the
cities, and Italian urban wards (21).
In 1920 the least Democratic voters were the rural
Norwegians, followed by the Swiss, the Lutheran German
and Dutch, the Finnish, the Swedish rural, the Belgians, the Welsh, the Italian rural, and the German
rural. When analyzing the ethnic returns for 1920,
critics have failed to perceive the large anti-Democratic vote that swept Wisconsin in this first postwar
election (22). Contributing to the flight from the
Democratic party was the candidacy of James M. Cox, the
Democrat who as governor of Ohio in April 1919 sponsored a bill in the Ohio legislature calling for
abolishment of Geman in schools because it was "part of
a plot by the German government to make school children
loyal to it" (23). In the Wisconsin voter's mind, Cox
was Wilson in sheep's clothing. The Republican National Committee during the campaign appealed to hyphenate
voters, reminding them that Wilson had declared war
against immigrants and then raped their homelands at
the Peace Conference. The jingoistic Cox outstripped
his opponents by inviting "every traitor" in America to
vote for Harding, and lost the Italians when he accepted Roosevelt's description of them as "fifty-fifty
citizens." Nor did the Democratic National Committee
help matters by charging in campaign pamphlets that the
Republicans appealed "to pro-Germans, hyphens, Bol-
shevists, and everything else un-American in the United
States" (24).
One of Wisconsin's "might-have beens" occurred in

1920 when Senator Irvine L. Lenroot declined being
nominated for the vice presidency. Upon the death of
Warren G. Harding in 1923, Lenroot instead of Coolidge
would have become president. That Lenroot would have
changed the course of history is unclear but it is
certain that the Scandinavians of Wisconsin would have
had in Lonroot their first American president (25).
Wisconsin in 1920 exercised the "politics of revenge."
The greatest vote loss to the Democrats occurred in
descending order from Swiss, Germans, Austrians,
Italian rural groups, Dutch Reformed, Welsh, Bohemians,
Belgians, and Norwegians. The Polish, Irish, and Dutch
Catholics, while eschewing their traditionally strong
support of the Democrats, were the least likely to
switch (26). The 1920 election was a genuine protest
against the Wilson peace (27). In 1922, when La Follette was pitted against William Garfield in a Senate
primary race, the Republican stalwarts tried to defeat
the fighting senator in the primary but he won overwhelmingly. The Democratic candidate, Jessie Jack
Hooper, got only 16 percent of the total vote in the
general election while La Follette walked away with 80
percent (a smattering went to splinter candidates).
Also in 1922, incumbent Republican Governor John J.
Blaine did nearly as well as La Follette, taking 76
percent of the vote against 10 percent for the Democrat, Arthur Bentley. The Socialist got 8 percent. In
1923 La Follette ran as a third-party candidate for the
presidency and won Wisconsin with 54.4 percent of the
total votes, the only state in which he polled a majority. At the pinnacle of his power, La Follete
enjoyed the support of Midwest labor, railway brother-
hoods, Nonpartisan Leaguers, and liberal progressives
in the Congress who campaigned on his behalf. But it
was the ethnic voters in Wisconsin who turned in the
most substantial majorities for their antiwar senator
(28). The Norwegians remained as faithful as they had
been before the war, with the exception of the city of
Stoughton in Dane County, which retreated. Belgian
rural areas, Canadians, and Italians remained supportive. Danish rural townships turned favorable
toward La Follette while Finnish and Swedish rural
voters held constant. Danish city voters and Swedish
villagers, however, diminished their support in 1924 as
compared to earlier elections. By far the largest
gains for La Follette came in the German areas that had

once been hesitant about his Progressivism. All rural
German groups in 1924 ranked above even the Norwegian
rural voters in giving La Follette more than 80 percent
of their votes. Since there was no Social Democratic
candiate for the presidency in 1924, it is conceivable
that some of the overwhelming vote for La Follette may
have included Socialist votes (29). Both Milwaukee
Mayor Daniel Hoan and Victor Berger were influential in
convincing the Socialists to support La Follette's
Conference for Progressive Political Action (the CPPA
party). In 1924, then, Wisconsin's ethnic voters found
a national candidate with whom they could register
their protest, which explains the Republican landslide
in 1920 and their generosity for La Follette's third-
party candidacy in 1924.

In looking at the opposition to La Follette among
nationality voters it turns out that the Welsh were the
most likely to oppose him during the 1920s. Urban
Yankees and Dutch Reformed also diminished their support as did Yankee and English rural areas. Traditionally strong Democratic groups, such as the Irish and
the Polish, in 1924 reported large pluralities for La
Follette. The solidly Irish voters of Erin Prairie in
St. Croix County broke ranks with the Democrats by
handing 86 percent of their ballots to La Follette. La
Follette was sustained by the prewar power of the
Scandinavians and Belgians, and now picked up Teutonic
groups, a few Irish, and some Polish (30). There were
occasions, however, when they charged that his Socialist support identified him with radicals and Reds (the
Red Scare) (31). Reasons why La Follette became the
lightning rod for anti-Bolshevik attacks reach back to
postwar years when be argued that Russia was moving in
the right direction and had a sacred right to determine
her own destiny (32).

Popularized as the agrarian reformer, La Follette in
1924 gained stronger support in urban areas than among
farmers except in his home state. Although he carried
no state but his own, La Follette enjoyed his strongest
support in those urban counties that were heavily populated by the foreign-born (33). In the 1920s he picked
up the ethnic backlash, especially the Germans, Swiss,
Bohemians, Austrians, and the Dutch Catholics. Having
voted overwhelmingly for La Follette in 1924, and for
Roosevelt in 1932, Wisconsin's ethnic groups might have
voted for Democrat Al Smith in 1928, except for the

fact that he was Catholic. The prewar Republican Scandinavians, being staunch Protestants, gladly voted for
La Follette in 1924, and they continued their shift
away from the Republican camp with the appearance of
Roosevelt. But in 1928 the Catholic candidacy of Smith
alienated them temporarily from the Democratic party
(34). Other factors such as wet-dry and urban-rural
issues also affected the 1928 outcome (35). Nevertheless no Yankee, British, Dutch Reformed, or Scandinavian areas in Wisconsin gave as much as 30 percent of
their votes to Smith in 1928. German Lutheran areas
went slightly over 30 percent for Smith, reflecting
probably the presence of German Catholic minorities
within the bounds categorized as German Lutheran. Only
the Swiss Reformed among all Protestants gave votes of
more than 50 percent to Smith. Mixed (Catholic and
Protestant) German areas voted about 50 percent in
favor of Smith. The Wisconsin Catholics--German,
Irish, Polish, and Italian--voted heavily in favor of
Smith. Religion was a factor in 1928. Already in 1900
thriteen of the fifteen most Democratic groupings were
Catholic while fourteen of the fifteen most Republican
units were Protestant (36).

Before turning our attention specifically to the
Roosevelt era and World War II, we should summarize
prohibition as an ethnic issue. The crusade against
alcoholic beverages was bitterly fought in Wisconsin as
early as the 1850s but subsided when the Civil War
monopolized men's minds (37). It returned in 1872 when
the Graham law was signed by Republican Governor Cad-
wallader C. Washburn. In 1873 the Protestant Germans
bolted to the Democrats to defeat Washburn and repeal
the antiliquor law. In 1875 the Republicans won back
their losses by running Harrison Ludington, the popular
Republican mayor of Milwaukee who had earned the loyalty of Germans by refusing to enforce the Graham Law in
that city. In 1869, the national Prohibition party
made its debut with a candidate for the presidency.
Two of its prominent leaders, Samuel Dexter Hastings
and Eugene Wilder Chafin, had come from Wisconsin,
Chafin becoming its presidential candidate in 1904.
The party never did well in Wisconsin, although in 1886
its candidate, John M. Olin, received 17,000 or 6
percent of the state's votes. The Women's Christian
Temperance Union began in 1873 in Ohio, and received
from Wisconsin its greatest leader, Frances Willard, who

grew up near Janesville. The Anti-Saloon League, launched in Oberlin, Ohio, in 1893, functioned as an umbrella for all temperance groups (38).

By the turn of the century Maine, Kansas, and North Dakota were dry; by 1914 fourteen states had gone dry; by 1916 there were twenty-three, and in 1918, thirty-two. Local dry spots showed up in Wisconsin during the 1880s but the real thrust came only in 1918. When World War I began, Wisconsin lagged well behind the nation, with only 45 percent of its people living in dry territory versus 71 percent for the nation. Precipitating the passage of prohibition was the war. In 1917, Congress passed a law forbiding the manufacture of liquor from grain; later that year the law took the form of a Prohibition Amendment submitted to the states. In the Senate, La Follette favored submission to the people not because he favored prohibition but because as a Progressive he believed in the popular referendum; the Swedish Lenroot was moderately in favor of prohibition. In the House, six Wisconsin members voted for and five against submission. Sponsored by Minnesota's Norwegian-American Andrew J. Volstead (Wraalstad), the Volstead Act became the Eighteenth Amendment on January 18, 1919, when the needed thirty-sixth state ratified it. Quickly the number of states ratifying rose to forty-five, including Wisconsin. At midnight on June 30, 1919, the legal manufacture and sale of intoxicants ceased and on July 1, 1919, some 10,000 saloons and 137 breweries in Wisconsin all closed. At the time, brewing was the fifth-largest industry in the state.

Only a minority of Wisconsin's citizens favored prohibition but in July 1919, Wisconsin passed the Mulberger Act, which established a prohibition commissioner to enforce federal provisions within the state. At first the commissioner had only $15,000 per year for enforcement, but that figure rose to $60,000 in 1922. In this his best year the commissioner procured more than 4,000 convictions and fines of over half a million dollars, and by the end of 1927 more than $2.5 million in fines had been collected. As early as 1923, however, the prohibition tide in Wisconsin turned when courts limited the commissioner in the methods he could use to secure evidence. In 1926 a referendum passed asking that the Volstead Act be amended to allow the manufacture of beer. In another referendum in April

1929, Wisconsinites voted 350,000 to 200,000 to repeal the state's prohibition law, and in May the legislature did repeal it, abolishing also the commissioner's office.
There is little question that prohibition was deeply entwined with the ethnic elements in Wisconsin. Clifton Child has demonstrated that, hopelessly splintered along relgious and political lines, the Germans united in their antiprohibition convictions (39). Always an abomination, the movement became an imminent threat after 1900, spurring formation of the hugh German-American Alliance. This organization, although perceived by the unsophisticated as an agency for the furtherance of German political aims in the United States, was powerful in 1914 only because of its struggle against the Anti-Saloon League. The German-American Alliance, with its 2 to 3 million members, was heavily subsidized not by the German government as its opponents charged, but by American brewers, virtually all of whom were German and who in the early 1900s saw not only their life-style but their economic existence threatened.
Led by her uncompromising wet governor, John J. Blaine, Wisconsin in several stages beginning in 1923, in 1926, and in 1929 dismantled prohibition as far as a state by itself could accomplish it. In 1932 the Democratic party called first for the legalization of wine and beer and then for repeal of the Eighteenth Amendment. Federal legislation to accomplish this was introduced in December 1932 by Wisconsin's former governor and now Senator John J. Blaine. Delegates elected to repeal the legislation in Wisconsin captured 82 percent of the vote and in April 1933 cast their unanimous decision for removal of prohibition. Wisconsin thus became the first state after Michigan to announce its acceptance of the new Twenty-First Amendment. On December 11, 1933, a special session of the Wisconsin legislature convened to specify new rules and taxation for the manufacture and sale of liquor (40).
Just how much of the 1932 Roosevelt plurality in Wisconsin may be attributed to the liquor question and therefore to the German population in Wisconsin is not easy to ascertain. Clearly the election was much more than some kind of referendum on prohibition. Nevertheless, it is worth noting that whereas Roosevelt carried the nation with 57 percent of the vote, in Wisconsin he

secured 63.5 percent, almost 20 percent higher than Al Smith's 44 percent. Urban ethnic groups were the largest in their swing toward the Democratic party, with Milwaukee voting 78 percent in its favor. The five Polish wards cast 92 percent of their votes for Roosevelt while the ten German wards equaled the 78 percent city-wide figure. The next ten largest cities in Wisconsin went 62 percent Democratic but the strongest support of all came in the rural areas. The rural Polish went 97 percent for Roosevelt, followed by the Belgians with 94 percent, Austrians, 93 percent, Bohemians, 90 percent, Irish, 90 percent, Swiss Reformed, 87 percent, Dutch Catholic, 86 percent, Norwegian and Danish, 71 percent, followed in descending order by the Welsh, Yankee, English, Finnish, and Swedish, who voted 57 percent Democratic. The Dutch Reformed gave FDR only 35 percent, in spite of his Dutch name (41).

The postwar decade of course witnessed many events other than prohibition that affected ethnic life in Wisconsin. Fighting Bob La Follette died in 1925, but his sons, notably Philip F. La Follette, tried to carry on. Beginning in 1928, another patriarchial family came into its own, that of German-American Walter J. Kohler, who was elected as a stalwart Republican governor by a margin of 55 percent in 1928. Victor Berger, the timeless Socialist, died in August 1929 after predicting that his Milwaukee movement would not survive him. Bigotry was an issue in several elections, notably when Catholic Roy Wilcox ran against Blaine for governor in 1920. The religious issue reared its head in 1928 with the Al Smith candidacy, again in 1946 over a school but referendum, and especially in 1960 with the candidacy of John F. Kennedy (42).

Other complicating issues in the 1920s were the fading Nonpartisan League and the Ku Klux Klan, which found fertile soil in Wisconsin. The Klan accentuated Americanism and struck a hostile stance toward the Catholic Church, Jews, Negroes, and especially foreigners. In that sense it represented a revival of Nativism, couched as it was in Protestant values. Wisconsin never had more than 40,000 Klan members although the Klan sometimes attracted crowds of 20,000 or more. Milwaukee, Kenosha, and Racine counties had the heaviest representation, areas that received the largest numbers of twentieth-century immigrants: Poles, Italians, and Russian Jews. German Socialists sometimes embarrassed Victor Berger by joining the Klan and mocking the Catholic clergy. The Klan also thrived in the Fox River Valley, in Dane, Green, and Rock counties, and in Eau Claire and La Crosse counties, all of which harbored sizable numbers of ethnic stock. In Rusk County, members joined because they found the Poles ready targets. In Madison they joined to attack the Italians, who had been brought in as marble workers on the new state capital (43). In general the Klan appealed to the secular Germans who found its fraternalism a satisfying substitute for the German clubs of old.

Immigrants in the 1920s gradually settled the cutover of northern Wisconsin in part through the efforts of the state Department of Agriculture, which boasted in 1923 that it had been in touch with 10,000 new settlers. Thousands arrived, tried to convert the wilderness to dairy farms, then returned promptly to the cities, leaving their mute, dilapidated structures scattered across the northern granitic dome (44). Earlier the American Colonization Company had established cutover colonies with people from Europe. Organized by the German Frederich Weyerhaeuser in 1906, this company sought to dispose of a million acres through two of its German directors, Frederich Von Pilis and George Claussenius. Von Pilis, a director of the North German Lloyd Steamship Line, opened offices in Bremen and Berlin and sent immigration agents to Finland, Russia, Poland, Denmark, Norway, and Sweden. Often when immigrants came to the northern counties, they settled together in cohesive religious and ethnic communities. Bohemians, Poles, and Lithuanians as well as Finns and Swedes followed a colonizer. Regardless of nationality or religion, the new arrivals failed. Their task with only horse-powered stump pullers and walking plows was too difficult. Dynamite did not become available until most had already given up the land for a job in an industrial center.

Coming directly to the industrial centers in the twentieth century were large groups of Mediterranean immigrants, including many Greeks. Beginning in 1905, small colonies of them arrived in Sheboygan, Milwaukee, Kenosha, Racine, and Waukesha. A few others sprang up in Fond du Lac, Oshkosh, Green Bay, Madison, and La Crosse. Domination of Greece by the Ottoman Empire until the conclusion of World War I and the niggardly soils in the homeland caused the religious and economic oppression that impelled Greeks to seek new homes in Wisconsin (45). According to the 1920 census, the total Greek population in Wisconsin stood at just 3,833, almost 2,000 of whom lived in Milwaukee County (46). By 1930 the state's Greeks had declined to 2,900, representing only 0.7 percent of the population, and dropped further by 1940. The Greeks were especially active as confectioners, restauranteurs, coffeehouse operators, small grocers, barbers, and saloon keepers. They also ran laundries and wholesale tobacco businesses. Like many immigrants from the Mediterranean, the Greeks who arrived prior to World War I apparently intended to return to their homeland once conditions there improved. After the war, under pressure to Americanize, they eschewed their instinctive Hellenism. Before World War I most of the proprietors named their establishments after themselves. After the war, like so many thousands of immigrants, they either Anglicized their names or retitled their enterprises: Liberty Restaurant, Busy Bee Lunch, Sanitary Laundry, and the like. Perpetuation of the Greek language was easy before the war, when private Greek schools thrived, but difficult thereafter, when Americanization swept them into oblivion.

Not only Greeks but also Germans switched appellations and disguised identities. The magnitude of the name change is evident when we compare the census reports of German born in Wisconsin in 1910 with the postwar census of 1920. In 1910 Wisconsin had a German-born population of 233,384, a figure that rises to 396,640 if we include those for whom both parents had been born in Germany. There were 38,691 born in Austria. In 1920 there were reported to be only 151,250 individuals in Wisconsin who had been born in Germany and 19,641 in Austria. This represents a decline of 35 percent for the Germans and 50 percent for the Austrians. Considering that immigration from Germany to the United States stayed near 30,000 per year through 1914, the dramatic drop of Germans and Austrians cannot be accounted for by deaths and move-aways. The Belgian-born who had almost entirely ceased immigrating to Wisconsin by 1910, declined from 1910 to 1920 by only 15 percent. Foreign-born immigrants from Holland actually increased over the period. Hungarians declined by only a fraction. The Italian-born in-

creased from 9,273 to 11,187. The Swiss declined from
8,036 to 7,797. Clearly the Germans and the Austrians,
made to register as enemy aliens during the World War
if they had not yet acquired citizenship, underreported
their country of birth in the 1920 federal census.

Being wary of the census taker, however, did not
mean that Germans were no longer sympathetic with their
homeland. Once the war was over, thousands joined the
relief effort undertaken on behalf of blood brothers
across the sea. When some senators tried to bar
defeated Germany from receiving United States credits,
Senator La Follette rose to tell the Upper Chamber that
excluding Germany from aid should "make you as an
American writhe and cringe in shame that you did it"
(47). Popular in Wisconsin, La Follette's speech
carried little weight in the Congress because he was at
the moment himself under threat of censure for his
speech to the Nonpartisan League in St. Paul in
September 1917. The nation wanted to believe that La
Follette represented German power in the United States.
He had even been burned in effigy on the campus of the
University of Wisconsin, where the faculty almost to a
man signed a petition condemning him for giving "aid
and comfort to Germany." When his censure finally came
up for a vote after the war, the Republicans were in
control of the Senate by one vote--La Follette's--and
the matter was dropped. But Congress could not be
persuaded to aid Germany's widows and orphans.

German-Americans therefore fell back on private
resources and churches took an active role in supplying
aid. The Milwaukee post office reported sending over
100,000 packages to Germany over an eighteen-month
period ending November 1920. The New York City post
office said it was "besieged by Teutons." Cautious of
charges of disloyalty, the Luthern Church at first sent
aid only to Lutherans in Poland, Hungary, and Romania
but gradually shifted some to Germany as well. Relief
was carried on by Herbert Hoover's quasi-private American Relief Administration, which distributed contributions from European nationals in the United States.
Himself a Quaker, Hoover worked closely with the American Friends Service Committee. Supported by the Nation
(whose second-generation German-American editor at the
time was Oswald Villard) and other liberal journals,
the German-language Milwaukee Herald pointed out that
the German people had been made victims of the Versail-

les Treaty and the Allied blockade, the "biggest atrocity of the war."

One of the most interesting forms of aid from Wisconsin to Germany in the postwar period occurred when the churches in Dodge and Jefferson counties organized campaigns to solicit milk cows for German orphanages to replace those that had been surrendered to France under the Versailles Treaty (48). The ocean steamer West Arrow was equipped to carry the live cows, of which at least three shiploads were delivered, all handled by the American Dairy Cattle Company with headquarters in Chicago. The first shiploads came from Indiana, Kansas, and Texas and departed from Galveston. Later shipments came from South Dakota and Wisconsin via Baltimore. Opposed by the American Red Cross and in particular by the American Legion, German-American farmers of the Dakotas and of Ixonia and Lebanon, Wisconsin, braved heady opposition in order to send their cows to Germany in the spring of 1921. During the night of March 23, the American Legion and their cohorts stampeded the cows that were being held in Scotland, South Dakota, for entrainment to Wisconsin. Some were killed, others aborted their calves, one was shot, and about twenty-five were scattered and never found. Those youthful German-Americans who traveled with the cows as caretakers had something of a lark at the many receptions arranged for them by the appreciative Germans.

As devastating inflation hit Germany in the 1920s and as Europe struggled through various phases of newly found democracies, Wisconsin ethnic groups waited silently. The economy boomed in the United States and few could have predicted the devastating depression that would befall them in the 1920s. Its economic pressures would further the process of assimilation as we shall see in the next chapter.

Chapter Nine
The Depression, World War II, and the Cold War

The central concern in Wisconsin as elsewhere during
the 1930s was not ethnicity, not war or its threat, not
even Americanization, but the brutality of the Great
Depression. The number of Wisconsin wage earners fell
from 264,745 in 1929 to 116,525 in 1933, a drop of more
than 50 percent. Wage payments fell by 60 percent.
The farmer was only a bit more secure, having some of
his own food. Using an index of 100 in 1929, the
prices for commodities Wisconsin farmers sold fell into
32 at the nadir of the depression in 1932–33. The same
index for products they had to buy fell to only 71.
Nothing but soup kitchens sprouted. Breadlines
lengthened and the jobless took to the highways.
Making matters much worse was the drought that settled
on the Midwest and lasted for half the decade (1).

In the 1930s Wisconsin's population clustered along
the great Lakes with Milwaukee as its magnet. Population also increased in the Fox River Valley and in Dane
and Rock counties. Immigration had slowed during World
War I but in 1930 Wisconsin still had a larger than
average number of foreign-born. As a percentage of its
total population, however, Wisconsin's foreign-born
slipped from 22 percent in 1910 to only 13 percent in
1930, when half of the people over sixty-five fell into
this 13 percent. In terms of foreign stock (one or
both parents of foreign birth) in 1930 Wisconsin had
1,447,367, which was a little over half of the entire
population of 2,939,006. Those of German background
accounted for 43 percent of the foreign stock. Many
forces came together in the 1920s and 1930s to wash out
ethnic islands that still persisted in rural areas and
in urban centers. Movies and especially the automobile
diffused insularity. In 1920 Wisconsin had only 718
miles of paved roads. Ten years later there were 3,660
paved miles and 84 percent of all farm families had an
automobile. By the Great Depression interethnic

marriage had become both the cause and the result of assimilation (2). Education had improved but in 1930 most rural children still went to one-room schools. Free high schools were provided by a 1921 law but high schooling for rural children in 1930 lagged more than 2.5 times behind that for urban children. The radio had just begun beaming voices into the hinterlands, which helped level rural-urban, foreign-native dichotomies. Electricity was available to most city households by 1930 but to only about 15 percent of rural homes. Ten percent more had wind systems and batteries. Deprivation of electrical power in the countryside tended to widen the gap between urban and rural life and affected the rate of assimilation both by driving people off the farms and by impelling those left behind to rely on themselves rather than on new appliances. Like the railroads of an earlier era, electrical utilities required infusions of capital to extend services to the far corners of the state. During the depression, capital was not available. Wisconsin followed its appetite for Progressivism, instituting a regulatory commission, but it could not order expanded service (3). Labor was now regarded with wariness nearly as much in the rural areas as in industrial centers. Newer immigrants belonged for the most part to the work force and were therefore suspect. The Socialists persisted in Milwaukee.

Mayor Daniel Hoan found in Milwaukee in the 1930s a cooperative spirit between Germans and Poles who were anxious for municipal reform. The Poles, at this time the poorer element in the community, accepted any support to get aldermanic and municipal posts. From 1932 to 1936 a Polish Socialist who served as chief of police was known as "the Czar of Milwaukee" (4). But the Socialist base was not the Polish but the German population throughout the 1930s. Mayor Hoan repeatedly won re-election until 1940, when Carl Zeidler, an ethnic German, defeated him by forging a coalition with the Polish wards. Although Carl resigned to enlist in the army and was killed in action in the Pacific, his brother, Frank Zeidler, kept on winning the mayoralty on the Socialist ticket through 1952. His Polish opponent in that year carried only one ward.

The second-generation Austrian-American Walter J. Kohler, from a family of plumbing magnates in Sheboygan, took control of the governor's chair in 1928, but

young Phil La Follette successfully challenged him in
the 1930 Republican primary, passing Kohler by 128,000
votes. Meanwhile, his brother, Robert La Follette,
Jr., in 1928 had comfortably won re-election to the
United States Senate. In 1931, therefore, Wisconsin
was back in the hands of Progressives, brothers who
enjoyed the broad ethnic support won by their father.
In 1932, however, the Democratic German-American
Schmedeman swept over Phil La Follette on the coattails
of Franklin D. Roosevelt. Phil and Bob La Follette
were promptly invited by Roosevelt to join the Democratic party, but instead they created their own, the
Farmer Labor Progressive League, which was stretched a
bit to incorporate Socialist party support. Young Bob
was re-elected in 1934 and again in 1940 in the United
States Senate, but was defeated in 1946 by a narrow
margin of 5,000 votes by the then-unknown Joseph R.
McCarthy. Phil La Follette was re-elected governor in
1924 and 1936, serving until January 1939. Phil's
downfall started when he became enamored of the success
of Adolf Hitler in mobilizing public opinion to lift
Germany out of its depression. Hoping to generate
similar purpose among Wisconsin's faltering Progressives, La Follette staged a 1936 rally in the Stock
Pavilion at the University of Wisconsin. In the center
of a circle, representing unity of the people, was a
huge cross said to represent the power of the ballot.
La Follette stumbled irreparably when critics saw in
the imagery an attenuated Swastika (5). In 1938 he was
defeated by a Milwaukee industrialist, German-born
Julius P. Heil, who was re-elected for a second term in
1940. Disconsolate, Phil now led a crusade for isolationism, speaking frequently for the America First
Committee. When war broke out, he enlisted in the army
and served under MacArthur in the Pacific (6).

During the depths of the depression, ethnicity in
Wisconsin, as witnessed in the 1936 presidential
results, was far from dead. Roosevelt barely increased
his Wisconsin voter appeal--to 63.8 percent from his
63.5 percent in 1932. By 1936 the returns in Wisconsin
were already shifting in proportion to ethnic loyalties. The Polish wards of Milwaukee showed gains for
the New Dealer but he lost ground in virtually all
rural areas. The Finns, as usual, cast their ballots
for Union or Communist party candidates. Swedes and
Dutch Reformed increased their support but since these

areas were never highly populated they had little
effect on the outcome. Roosevelt's most severe losses
came from the Dutch Catholic, German Catholic, and
Bohemian rural areas. He also suffered slippage in the
Irish, Italian, German Lutheran, and Austrian rural
areas as well as in two Danish villages. In 1936
Roosevelt's anti-Germanism was apparent and it cost him
the disaffection of Wisconsin's Germans (7).

In 1936 William F. Lemke's Union party candidacy
appealed to Wisconsin voters, especially German and
Dutch Catholics, Bohemians, and Irish (8). Lemke
hailed from neighboring North Dakota, enjoyed the
spellbinding support of Father Charles E. Coughlin (the
"Detroit Fascist" priest, in the words of opponents),
and like his contemporary in Nazi Germany, used the
airplane better than any presidential candidate until
1960 to appear nearly everywhere simultaneously. A
German-American, Lemke was born of Prussian immigrants
to Minnesota's most German and most Catholic county
(Stearns), who moved to North Dakota shortly after
William's birth. Here Lemke served as legal counsel
to, and an officer in, the Nonpartisan League and later
as attorney general in North Dakota before being
elected to Congress. Wisconsinites respected Lemke for
authoring the Farm Mortgage Act, which helped farmers
facing foreclosures. He garnered strong support in
Wisconsin's central counties, notably Marathon, where
the Germans were numerous. At Marathon Park in September 1936, he spoke before an estimated 4,000, promising
to "kick the brainless trust out of Washington," assur-
ing that Father Coughlin would be welcomed in the Lemke
White House (9). Lemke also appealed to the growing
number of isolationists among Wisconsin's ethnic groups
by linking the New Deal to communism and himself to
Americanism. His Union party opposed internationalism
in any form and "advocated that we eat, drink, wear and
buy American products" (10). Wisconsin's Germans also
loved to hear Lemke twit Roosevelt for his fear of
foreignism (meaning German) and to call Eleanor the
"pink-tea socialist." When the ballots were counted,
Lemke got more than 10 percent of the national vote in
thirty-nine counties. In twenty-one of the thirty-
nine, Catholics represented more than 50 percent of the
voters. In thirty-eight of the thirty-nine, the pre-
dominant nationality was German. Only four cities gave
Lemke 10 percent of their votes but these were heavily

German and Catholic: St. Paul, Dubuque, Cincinnati,
and Boston (Irish Catholic) (11).

In the election of 1940 Roosevelt losses of 40 to 50
percent occurred in the German rural areas and in the
lone Austrian township. Belgians, Irish, and Italians
abandoned him as did, to a lesser degree, Bohemians and
Swiss. By 1940 even the Scandinavians (with the exception of the Finns) were fading. In the twenty-two
counties where Roosevelt in 1940 suffered a drop of
more than twenty percentage points voters had given
Phil La Follette 45 percent of their votes for the
governorship in 1936. In 1938 La Follette lost all but
one of the same counties. President Roosevelt carried
Wisconsin in 1940 but his margin was extremely close
and his average losses by counties (17 percent) were
greater than in any other state (12). During World
Wars I and II, Germanic groups moved away from the
Democratic party, which they held responsible for
America's hard line against Germany. Moreover, as
Samuel Lubell has pointed out, Swedish-Americans in the
early years of World War I were as fiercely antiwar as
German-Americans while the Norwegians were only slight-
ly less so. The Swedish-American press and clergy
assailed Russia in 1914 as Sweden's traditional enemy
while Germany was considered a champion of Protestant
and Teutonic civilization. In 1916 and 1920 Wisconsin
voters carried their feelings into the ballot booths.
Once again in 1940 these groups were disappointed.
Some German-Americans now turned isolationist. Jewish,
Polish, and Norwegian voters found fault with Hitler's
anti-Semitism, his invasion of Poland in 1939 and of
Norway by the time of the 1940 elections. In the
presidential race of 1944, FDR lost Wisconsin, proving
that the defection of ethnic voters that began in 1936
intensified with each successive election. By 1944 the
Progressive party of the La Follettes had largely subsided and Milwaukee socialism was practically dead.
Moreover, the war effort greatly distorted Wisconsin's
unique character by uprooting her people either for the
battlefield or for the work force in big-city defense
plants.

A United States Nazi _Sturm-Abteilung,_ begun in 1923,
advanced steadily until 1932, when the movement had
many local units, newspapers, and magazines in major
cities of the German belt (13). Following Hitler's
ascent to power in 1933, the "Society of the Friends of

New Germany" was organized, which published <u>Das neue
Deutschland</u>. In 1935 the German government forbade
German citizens in the United States from joining the
"Friends." Thus, in 1936 it changed its title to
<u>Deutschamerikanische Volksbund</u>, Bund for short. Led by
Fritz Kuhn, the Bund was very active in the following
years but the release of material assembled by the
Martin Dies Committee on Un-American Activities in 1939
caused it to decline rapidly. Kuhn was arrested for
embezzling funds, imprisoned, and eventually deported
to his native Munich where he died.

Most Germans in Wisconsin, it would appear, were
oblivious to the Bund's existence. Nevertheless in the
Milwaukee suburb of Grafton there was a sizable number
of Bundists who met regularly at Camp Hindenburg (14).
Established in 1937 on twenty acres along the Milwaukee
River in Grafton, the Bund staged outings, rallies, and
picnics. In 1939 the Wisconsin Federation of German-
American Societies, a group founded primarily to counter the Bund, preempted the lease on the twenty acres
and founded Camp Carl Schurz in its place. The Baud,
through a front organization called the Grafton Settlement League, purchased land about a mile away on the
river and reopened Camp Hindenburg on May 31, 1940.
Next the American Legion established a task force to
take down license-plate numbers of automobiles parked
in the vicinity to discover the identities of individuals
involved. As a result of a government lawsuit in 1942,
the names of the stockholders of the Grafton Settlement
League were made public. Meanwhile the Bund held
rallies in Milwaukee and Kenosha using Highland Café as
a meeting place. Shortly after the United States
entered World War II, the Bund dissipated (15).

With the death of President Roosevelt in 1945,
ethnic voters in Wisconsin began their trek back to the
Democratic party. Samuel Lubell has shown that by
virtue of his death, Roosevelt removed the roadblock to
a successful victory for the Democratic party, which
now realigned itself with the German stronghold of the
Midwest, especially Wisconsin (16). German precincts
that voted heavily for Dewey in 1944 fell handily to
Truman in 1948. Over a dozen rural Wisconsin counties
lost by Roosevelt in 1940 and 1944 returned to the
Democratic fold in 1948, enabling Harry Truman to carry
Wisconsin by 4.4 percent in 1948. In the gubernatorial
race of 1950, however, Republican Walter Kohler, Jr.,

son of the former governor of Austrian-American ancestry, triumphed over the Democrat Carl Thompson. In
1950, as previously, Republican voters were the Dutch
Reformed, native stock, and German Lutherans. Also
favorable to the Republicans were the English, Welsh,
Swedish, and Danish as well as the Belgian and some
German Catholic rural dwellers. Democratic adherents
were the Polish, Finnish, and Irish. The flexibility
of the German Catholics along with the Italians, Swiss,
Norwegians, and Bohemians made the 1948 switch to
Truman a reality (17).

After the cessation of hostilities, one of the many
new faces on the Wisconsin political landscape was
Joseph R. McCarthy, who was born on November 14, 1908,
of Timothy and Bridget McCarthy, Irish Catholics.
After graduation from the Jesuit Marquette University
in Milwaukee, young Joe practiced law at Waupaca ánd
Shawano before being elected to the bench in 1939.
Three years later in 1942 he left his judgeship to
enlist as a private in the United States Marine Corps,
in which he reached the rank of captain as a result of
campaigns in Guadalcanal, Munda, and Bougainville (18).
McCarthy won the Republican senatorial primary held on
August 13, 1946, against Senator Robert M. La Follette,
Jr., by the slim margin of 5,378 votes, thus ending
forty-six Senate years of the La Follettes. Paradox-
ically, La Follette placed more emphasis on the Communist menace than did McCarthy, whose name was destined
to become synonymous with the Cold War Communist scare.
Claiming after his defeat that he always endured rather
than enjoyed public life, La Follette in fact found
private life the more unendurable and at the age of
fifty-eight in February 1953 committed suicide (19).

Joe's grandfather Stephen McCarthy was born in Ireland and came to the United States about 1850, buying
land in Outagamie County in 1855. In 1862 Stephen
married Margaret Stoffel, whose parents had immigrated
from Bavaria, and raised many children who also farmed
in the area. The McCarthys made up an Hibernian island
in a sea of German and Dutch farmers, an enclave that
came to be known as the Irish Settlement. Three-
quarters Irish and one-quarter German, Joe was the
fifth child. In the country school he attended, the
children of German background heavily outnumbered the
McCarthys. Later Joe raised chickens on his father's
farm until a series of disasters ruined him in 1928.

In 1929, at the age of twenty-one, he enrolled as a
freshman in high school but in just one year completed
all subjects for a diploma through sheer "will power,
unusual ability, and concentrated work" (20). Senator
Joseph McCarthy would have remained an unknown and
ineffective senator from Wisconsin had he not found a
cause that happened to please his constituency. By
1950 several things had outraged German and Irish
Catholics. One was that the United States government
seemed powerless against the rising threat of communism
in Europe. Ever since the 1930s the official Catholic
Church had been sympathetic toward Germany because it
offered the best hope against atheistic communism.
German farmers in Wisconsin liked the Republican slogan
"Get the reds out of the government and the government
out of the red." They could not understand why the
United States was giving aid to Communist Tito of
Yugoslavia and refusing it to the Catholic Franco of
Spain. Paranoia in Wisconsin over the Communist threat
was exemplified in heavily German Marathon County when
a nationally advertised "Day under Communism" was
staged in the town of Mosinee on May 1, 1950. At
daybreak, under the auspices of the Wisconsin American
Legion, Mayor Ralph Kronewetter was arrested and with
police chief Carl Gewiss liquidated. Townsfolk witnessed censorship, atheism, book burnings, executions, and
ate nothing but black bread while a Council of People's
Commissars proclaimed victory over capitalism. National television, newsreel cameras, and the world's press
reported the event widely (21).

McCarthy seized the opportunity! As a senator grop-
ing for an issue he demanded 100 percent Americanism as
fanatically as World War I advocates, for Americanism
now captivated ethnic voters with promises of saving
their homelands. By 1952, when McCarthy was up for re-
election, he was able to carry the state handily,
polling between 61 and 78 percent in most counties.
Some of his success can be ascribed to Eisenhower,
whose campaign the Republicans had specifically designed to capture the ethnic vote. After analyzing why
they had lost in 1948, the Republican National Committee
organized an Ethnic Origins Division in 1952. Strate-
gists made detailed studies of the distribution of
Americans of foreign origin broken down by politically
strategic states, cities, and congressional districts.
The committee also gathered data on the foreign-lan-

guage press, ethnic churches, and societies, and cut
phonograph records that featured a political tract in
the foreign language, "The Star-Spangled Banner," and
the respective national anthem for the country of
origin (22). The committee sought also to counter
anti-Eisenhower feelings among Wisconsin Poles for his
acceptance of the Soviet Order of Suvarov and for
taking a grant from the Communist government of Poland
to establish a chair of Polish literature while he was
president of Columbia University. The Germans in Wisconsin resented Eisenhower for the Carthaginian armistice he had imposed on Germany and for the "heartless
exiling of some 200,000 Germans to Russia for slave
labor." Gradually, however, the General redeemed himself by insisting that West Germany be brought into the
North Atlantic Treaty Organization.

The Wisconsin primary by 1952 had become the testing
ground for fledgling candidates for the presidency.
Although McCarthy was oblivious to the Communist
threat previously, the man he defeated in the Republican primary in 1946, Bob La Follette, had written about
it McCarthy-style in a widely publicized 1947 article
in Collier's entitled "Turn the Light on Communism."
Astonishingly La Follette and not McCarthy was the
first to claim that he knew "from firsthand experience
that Communist sympathizers had infiltrated into committee staffs on Capitol Hill in Washington" (23). He
presented no concrete evidence to support his allegations. Known until 1950 only as the man who had beaten
La Follette, McCarthy launched his wrenching crusade
against Communists in government as if to mirror La
Follette, whom he considered a potentially formidable
opponent for the 1952 senatorial campaign. Any number
of superficial pundits wanted to see in McCarthy the
political heir of "Fighting Bob" La Follette. Invited
in 1951 by Vance Packard, editor of American Magazine,
to write a hard-hitting piece against Senator Joseph
McCarthy and his methods, Young Bob declined. When the
Truman adminstration tried to recruit him for various
jobs, including the chance to run as a Democrat against
McCarthy in 1952, he again refused (24). When both
Eisenhower and Stevenson sought his help in the presidential campaign he rejected all offers. Some said La
Follette feared McCarthy would call him to testify
about the article in Collier's. He never did.

The Wisconsin primary by 1952 had become the testing
ground for fledgling candidates for the presidency.
Governor Earl Warren, General Dwight D. Eisenhower,

Senator Robert Taft, and Harold Stassen all entered the
primary. The 1948 favorite-son hopeful, General Douglas MacArthur, had been recalled in 1951 and in 1952
threatened to run in the primary but did not become a
candidate (25). The Democrats hoped Republican Walter
Kohler would become McCarthy's opponent but in the end
he refused and stood for re-election as governor. That
fall Eisenhower campaigned nervously, and occasionally
with McCarthy on the same platform, obliquely rejecting
McCarthy's methods while asking his audience to support
the whole ticket (26). McCarthy dismissed the Democra-
tics with the suggestion that if Adlai E. Stevenson
rather than Nixon had served on the House Un-American
Activities Committee, Alger Hiss might be Secretary of
State or a presidential candidate himself. In a nationally televised speech in support of the Republican
ticket, McCarthy made the calculated slip, "Alger--I
mean Adlai" (27). When the balloting was finished
analysts at the national level concluded that recip-
ients of McCarthy's support had actually been impaired
(28). In states other than Wisconsin, those candidates
whom McCarthy backed ran 5 percent behind the Republican norm. In Wisconsin, however, McCarthy was unques-
tionably a favorite son. Conservative Catholic voters
were particularly enthusiastic about him, especially
those with an isolationist tinge. The Irish, Poles,
Catholic Germans, and Czechs strongly supported him.
It would appear that McCarthyism in Wisconsin emerged
as a latent revenge of ethnic voters against Roosevelt
policymakers who had propelled America into a war
against Germany only to lose the advantage to Communist
Russia, the real terror for Catholic ethnics in Wisconsin. In not one of the counties harboring large German-
American settlements that Lubell had visited did a
single person believe that any accommodation with the
Soviet Union was possible (29). The Germans and Poles
in Wisconsin were less than pleased that all of Poland
and half of Germany had fallen behind the Iron Curtain.
During the spring of 1954, Wisconsinites led by
Leroy Gore, the redoubtable newspaper editor and publisher of the Sauk Prairie Star at Sauk City, initiated
a petition to recall Senator McCarthy. By the June 5,
1954, deadline, recall supporters had collected about
400,000 signatures, although the exact total will never
be known. When the Sauk county district attorney sub-
poenaed them, campaigners whisked many away and buried

the rest on local farms. Journalists counted 335,000
in the Chicago Hilton and 50,000 in Minneapolis (30).
In the recall movement, ethnicity played conflicting
roles. Arthony Gruszka, the Milwaukee editor of the
Wisconsin Republican, created the "Wisconsin Poles for
McCarthy Club" to keep Polish Americans from signing
but Casimar Kendziorski, a wheelhorse Democrat in Milwaukee's Polish community, denounced the club, and
urged support of the "Joe Must Go" movement. Poles
were still voting Democratic and were therefore willing
to bid good-bye to any Republican. Farmers across the
state turned out in droves against McCarthy, factory
workers of all ethnic stripes favored the recall, and
tradespeople threw their support behind the movement.
State labor leaders were slow to voice official support
for recall, but eventually the pressure of locals
brought them to take a stand.

Notably silent were Wisconsin's pulpits. Not a
single group of Catholics, Protestants, or Jews endorsed the recall. Protestant clergymen had already
been attacked by the senator and feared new outbursts.
Catholics apparently tried to maintain the spirit of
separation of church and state, for they wanted state
aid for busing and indirect school subsides. In addition, McCarthy was Irish and Catholic. The recall
movement must be characterized as a genuine, grass-
roots effort in which ethnicity lined up on both sides.
Although the recall failed, the message nevertheless
reached Washington. For his behavior toward committees
of Congress, but not for his abridgment of civil liber-
ties, McCarthy was censured by the Senate on December
2, 1954, in a 67-22 vote, the Democrats voting unanimously in favor, the Republicans splitting evenly, 22
on each side. As rapidly as his star had risen, it now
plunged into oblivion. On May 2, 1957, he died of a
liver ailment that was hastened by heart trouble, her-
nia, and excessive alcoholism (31). Before McCarthy
was buried on May 7 at Appleton, 25,000 people filed
through St. Mary's Catholic Church to visit the bier.
In death many praised him. Others, like the editors of
the Wisconsin State Journal, found that while McCarthy
had made Americans dramatically conscious of Communists, he had also made them aware of "conscience, the
need for fair play, and the basic American right to
assumption of innocence until proven guilty" (32).

McCarthy in the long run did not serve Wisconsin or

the ethnic groups in the state very well. Nor was the Republican party served. After Joe's passing the Grand Old Party disappeared from Wisconsin power posts and to this day has never memorialized him. His opponents on many levels, especially the Democrats on the political stump, could finally unite on one issue: their opposition to McCarthy. Joe's death also conveniently marks an end to the Cold War. Following him in Wisconsin were a new breed of leaders and vastly different issues: the Kennedy years and the Vietnam War. Questions of Communist conspiracies and the dreadful plight of people in East European countries, whence so many of Wisconsin's immigrants had derived, now turned to a much more distant immigrant group. The issues of the 1960s were to be not communism and the oppression of Europeans, but civil rights and the lack of freedom for black Americans. How Wisconsin would behave through this new struggle is the story of our next chapter.

Chapter Ten
Ethnic Trends in Wisconsin, 1958–1980

After the McCarthy era, attention shifted away from issues of the Cold War, especially once the erection of the Berlin Wall in 1961 had dashed all hopes of rolling back the Iron Curtain to free ethnic brothers in Europe. Most nationality groups in Wisconsin acquiesced to the status quo and their contact with relatives in Europe diminished. After 1961 the super powers tried to woo the Afro-Asian peoples as they emerged from colonialism. By refusing to be controlled by either Western- or Eastern-bloc powers, Third World nations enkindled black pride in America, which ultimately inspired all ethnic groups in Wisconsin to search for their ancestral identities. Sparked by the enthusiasm of the Kennedy administration, progress for black and white ethnicity reached a zenith during the Johnson years, just as the nation was being wrenched by the Vietnam debacle. "Americanism" now came to mean monolingualism and monoculturalism, for Wisconsin's young people by 1970 had been "cleansed" of their European accents. Ignorance of a foreign culture was now taken for granted, even openly advocated.

In Wisconsin politics after McCarthy there were gaps to be filled. William Proxmire, a Democrat who in 1949 had moved to Wisconsin from Illinois and had run thrice unsuccessfully for governor, was elected to fill the senate vacancy left by Joseph McCarthy in 1957. Proxmire's victory over Republican Governor Walter J. Kohler inspired some to see in his election a rebirth of the La Follette politics of a half-century earlier. Proxmire seemed the appropriate successor to a family legacy that had been so rudely interrupted by McCarthy. His strategy for success, like Fighting Bob's, lay in a trek to the grass roots, a tireless campaign that rekindled the Democratic party in Wisconsin. Democrat Gaylord Nelson rode to the governorship in 1958 and to a senate seat in 1962 (1). Both Democratic senators

remained in power until Nelson was overwhelmed in the
Reagan landslide of 1980. About 50 percent of the
Germans and 78 percent of the Poles and East Europeans
supported Proxmire, but the exact reasons for the
success the two senators enjoyed remains for further
investigation. The same applies to analyzing the
achievements and perennial successes of Democratic
congressional standbys, among them Fourth District
Clement Zablocki, a Milwaukee-born Polish American (who
died in office on December 3, 1983), and the powerful
Congressman Henry S. Reuss, a Milwaukee-born German-
American who served Wisconsin's heavily German Fifth
District from 1954 to 1982. Called to Hyannis Port in
the summer of 1960, Reuss headed the ethnic voters
division of the Kennedy campaign, latter served presidents as an adviser on Germany, and helped initiate a
Peace Corps for the Federal Republic of Germany in
1963.
On the field of national politics, Wisconsin in 1960
exercised a decisive role in the selection of John F.
Kennedy, a choice in which ethnic voters had a say.
The setting was the Democratic primary in which Kennedy
squared off against Hubert H. Humphrey from neighboring
Minnesota. When the results of the April 5 primary
were known, Kennedy had won in six of the ten cogres-
sional districts, with 56.3 percent of the statewide
vote (2). Except for John Giacomo, the streetworker
official, ethnic-charged labor leaders like George
Haberman, president of the state AFL–CIO, Harvey Kitz-
man, regional director of the UAW, and Sam Rizzo, the
Racine director of the state Machinists' Union, all
supported Humphrey. Kennedy won in only thirty-three
of the seventy-one counties, for Humphrey captured the
West and North, which were influenced by Minnesota news
media. Humphrey did best among Scandinavians while
Kennedy excelled in the Polish, German, and Bohemian
Fox River Valley and in the industrial centers of
Milwaukee, Racine, and Kenosha, where recent immigrants
and their children held the balance of power. Only
three of the nineteen most Democratic counties failed
to report a majority for Kennedy, while seven gave him
more then 60 percent. All of the latter were Catholic
and German. Residents in these counties reportedly
looked on Kennedy as a good Democrat who bore the image
of an immigrant (Irish). James Bartlett in the <u>Green
Bay-Press</u> ascertained that Republican counties of the

South and Southwest (Yankee, English, and Scots)
opposed Kennedy (3). The Scandinavians quite naturally
favored Humphrey both for his liberalism and his missionary image.

Like so many national presidential hopefuls before
him, George Wallace came calling in the Wisconsin
primary of 1964. Once again it was the La Follette
open primary together with early timing that made
Wisconsin attractive for testing bipartisan support for
an upstart candidate. As if pitching his campaign like
Kennedy before him to the white, ethnic, Catholic
voter, Wallace concentrated on Milwaukee and the Fox
River Valley. In 1964 civil rights was the national
issue. Democratic blue-collar voters in South Milwaukee resented Governor John W. Reynolds's unsuccessful
attempt in early 1964 to get the Wisconsin state legislature to pass an open-housing law. In the primary,
Reynolds now squared off against Wallace, giving a
national significance to the outcome (4). Wallace had
gained notoriety for his stand against civil rights in
1963. Following speaking engagements on America's best
campuses, Wallace appeared at the University of Wisconsin in Madison just nine days after the House of Representatives passed the sweeping new Civil Rights Bill.
On this and other visits he learned how easy it was to
enter a Wisconsin primary. On the filing deadline of
March 6, therefore, Wallace flew to Madison and entered
as a Democrat for the April 7 contest. Immediately he
welcomed support from the John Birch Society and challenged Governor Reynolds to a television debate on
civil rights. The latter declined.

The reactions of Wisconsin in 1964 contradicted
those of 1960, when Kennedy won because of the support
he received from ethnic Catholics. Catholic newspapers
editorialized against Wallace; hotels refused to lodge
him and his entourage; pickets greeted him everywhere.
Following in Kennedy's footsteps Wallace moved through
the conservative Fox River Valley praising Joe McCarthy
and ascribing the Civil Rights Bill to the Communists.
He hoped desperately to resurrect the former coalition
of ethnic and religious voters to work a political
miracle. He even brought from Alabama a bevy of
Polish, Greek, Slovakian, German, Italian, and Jewish
campaigners to excite Wisconsin voters of non-English
background.

Wallace's greatest success was achieved with south-

side Milwaukeeans who spoke English with noticeable
Polish or East European accents. Most of them had
struggled to purchase their own homes in spite of low
levels of education and modest factory pay. Most had
rendered distinguished service to the United States
during two world wars. Most of their communities had
been augmented after 1945 by a large influx of displaced persons who came because of the failures (in
their minds) of American foreign policy toward the
Communist onslaught in Eastern Europe. In 1964 their
children overwhelmingly were still enrolled in all-
white public and parochial schools. What these Milwaukeeans had accomplished had cost enormous personal
sacrifice.

During Wallace's 1964 campaign, the popular gathering spot was Serbian Hall, which was operated by the
St. Sava Serbian Orthodox Church. For their part, the
Milwaukee Serbs and Croations clustered around several
churches in Milwaukee and in two of the close suburbs,
Cudahy and West Allis. Cudahy was the home of the
Patrick Cudahy Meat Packing Company while West Allis
was the base of Allis-Chalmers Corporation, where large
numbers of the slavic population of Milwaukee found
jobs. Not until the twentieth century did the Serbs
found a colony in Milwaukee, after arriving from the
Austro-Hungarian states of Slavonia, Lika, Vojvodina,
Bosnia, and Hercegovina. Numbering 2,500 in 1910 they
began to organize fraternal societies and their own
church. By 1916 they had increased to 5,000 and established a chapter of the Serbo-American National Defense
League. Of peasant origin, they lacked the skills for
socioeconomic upward movement. Among them were Serbian
Socialists who agitated on the labor front. In 1916
many with a nationalist frame of mind left Milwaukee to
serve on the Salonika front, while others came to the
United States only after World War II.

St. Sava Serbian Orthodox Church erected American
Serb Hall on the corner of Oklahoma and 51st Streets in
1949 and in 1956 added a new cathedral built in the
style of a medieval Serbian monastery. In suburban
Cudahy the members of St. Nikola Parish were for the
most part post-World War II immigrants who actively
taught their youth the Serbian language along with
relgion in Saturday and Sunday schools of the parish.
At the Milwaukee site, a new cultural center adjacent
to St. Sava's was completed in 1973. Here and in

American Serb Hall, over twenty-five parish organizations meet regularly to carry on ethnic traditions. At
Serb Hall the entire Slavic public had access to the
bars, the bowling alleys, and the great meeting room,
which can be scheduled for a wide range of activities.
Living in close proximity to but not necessarily in
strict harmony with the Serbs, Poles, and Croations
were the Slovenians, whose immigrant stock population
in Milwaukee and West Allis reached about 25,000 by
1950. They supported thriving Slovenian churches as
well as parochial schools in both Milwaukee and West
Allis (6).

Of course the largest Slavic element in South
Milwaukee is the Polish. In 1964, when George Wallace
arrived to meet his audience in Serb Hall, he was
greeted by the most enthusiastic audience of his primary campaign. As he entered, the overflow crowd burst
forth spontaneously singing the first stanza of "Dixie"
in Polish, the reverberations of which were heard in
both Madison and Washington, D.C. Immediately Governor
Reynolds and President Lyndon B. Johnson arranged for
Postmaster General John A. Gronouski to fly in from
Washington and campaign nonstop among his fellow Poles,
especially in the Fourth District. Born of an Irish
mother and Polish father, Gronouski grew up at Oshkosh
and in August 1963 became the first cabinet member of
Polish extraction in history, a gesture designed by
Kennedy to placate Polish Americans who had deserted
the Democratic party on account of the civil rights
movement. To shore up the Polish-American vote, Presi-
dent Johnson in 1965 appointed Gronouski ambassador to
Poland (7). In 1964 Gronouski visited Polish and East
European voters not only in Milwaukee but also in Green
Bay, Sheboygan, Madison, and the Fox River Valley.
Everywhere he went Wisconsin ethnic organizations were
persuaded to endorse Reynolds. They included the Milwaukee County Citizens´ Committee, which had representatives from the Polish National Alliance, the Polish
Roman Catholic Union, and many others. Nevertheless,
Wallace gained support from the rank and file by reit-
erating that the Civil Rights Bill would inevitably
destroy their neighborhoods and their schools.

The Poles of Milwaukee´s south side were a special
group. Bounded by Oklahoma on the South, 27th on the
West, and Greenfield on the North, they constituted a
New World Polonia unto themselves. There was a sizable

ward of Poles on the north side of Milwaukee, too, but
the north-side Poles behaved and voted differently.
Republican Governor John Blaine captured large numbers
of the south side but few north-side Polish votes as
far back as the 1920s (8). Support for Socialist
candidates likewise was confined exclusively to the
Polonia on the south side. Polish voters on the north
side consistently remained Democratic. The south-side
Polish community according to the 1905 state census was
concentrated in Wards 11, 12, and 14, the most densely
Polish being the 14th. The north-side Poles were in
Wards 13, 15, and 18. In 1905 Ward 14 had the highest
density (thirty-six persons per acre) and the highest
local death rate (15.1 per thousand) of any area in the
state. Water supplies were usually independent for
each dwelling but separate toilet facilities were rare.
Below-grade habitation was not uncommon and in numerous
cases basement families lived in one room (9). It
appears, however, that the pyramiding of housing derived not from any failure to appreciate hygienic living or from an inability to afford something better.
The real reason was the intense desire of the Polish
immigrant to own his own home in the ethnic community.
Milwaukee had always had an exceptionally high rate of
home ownership when judged by state and national standards. But owner occupancy in the 14th Ward in 1940
exceeded the average for the city, suggesting that the
first-generation Polish families placed an unusually
high priority on home ownership. Overcrowding persisted as late as 1940, when 47 percent of the inhabitants
of dwelling units were either sharing bathroom facilities or had none at all, twice the city average.
Between 1940 and 1970, however, the rate of ownership
continued to rise while congestion declined. In the
period leading up to the Wallace appearance, the percentage of units lacking bathroom facilities fell below
8 percent and the number of persons per household was
reduced to 2.9, reflecting the fact that Poles who had
doubled families in one house to support a mortgage had
realized their goals (10).

A few Polish political leaders, such as Leo Krzycki,
in the 1930s tried to reach out beyond the Polish 14th
Ward by calling on farmers to unite with urban laborers
under a Socialist banner to overthrow the corrupt capi-
talist system. After World War II, Krzycki received
Communist Poland's highest civilian honor, an indica-

tion of how much he was revered in his old homeland, although in the end this accolade proved to be a bit much for the Milwaukee Poles (11). Between 1910 and 1940, also, Milwaukee Poles had elected twenty-three of their own aldermen, seven of whom were Socialists. The last was not defeated until 1936 when other Poles swamped him in landslide victories. Usually the office of municipal comptroller was held by a Pole, for example, by Louis Kotecki from 1912-33, and bore the popular title of "Polish Mayor." The abject living conditions of the Poles in their early life in Milwaukee, coupled to a maverick attraction of the south-side Poles for socialism, seems to explain their 1964 enthusiasm for George Wallace. When they temporarily toyed with socialism as a solution to their problems the Catholic Church turned critical. In the early twentieth century Archbishop Sebastian G. Messmer prohibited Catholics from joining the Socialists under pain of excommunication. Polish clergymen steadily hammered the message that "a good Catholic is a good Democrat." The stormiest protagonist among them, Wenceslaus Kruszka, called socialism "the seduction of a serpent" (12). In 1964 pulpits rang out against Wallace with equal vigor, and a parallel lack of effect.

In contrast to the silence of the pulpits during the McCarthy elections, priests, nuns, and many laymen cried out against the segregationist positions of George Wallace. But in the face of their mentors, the south-side Poles rekindled their spunky Socialist streak to defy their leaders and vote for the mischiefmaker. Underlying the issue was the fear that their hard-won economic gains would be eroded by the civil rights movement. The Poles of Portage, Brown, Trempealeau, and Marinette counties were not especially generous with votes for Wallace in 1964. Their economic situations were substantially different from those of Polish south-side Milwaukee.

When the polls closed on April 7, 1964, George Wallace had won 266,136 votes compared to 522,405 for John W. Reynolds statewide. A significant crossover vote is indicated by the fact that unopposed Republican John W. Byrnes got only 299,612. The traditionally Democratic districts of Milwaukee, populated by working Poles, Italians, Serbs, Croatians, and others, gave Wallace his greatest boost. He also won majorities in comparable precincts in Racine and Kenosha (13). In

most counties Wallace ran third behind both Reynolds
and Byrnes, but in eight he ran second: Douglas, Iron,
and Vilas in the rural far north (counties with many
Poles, Italians, and Finns) and Milwaukee, Kenosha,
Racine, Waukesha, and Ozaukee in the southeastern lakeshore district. In the post-World War II period, these
two sections--the industrial Southeast and the shipping
and mining Northwest--were home to the most recent
influx of white ethnics. Reynolds's greatest loss from
his 1962 returns occurred in the thirty-three precincts
of the Polish 14th Ward of Milwaukee. This was the
heavily Democratic Fourth Congressional District,
represented in the House of Representatives by Clement
Zablocki, who in 1975 would receive an honorary LL.D.
from the Jagiellonian University of Krakow, Poland.
Reynolds won overwhelmingly in the black precincts of
Milwaukee. Wallace ran well in the German, affluent
Ninth Congressional District, which has Wisconsin's
highest per-capita income and is rimmed by Negro neighborhoods. The Sixth Congressional District, staunchly
German, includes the cities of Oshkosh, Fond du Lac,
and Sheboygan as well as Washington and Ozaukee counties. In the Sixth, Wallace compaigned vigorously and
won only 23 percent of the vote, well below his state
average of 34 percent (14). At the behest of ethnic
and Republican protest voters, George Wallace carried
on a twelve-year effort to influence national politics.
Not until 1976, when Jimmy Carter was endorsed by both
Wallace and Martin Luther King, Sr., did his struggle
finally end.
    Beginning with the year 1950 Wisconsin harbored new
ethnic groups who were statistically insignificant in
previous decades. This was the result of post-World
War II immigration under the Displaced Persons Act of
June 29, 1951 (15). While the original act authorized
only 205,000 DPs to immigrate from war-occupied zones
of Germany, Italy, and Austria, amendments brought the
total to over 440,000 by 1952. Nearly 10 million
ethnic Germans from various nations had flooded into
Germany ahead of the Red armies. Immediately after the
collapse of Hitler's Germany, Czechoslovakia, Poland,
Romania, Yugoslavia, and Hungary expelled all remaining
German minorities (<u>Volksdeutsche</u>). Communist Poland
followed with the expulsion of Germans (<u>Reichsdeutsche</u>)
who had formerly lived east of the boundaries formed by
the Oder and Neisse rivers (16). Under similar legis-

lation refugees arrived in the United States from
Hungary in 1956 and after 1960 over 165,000 came from
Cuba.

A great many displaced persons who reached Wisconsin
were ethnic Germans. While some were farm workers and
remained on the land, the majority drifted toward large
cities after their obligations to rural sponsors had
been met. In comparing the foreign-born and foreign-
stock populations of the state for 1940, 1950, and 1960
it does not appear that the relative proportion of the
various ethnic groups was significantly altered by the
influx of DPs. By 1960 the foreign-stock population of
Wisconsin was put at 914,102, of which 326,313 or 36
percent were from Germany. The next-highest number was
10 percent (93,663) from Poland. Below Poland came
Norway (73,505), followed by Sweden (36,352), Austria
(33,446), Czechoslovakia (33,227), Italy (31,673), and
the USSR (29,733). In terms of foreign-born in 1960,
Germany furnished 43,554, 2.5 times the closest compet-
ing nation, Poland, which had 17,695. There were 8,693
born in Norway, 8,479 in Italy. The Austrian-born
(8,441) identified culturally with the Germans. In
1960 Wisconsin also had foreign-born totals of approximately 2,000 each from Lithuania, Latvia, Finland, and
Greece. There were 3,600 Swiss and a like number of
Hollanders, with 4,400 Danes and 1,020 from Belgium.
Mention should also be made of the 13,101 Irish-born
and 5,753 from England. In 1960 Wisconsin did not have
a sizable Mexican or Cuban population, 1,880 and 53,
respectively.

About 7,500 Polish, Latvian, Ukrainian, Lithuanian,
and Estonian DPs also settled in Wisconsin (17). Latvians reportedly made up 40 percent of the contingent
(although the United States census for 1960 reports
only 2,093 foreign-born Latvians plus 2,981 of Latvian
stock in Wisconsin). There were, however, 2,471 of
Lithuanian birth and 7,442 of Lithuanian stock but only
230 Estonians in 1960. Milwaukee had the largest Latvian community, with about 2,000. Fond du Lac had 300,
and about 120 lived in Madison. Earlier Latvian immigrants to Wisconsin, mostly men, had settled in the
northern counties, where they worked in forestry and
clearing farmland of stumps and stones (18). Like
their Finnish cohorts in the northern counties, these
Latvians were anti-Czarist and pro-Communistic because
of the hope socialism held out to them at the time they

left their homeland. They arrived to settle between
1897 and 1922 in Lincoln and Langlade counties in the
vicinity of Merrill, at least 500 coming between the
initial date and 1908. Most were from southwestern
Latvia or northwestern Lithuania, which, along with
Estonia, were provinces of Czarist Russia until 1918.
Farm hands or renters when they left, these Latvians
were poor even though some had spent time working in
the eastern United States. Most came to Wisconsin
because Boston-based Latvian leaders established a
Latvian farm colony in Wisconsin. Gradually the settlers founded an Evangelical Lutheran Church (although
of course the Socialists among them were excluded from
it), a Latvian Welfare Association, and their own meeting hall, which fell victim to an arsonist. Predominantly male, they had to import fiancées from other
Latvian colonies (notably Chicago, Philadelphia, and
Baltimore), as well as newspapers and books. Many of
these Latvians would gladly have returned to Europe
except that they faced automatic imprisonment from
Czarist authorities. In the 1930s they were declared
unwelcome because the new Latvian government feared
these Communistic Latvians might endanger the new autonomous free state.

The Latvian DPs of the 1950s, by contrast were
strongly anti-Communist because they had experienced
Red rules before departing their homeland. They were
also markedly different from the earlier group in educational background, the latter being almost exclusively professionals from the urban centers and not from
the peasant classes, as were those who had settled in
northern Wisconsin. Smitten initially with a "suitcase
mentality," the latter-day arrivals have now given up
plans of returning to Latvia as soon as the political
climate there improves. Most have acquired American
citizenship without surrendering Latvian traditions and
speech.

Two separate Croatian communities developed in
Wisconsin, one in Milwaukee, the other in suburban West
Allis (19). Some arrived early in the twentieth century and founded the Catholic Church of the Sacred
Heart in 1917, on the near north side near the Schlitz
Brewery. Struggling with financial hardship through
the 1930s and an encroaching black population in the
1940s, they moved the church to 49th and Wells in 1949,
but they themselves dispersed throughout the Milwaukee

area. Factory workers and laborers for the most part
from Slavonia, many are trilingual--German, Croatian,
and English. Besides the church organizations, which
include the usual parochial school (in which, however,
only 10 percent of the pupils are Croatian today),
there are lodges, the Croatian Fraternal Union and the
Croatian Catholic Union, a radio station, dance groups,
and a Croatian Central Committee, which coordinates all
others. Estimates put the number of Milwaukeeans of
Croatian background as high as 20,000. The Croatians
in West Allis are visible in their congregation of St.
Augustine, which began in 1929. They constructed their
own church in 1939 at 6700 West Rogers Street. A
parochial school was not built until 1954 but was
expanded in 1963. Today the parish is used also by the
Polish settlement to the extent that Croatian activities are available only at Sacred Heart. Several weekly radio broadcasts in Serbian and Croatian offer
music and political commentary--from Racine and Chicago. The DPs who fostered Serbian and Croatian languages after 1950 have of late been unable to maintain
them.

Another group of DPs that arrived in Wisconsin
around 1950 is called the Danube Swabians. Their
origin dates back to the early eighteenth century, when
Prince Eugene led the combined armies of Germany and
Austria to drive Turkish forces out of southeastern
Europe. In his wake, German farmers were encouraged to
colonize lands bounded by the Rivers Danube, Risza, and
Maros and the Carpathian Mountains beginning in 1722.
A new impetus to migration came between 1763 and 1770
under Empress Maria Theresa and Emperor Joseph II.
When the Austro-Hungarian Empire dissolved after World
War I, local nationalism put increasing pressure on
these Germans, now numbering over a million. The
invading Red armies at the close of World War II forced
nearly all Germans, except for a few pockets in Romania, to depart in 1945. Several hundred thousand came
to the United States. Here they usually joined post-
World War I immigrants in urban colonies, and Milwaukee
has one of the largest. Statistically they are difficult to isolate because their numbers are incorporated
in the 1970 census totals of foreign-born from Yugoslavia (6,850), Hungary (3,717), the USSR (5,961), and
"other Europeans." For example, the 1970 Wisconsin
statistics report only 1,384 speakers of Russian yet

they report 5,961 persons born in the USSR. In 1970 there were only 30,448 persons who had been born in Germany but 47,303 foreign-born in Wisconsin who spoke German as their mother tongue. Some of these are accounted for by the 5,652 who were born in Austria but most were Danube Swabians or <u>Volksdeutsche</u> (ethnic Germans with other than German citizenship). Accustomed from their European experience to maintaining their island culture within a majority of the assimilated (Russians, Romanians, Yugoslavs, or Americans), these Germans assiduously adhere to their German language and traditions. They are strongly organized in clubs, maintain special Saturday schools to teach their progeny Germany, and own a central meeting hall, the <u>Schwabenhof</u>, in Milwaukee. Under the aegis of this large organization, families and groups from special geographic areas enjoy social activities among their own kind (20).

Three-quarters through the twentieth century, Wisconsin's ethnic groups remain constituted as they were when the century dawned. The state was, more than any in the Union, a German state. New York always had more German-born than other states—18 percent of the national total in 1880—followed by Illinois with 12 percent, Ohio with 10 percent, Wisconsin with 9 percent, and Pennsylvania with 8.6 percent. But in terms of percentage of the total population, Wisconsin always had the greatest proportion. Germans in Wisconsin were three times more numerous than their share of the total national population in 1910 when at least ten contiguous counties had 35 percent or more first- and second-generation German populations. The states of Minnesota, Iowa, Nebraska, and Texas each had at least one such 35 percent German county in 1910. Milwaukee always had decisively more Germans on a proportional basis than any other city in America (21). The reports on mother-tongue usage exemplify a similar situation. In 1970 there were 4,417,731 people living in Wisconsin. Of these, 3,279,289 spoke English as their mother tongue. An astonishing 464,453 still spoke German as their first language followed by speakers of Polish (108,192). In 1970 only 24,035 spoke Spanish natively, fewer than those who grew up speaking Italian (24,221).

Spanish-speaking migrant workers became numerous in Wisconsin agriculture during World War II but their numbers declined sharply following the mechanization of

vegetable harvesting methods in the late 1960s (22).
Originally Belgians were the primary source of labor.
Beginning in the early 1900s the Germans from Russia
supplied the main work force, especially in the production of sugar beets. During the 1940s and 1950s
migrant workers were brought in from the British West
Indies. Many field hands came from cities such as
Sheboygan, Milwaukee, Chicago, or St. Louis, and eventually became permanent farmers and landowners. The
West Indians were always considered sojourners (23).
With World War II came a campaign to increase the
production of food for the war effort just as domestic
workers were being siphoned off by the draft and the
lure of high pay in defense plants. Through the Emergency Farm Labor Program (1943-1947) Wisconsin recruited male workers from Jamaica, the Bahamas, British
Honduras, and Mexico. As late as 1945 only 1,300 of
the 6,700 foreign agricultural laborers employed in
Wisconsin were Mexicans. At least 3,500 were German
(together with a few Italian) prisoners of war, captured after the 1943 surrender of the <u>Afrika Korps</u> in
Tunisia (24). Immediately following World War II, the
prisoners left and Wisconsin growers recruited 85 percent of their workers from pools in the United States.
Many of these were Texas Mexicans who were known in
Wisconsin already in the 1920s and 1930s. The shift
away from importing foreign workers occurred because
the emergency program of the federal government lapsed
and the Wisconsin State Employment Service took over
coordination of migrant labor programs (25). Foreign
and domestic workers in Wisconsin during the 1950s
hovered around an annual average of 12,000, mostly
under the impetus of the Bracero Program. After 1963
this program between the United States and Mexico
lapsed and far fewer foreigners were available. The
number declined rapidly from a peak of 15,000 reached
in the mid-1950s because of mechanization of harvest
operations in sugar beets, potatoes, snap beans, and
cherry picking. By 1980 the use of migrant workers in
Wisconsin's rural areas had ceased (26).
     Not technically foreign-born but contributing to the
approximately 25,000 mother-tongue speakers of Spanish
in Wisconsin in 1970 are members of the Puerto Rican
community. Present to some degree in all industrial
cities in southeastern Wisconsin, they are perhaps most
numerous in Milwaukee. According to a survey done in

1976 Puerto Ricans have lived in Milwaukee for about a
quarter of a century. They began settling along State
Street from Jefferson to 35th in the Northeast, in the
Mexican and Chicano area on the South, and on the West
between 12th and the Menomonee River Valley. Migration
began in the late 1940s but did not achieve 2,000 until
1952 as a result of Wisconsin State Employment Service
recruiting on the island, mostly for foundries and
tanneries. Families have long since joined the original laborers and, except for returnees during periods
of economic downturn, have perpetuated their ethnic
community. According to a recent survey 80 percent of
the Puerto Rican population report being Catholic (27).
Most speak only Spanish and enjoy the services of
Spanish newspapers, radio, and television programs.
Because of the language barrier, 85 percent work in
factories and exhibit indifference toward politics.
But bilingual programs in the Milwaukee public schools,
in which 80 percent of the Puerto Rican children are
enrolled, hold out promise for improving the socioeconomic situation.

Similar circumstances obtain for the Mexican population in Milwaukee. A different experience prevailed
for early refugees from the Cuban Revolution because it
removed the upper- and middle-class strata from dominant positions in Cuba after 1962. In Milwaukee, these
Cubans exercised determined individualism to attain
high worldly goals (28). A quite different group of
Cubans arrived at the processing center of Fort McCoy
during the summer of 1980 but their fate in the assimilative cauldron is yet to be determined. No in-depth
studies of the Spanish-speaking communities of Wisconsin have been undertaken except for Racine, where
scholars have statistically compared Mexican-Americans
with Negro and Anglo samples to shed light on the
assimilative process (29). The investigation illustrates how the end of agricultural employment in
Wisconsin has created certain problems for this ethnic
group in the urban setting. Much more study is called
for on this aspect of ethnicity. The same can be said
for the Vietnamese. Except for offical statistics and
newspaper reports, we know next to nothing about Southeast Asians in Wisconsin.

Numerous factors in the economy and in the evolution
of larger cities, which are incessantly absorbing the
state's rural population, account for changes evolving

in the established patterns of ethnic life in Wisconsin. We know nothing about the possible conflicts of new Asian immigrants with the Mexican migrant workers or with new Cuban refugees, not to mention black Americans. Schools continue their assimilative function but, as elsewhere in the United States, have achieved racial balance only by dislocating neighborhoods. The drums on distant Indian reservations have also been heard in Wisconsin, not only in the rural North but also in Milwaukee and in the legislative halls of Madison. Spanish-speaking migrants periodically prick the legislative conscience and from time to time the state government tries to alleviate problems. The permanent impact of the Spanish and Asian presence in Wisconsin awaits serious study. There are many German, Norwegian, Danish, Polish, and other festivals but the precise ethnicity or lack of it in each of them is blurred by the community boosterism that usually accompanies them. Much more study will be necessary to establish the status of Wisconsin's ethnicity in the last decades of the twentieth century.

Appendix

Location of Wisconsin's Major Immigrant Populations in 1910

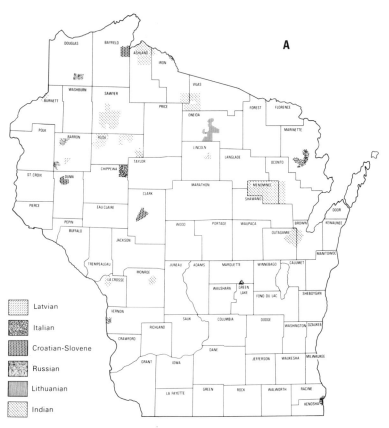

Legend:
- Latvian
- Italian
- Croatian-Slovene
- Russian
- Lithuanian
- Indian

Illustrations by the cartography department of the University of Minnesota.

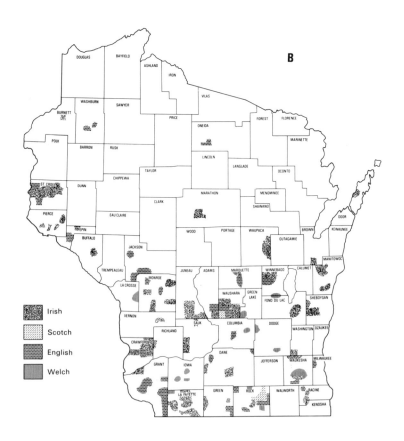

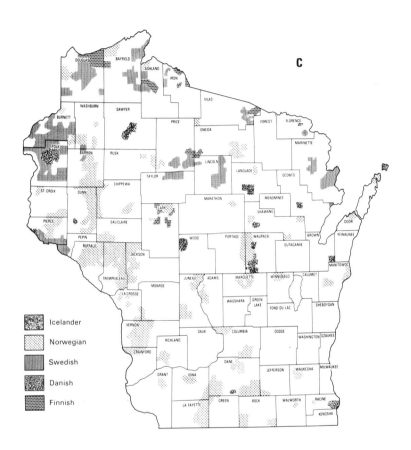

C

Icelander

Norwegian

Swedish

Danish

Finnish

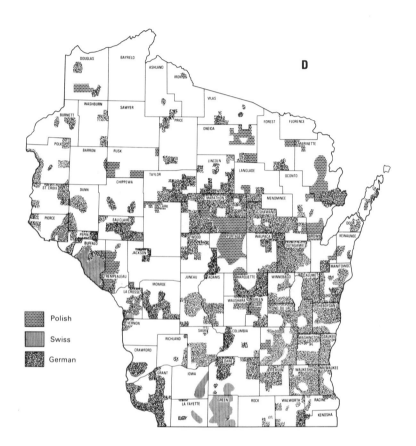

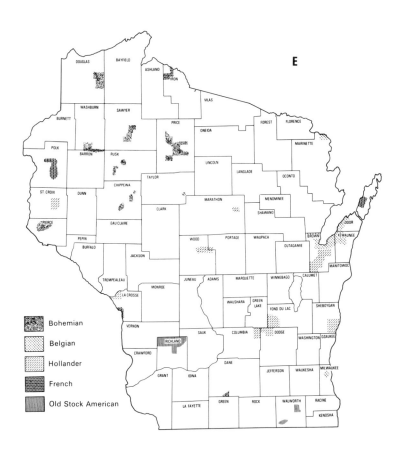

Bohemian

Belgian

Hollander

French

Old Stock American

Notes and References

Five works that appear frequently are abbreviated in the notes:
Collections of the State Historical Society of Wisconsin: Collections SHSW
Historical Messenger of the Milwaukee County Historical Society: Messenger MCHS
Proceedings of the State Historical Society of Wisconsin: Proceedings SHSW
Transactions of the Wisconsin Academy of Sciences, Arts and Letters: Transactions WASAL
Wisconsin Magazine of History: WMH

Preface

1. Old World Wisconsin, a 47-page pamphlet published in 1973 by the Department of Landscape Architecture, School of Natural Resources, and the College of Agricultural and Life Sciences, University of Wisconsin-Madison.
2. Irene Hanson, "European Village," Lore 29 (1979):1-36.

Chapter One

1. Alice E. Smith, The History of Wisconsin, vol. 1: From Exploration to Statehood (Madison: SHSW, 1973), pp. 95-121.
2. Kathleen Neils Conzen, Immigrant Milwaukee, 1836-1860 (Cambridge: Harvard University Press, 1976), pp. 15 ff., and William George Bruce, "Old Milwaukee," WMH 27 (March 1944):295-309. An excellent survey of early immigrants in Wisconsin is chapter 1, "Wisconsin's Immigrants," by Richard M. Bernard, in The Melting Pot and the Altar: Martial Assimilation in Early Twentieth Century Wisconsin (Minneapolis: University of Minnesota Press, 1980), pp. 3-41, including maps and charts.
3. Milwaukee Sentinel, October 9, 1839, in Conzen,

Immigrant Milwaukee, p. 15.

   4. Mack Walker, Germany and the Emigration (Cambridge: Harvard University Press, 1964), especially pp. 157 ff.

   5. Anna Adams Dickie, "Scotch-Irish Presbyterian Settlers in Southern Wisconsin," WMH 31 (March 1948):291-304.

   6. Conzen, Immigrant Milwaukee, p. 21. See also Harry H. Anderson, "Early Scandinavian Settlement in Milwaukee County," Messenger MCHS 25 (March 1969):2-19.

   7. Harry H. Anderson, "Norwegian Shipbuilding in Early Milwaukee," Milwaukee History 1 (Spring/Summer 1978):81-104.

   8. Henry S. Lucas, "Reminiscences of Arend Jan Brusse on Early Dutch Settlement in Milwaukee," WMH 30 (September 1946):85-90; Sipko F. Rederus, "The Dutch Settlements of Sheboygan County," WMH 1 (1917-1918):256-65; and Henry S. Lucas, "The First Dutch Settlers in Milwaukee," WMH 30 (December 1946):174-83.

   9. William George Bruce, "Old Milwaukee's Yankee Hill," WMH 30 (March 1947):289-91.

   10. Louise Phelps Kellogg, "The Story of Wisconsin 1634-1848. Foreign Immigration in Territorial Times," WMH 3 (1920):314-26, and "Immigration," by Robert and Mary Gard, in My Land, My Home, My Wisconsin (Milwaukee: Milwaukee Journal, 1978), pp. 8-12.

   11. Humphrey J. Desmond, "Early Irish Settlement in Milwaukee," WMH 13 (June 1930):365-74. See also Leo Rummel, O. Praem., History of the Catholic Church in Wisconsin (Madison: Knights of Columbus, 1976), pp. 97-105.

   12. Kellogg, "The Story," p. 136; Smith, Wisconsin, p. 489.

   13. Grant Foreman, "Settlement of English Potters in Wisconsin," WMH 21 (June 1938):375-96.

   14. Joseph Schafer, A History of Agriculture in Wisconsin, Wisconsin Domesday Book, 1 (Madison: SHSW, 1922), pp. 23-64, map p. 50. See also the illustrated 39-page pamphlet Phillips G. Davies, Welsh in Wisconsin (Madison: SHSW, 1983).

   15. James A. Bryden, "The Scots in Wisconsin," Proceedings SHSW 1901 (1901), pp. 153-58.

   16. Louis Albert Copeland, "The Cornish in Southwest Wisconsin," Collections SHSW 14 (1898):301-34. Statistics, p. 311.

   17. James I. Clark, The Wisconsin Lead Region:

Frontier Community (Madison: SHSW, 1955), 20 pp., and Joseph Schafer, The Wisconsin Lead Region (Madison: SHSW, 1932).

18. Kellogg, "The Story," p. 319, and Lieselotte Clemens, Old Lutheran Emigration from Pomerania to the U.S.A. The History and Motivation, 1839-1843. (Hamburg: Pomeranian Society, 1976).

19. Encyclopedia of the Lutheran Church (Minneapolis: Augsburg, 1965), 2:885, and J. J. Schlichter, "The Beginning and Early Years of the Mission House," WMH 25 (September 1941):51-72, and (December 1941):187-209.

20. W. F. Whyte, "The Settlement of the Town of Lebanon, Dodge County," Proceedings SHSW (1915), pp. 99-110.

21. Elda O. Baumann, "The History of Potosi," WMH 23 (September 1939):44-57. From this colony came one of Wisconsin's greatest historians and longtime editor of the Wisconsin Magazine of History, Joseph Schafer. Joseph was born on a farm at Muscoda in Grant County of German-born parents, Mattias Schafer and Anna J. Bremmer. See John D. Hicks, "Memorial to Joseph Schafer," WMH 24 (March 1941):249-52.

22. Ferdinand F. Doubrava, "Experiences of a Bohemian Emigrant Family," WMH 8 (June 1925):393-406.

23. Louise Kellogg, "The Story of Wisconsin," p. 320.

24. Chrysostom Adrian Verwyst, "Reminiscenses of a Pioneer Missionary," Proceedings SHSW (1916), pp. 148-85. Letters of Father T. J. Van den Broek in Collections SHSW 14 (1898):192 ff.

25. Leo Schelbert, ed., New Glarus 1845-1970, the Making of a Swiss American Town (Glarus: Tschudi, 1970). See also John Luchsinger, "The planting of the Swiss Colony at New Glarus, Wisconsin," Collections SHSW 12 (1892):333-82; John Paul von Grueningen, ed., The Swiss in the United States (Madison: Swiss-American Historical Society, 1940), pp. 31-33; and J. Q. Emery, "The Swiss Cheese Industry in Wisconsin," WMH 10 (September 1926):42-52.

26. Kellogg, "The Story of Wisconsin," p. 323; Claire Elaine Selkurt, "The Domestic Architecture and Cabinetry of Luther Valley--A Norwegian-American Settlement," unpublished M.A. thesis, University of Wisconsin, 1973; and Richard J. Fapso, Norwegians in Wisconsin (Madison: SHSW, 1977), a useful 39-page pam-

phlet, illustrated but undocumented. See also C. A.
Clausen, ed. & tr., A Chronicler of Immigrant Life:
Svein Nilsson's Articles in Billed-Magazine, 1868-1870
(Northfield, MN: Norwegian-American Historical Asso-
ciation, 1982).

    27. George C. Brown, ed., "A Swedish Traveler in
Early Wisconsin: The Observations of Frederika
Bremer," WMH 62 (August 1978):41-56.

    28. Rasmus B. Anderson, "The First Norwegian Set-
tlements in America, Within the Present Century," Proceedings SHSW (1898), pp. 150-67, esp. 164 ff., and
Albert O. Barton, "Muskego: the Most Historic Norwegian Colony," WMH 21 (December 1937):129-38.

    29. Maps in Mary Josephine Read, "A Population
Study of the Driftless Hill Land During the Pioneer
Period 1832-1860," unpublished Ph.D. dissertation,
University of Wisconsin, 1941, pp. 37, 94, 101, 148.

    30. Margaret Fuller, "The Promise of Milwaukee," in
Walter Havighurst, ed., The Land of the Long Horizons
(New York: Coward-McCann, 1960), pp. 287-88.

    31. Although the blacks are generally excluded from
consideration here, the reader's attention is directed
to Zachary Cooper, Black Settlers in Rural Wisconsin
(Madison: State Historical Society, 1977), a 27-page
pamphlet with a short bibliography.

    32. Jack J. Detzler, ed., `I Live Here Happily': A
German Immigrant in Territorial Wisconsin," WMH 50
(Spring 1967):254-59.

Chapter Two

    1. Guy-Harold Smith, "The populating of Wiscon-
sin," Geographical Review 18 (July 1928):402-21, esp.
403, and his, "The Settlement and the Distribution of
the Populaion in Wisconsin," Transactions WASAL 24
(1929):53-107.

    2. Maps in Smith, "The Settlement," facing p. 420.

    3. John Goadby Gregory, West Central Wisconsin
(Indianapolis: Clarke, 1933), 1:397-490, and 3:863-77.

    4. John I. Kolehmainen and George W. Hill, Haven
in the Wood: The Story of the Finns in Wisconsin (Madison: SHSW, 1965), pp. 27 ff., and Mark Knipping,
Finns in Wisconsin (Madison: SHSW, 1977), pp. 14 ff.

    5. Writers' Program of the Work Projects Adminis-
tration, Wisconsin, A Guide to the Badger State (New
York: Duell, Sloan & Pearce, 1941), p. 217. See also

John Arthur Valentine, "A Study in Institutional Ameri-
canization: The Assimilative History of the Italian-
American Community of Madison, Wisconsin," unpublished
M.A. thesis, University of Wisconsin, 1967.

6. Peter N. Laugesen, "The Immigrants of Madison,
Wisconsin, 1860-1890," unpublished M.A. thesis, University of Wisconsin, 1966. See also in general David
Mollenhoff, Madison (Dubuque, Iowa: Kendall Hunt,
1983).

7. John D. Buenker, "Immigration and Ethnicity,"
in Nicholas C. Burcket, ed., Racine: Growth and
Change in a Wisconsin County (Racine: Racine County
Board of Supervisors, 1977). See also Kristian Hvidt,
Flight to America: The Social Background of 300,000
Danish Emigrants (New York: Academic Press, 1975).

8. John D. Buenker, "Immigration and Ethnic
Groups," in John A. Neuenschwander, ed., Kenosha
County in the Twentieth Century: A Topical History
(Kenosha: County Bicentennial Commission, 1976), pp.
1-49.

9. Leo Rummel, O. Pream., History of the Catholic
Church in Wisconsin (Madison: Knights of Columbus,
1976), pp. 141-45.

10. Peggy Lautenschlager, "The West Siders:
Development and Disintegration of the Volga German
Community in Oshkosh, Wisconsin," senior thesis, Lake
Forest College, Ill., 1977.

11. Richard Sallet, Russian-German Settlements in
the United States, trans. La Vern J. Rippley and Armand
Bauer (Fargo: Institute for Regional Studies, 1974),
p. 55.

12. Ibid.

13. Guido A. Dobbert, "German-Americans between New
and Old Fatherland," American Quarterly 19 (1967):663-
80.

14. Justin B. Galford, "The Foreign Born and Urban
Growth in the Great Lakes, 1850-1950: A Study of
Chicago, Cleveland, Detroit, and Milwaukee," unpub-
lished Ph.D. dissertation, New York University, 1957,
and Louis J. Swichkow and Lloyd P. Gartner, The
History of the Jews of Milwaukee (Philadelphia: The
Jewish Publication Society of America, 1963).

15. Bayrd Still, Milwaukee, The History of a City
(Madison: SHSW, 1948); Conzen, Immigrant Milwaukee;
and Kathleen Neils Conzen, "Pattern of Residence in
Early Milwaukee," in The New Urban History, ed. Leo F.

Schnore (Princeton: Princeton University Press, 1975),
pp. 145-83.
    16. Jonathan David Mayer, "The Journey-to-Work,
Ethnicity and Occupation in Milwaukee, 1860-1900,"
unpublished Ph.D. dissertation, University of Michigan,
1977, pp. 66 ff.
    17. Conzen, Immigrant Milwaukee, pp. 134 ff. See
also Margaret Walsh, The Manufacturing Frontier: Pioneer Industry in Antebellum Wisconsin, 1830-1860 (Madison: SHSW, 1972) esp. pp. 185-88.
    18. See Conzen's chapter on "Vereinswesen," pp. 154
ff. See also other studies, e.g., Francis Magyar, "the
History of the Early Milwaukee German Theater (1850-
1868)," WMH 13 (June 1930):375-86, and Carl Heinz
Knoche, The German Immigrant Press in Milwaukee (New
York: Arno Press, 1980).
    19. Henry Morton Bodfish, ed., History of the
Building and Loan Associations in the United States
(Chicago: Building & Loan League, 1931).
    20. Bayrd Still, Milwaukee, p. 259, and Louise W.
Mears, "Milwaukee: A City of Good Foods," WMH 24 (June
1941):430-36.
    21. Robert G. Carroon, "Foundations of Milwaukee's
Polish Community," Messenger MCHS 26 (September
1970):88-96.
    22. Victor Greene, For God and Country: The
Rise of Polish and Lithuanian Ethnic Consciousness in
America, 1860-1910 (Madison: SHSW, 1975).
    23. William J. Galush, "Faith and Fatherland.
Dimensions of Polish-American Ethnoreligion 1875-1975,"
chapter 5 in Randall M. Miller and Thomas D. Marzik,
Immigrant and Religion in Urban America (Philadelphia:
Temple University Press, 1977), pp. 84-102, and Edward
R. Kantowicz, "Polish Chicago: Survival through
Solidarity," in Melvin G. Holli and Peter d'S. Jones,
eds. The Ethnic Frontier: Essays in the History of
Group Survival in Chicago and the Midwest (Grand
Rapids, Wm. B. Eerdmans, 1977), pp. 179-209.
    24. Anthony J. Kuzniewski, "Milwaukee's Poles,
1866-1918: The Rise and Fall of a Model Community,"
Milwaukee History 1 (1978):13-14.
    25. Roger D. Simon, "Housing and Services in an
Immigrant Neighborhood: Milwaukee's Ward 14," Journal
of Urban History 2 (August 1976):435-57, and Helena
Znaniecki Lopata, Polish Americans: Status Competition
in an Ethnic Community (Englewood Cliffs, N.J.: Pren-
tice-Hall, 1976), pp. 94 ff.

26. Alberto C. Meloni, "Italy Invades the Bloody Third: The Early History of Milwaukee's Italians," Messenger MCHS 25 (March 1969):34-46, and Rudolph Vecoli, "The Formation of Chicago's `Little Italies.'" Journal of American Ethnic History 2 (Spring 1983):5-22.

27. John Arthur Valentine, "A Study in Institutional Americanization: The Assimilative History of the Italian-American Community of Madison, Wisconsin," unpublished M.A. thesis, University of Wisconsin, 1967, pp. 16-17. Tables and appendixes. See also "The Italian Immigrants," in Rummel, History, pp. 112-14, and Rudolph J. Vecoli, "Contadini in Chicago: A Critique of The Uprooted," Journal of American History 51 (December 1964):404-17.

28. Alfred Vagts, Deutsch-Amerikanische Rückwanderung (Heidelberg: Carl Winter, 1960), pp. 14 ff., and Betty Boyd Caroli, Italian Repatriation from the United States (New York: Center for Migration Studies, 1974).

29. Marie Prisland, "The Slovenians, Most Recent American Immigrants," WMH 33 (March 1950):265-80.

30. United States Census, 1950, table 13.

31. Gwen Schulz, "Evolution of the Areal Patterns of German and Polish Settlement in Milwaukee," Erdkunde (1956), pp. 136-41. Thaddeus Borun, We, the Milwaukee Poles (Milwaukee, Nowiny, 1946), history and churches pp. 1 ff.; Kaszubas, pp. 121 ff., ward distribution pp. 154 ff. See also Klaus Bade, "Die Gastarbeiter des Kaiserreichs, oder, Vom Auswanderungsland des 19. Jahrhunderts zum Einwanderungsland Bundesrepublik?" Geschichte in Wissenschaft und Unterricht 2 (1982):79-93.

32. Roger D. Simon, "The Expansion of an Industrial City: Milwaukee, 1880-1910," unpublished Ph.D. dissertation, University of Wisconsin, 1971.

33. Mayer, "The Journey-to-Work," pp. 135 ff., 207 ff. See also in general, Harry H. Anderson and Frederick I. Olson, Milwaukee: At the Gathering of the Waters (Tulsa: Continental Heritage, 1981).

34. United States Census, and Galford, "The Foreign Born" pp. 288 ff.

Chapter Three

1. Kate Asaphine Everest, "How Wisconsin Came by Its Large German Element," Collections SHSW 12

(1982):299-334; Jürgen Eichhoff, "Wisconsin's German-Americans: From Ethnic Identity to Assimilation," German-American Studies 2 (1970):44-54; and Eichhoff, "German in Wisconsin," German Language in America: A Symposium, ed., Glenn Gilbert (Austin: University of Texas Press, 1971), pp. 43-57.

2. Joseph Schafer, Wisconsin Domesday Book, General Studies, vol. 4, The Winnebago-Horicon Basin: A Type Study in Western History (Madison: SHSW, 1937), pp. 142-257, esp. 204 ff. See also Peter McGraw, "The `Kölsch´ Dialect of Dane County, Wisconsin: Phonology, Morphology and English Influence," unpublished Ph.D. dissertation, University of Wisconsin, 1973.

3. Ernest Bruncken, "The Political Activity of Wisconsin Germans, 1854-1860," Proceedings SHSW 49 (1901):190-211, esp. 191. See also Ballard C. Campbell, "Ethnicity and the 1893 Wisconsin Assembly," Journal of American History 62 (June 1975):74-94, and Kathleen Neils Conzen, "Precocious Reformers: Immigrants and Party Politics in Ante-Bellum Milwaukee," Messenger MCHS 33 (Summer 1977).

4. Joseph Schafer, "Know-Nothingism in Wisconsin," WMH 8 (September 1924):14.

5. Ibid., p. 16.

6. A Forty-eighter is a German immigrant, usually well educated and often in sympathy with liberal, even radically socialistic principles, who either fled or was expelled from Germany as a result of the unsuccessful German (and European) revolutions of 1848.

7. Volumes 2, 7, 9, 12, 13, 14, 15, 16, 17, 20, 21, 22, 23, 25, 26, 27, and 29 of the Wisconsin Magazine of History offer articles and references to Carl and his wife, Margarethe. The best recent biography of Schurz is Hans L. Trefousse, Carl Schurz: A Biography (Knoxville: University of Tennessee Press, 1982).

8. Bruncken, "Political Activity," p. 193. See also Wilhelm Hense-Jensen, Wisconsin's Deutsch-Amerikaner bis zum Schluss des neunzehnten Jahrhunderts (Milwaukee: Germania, 1900-1902), 2 vols., pp. 96-140, esp. 118 ff.

9. Hense-Jensen, Wisconsin's Deutsch-Amerikaner, pp. 141-82.

10. Ernest Bruncken, "The Germans in Wisconsin Politics until the Rise of the Republican Party," Parkman Club Publications 9 (Milwaukee, October 13, 1896):225-38, and his "German Political Refugees in the

United States during the Period from 1815-1860,"
Deutsch Amerikanische Geschichtsblätter 3, no. 3
(1903):33-48; 3, no. 4 (1903):33-48; and 4, no. 1
(1905):33-59.

11. Karl Pflaume, "A German Farmer Views Wisconsin,
1851-1863," ed. Hartmut Keil, in WMH 62 (Winter 1978-
1979):128-43; Hense-Jensen, Wisconsin's Deutsch-Amerikaner, pp. 171-82.

12. C. C. Scholes and Amherst W. Kellogg, "Historical Fragments, the Chicago Convention of 1860," WMH 5
(June 1921):99-104.

13. Frederick C. Luebke, ed., Ethnic Voters
and the Election of Lincoln (Lincoln: University of
Nebraska Press, 1971); Hense-Jensen, Wisconsin's
Deutsch-Amerikaner, pp. 183-210.

14. Joseph Schafer, "Who Elected Lincoln," in
Luebke, Ethnic Voters, pp. 46-61.

15. Walter S. Glazer, "Wisconsin Goes to War April
10, 1861," WMH 50 (Winter 1967):147-64.

16. Richard N. Current, The History of Wisconsin
(Madison: SHSW, 1976), p. 299. See also Frank
Klement, "Copperheads and Copperheadism in Wisconsin:
Democratic Opposition to the Lincoln Administration,"
WMH 42 (Spring 1959):182-88.

17. Horn letter to Governor Alexander Randall,
April 18, 1861. About Horn, cf. Joseph Schafer, Wisconsin Domesday Book, General Studies, vol. 2, Four
Wisconsin Counties, Prairie and Forest (Madison: SHSW,
1927), pp. 236 ff.

18. Current, History of Wisconsin, p. 306.

19. Turners were members of the German gymnastic
societies that began in Germany in response to the
Napoleonic Wars. Founded by Friedrich Jahn to develop
a sense of patriotism among the German people, the
Turner movement was suppressed by Metternich in 1819.
In the 1820s, and especially after 1848, the Turners
were transplanted to the United States.

20. Sister M. Hedwigis Overmoehle, "The Anti-
Clerical Activities of the Forty-Eighters in Wisconsin
1848-1860," unpublished Ph.D. dissertation, St. Louis
University, 1941, p. 260, and William B. Hesseltine,
"Lincoln's Problems in Wisconsin," WMH 48 (March
1950):187-95.

21. Sister M. Justile McDonald, History of the
Irish in Wisconsin in the Nineteenth Century (Washington, D.C.: Catholic University of America Press,

1954), pp. 140 ff.
22. Milwaukee Sentinel, August 12, 1862, quoted in McDonald, History of the Irish, p. 141.
23. Theodore C. Blegen, Norwegian Migration to America (Northfield, Minn.: Norwegian-American Historical Association, 1940), p. 385, and Ingrid Semmingsen, Norway to America, A History of the Migration, tr. Einar Haugen (Minneapolis: University of Minnesota Press, 1978), pp. 32 ff.
24. Blegen, Norwegian Migration, p. 391, and Carol Lynn H. Knight and Gerald S. Cowden, eds., "Two Immigrants for the Union: Their Civil War Letters," Norwegian-American Studies 28 (1979):109-56.
25. Blegen, Norwegian Migration, p. 392, and Albert O. Barton, "Muskego: The Most Historic Norwegian Colony," WMH 21 (December 1937):129-38.
26. Semmingsen, Norway to America, p. 57. See also in general La Vern J. Rippley, "Official Action by Wisconsin to Recruit Immigrants, 1850-1890," Yearbook of German-American Studies 18 (Lawrence, Kansas: SGAS, 1983), pp. 185-95.
27. The Nordlyset, quoted in Richard J. Fapso, Norwegians in Wisconsin (Madison: SHSW, 1977), p. 36; Arlow William Anderson, "Venturing into Politics: The Norwegian-American Press of the 1850s," WMH 32 (September 1948):58-79.
28. Current, History of Wisconsin, p. 313, Frederick I. Olson, "Milwaukeeans in State Politics: A Look at the Record," Messenger MCHS 32 (1976):124-28.
29. Peter Leo Johnson, "Port Washington Draft Riot of 1862," Mid-America 1 (January 1930):219-22; Mary D. Meyer, "The Germans in Wisconsin and the Civil War: Their Attitude toward the Union, the Republicans, Slavery, and Lincoln," unpublished M.A. thesis, Catholic University of America, 1937, pp. 45-46; Craig L. Kautz, "Fodder for Cannon: Immigrant Perceptions of the Civil War--The Old Northwest," unpublished Ph.D. dissertation, University of Nebraska, 1976; and Benjamin J. Blied, Catholics and the Civil War (Milwaukee: By the Author, 1945).
30. Current, History of Wisconsin, p. 316; Lawrence H. Larsen, "Draft Riot in Wisconsin, 1862," Civil War History 7 (December 1961):421-27; John W. Oliver, "Draft Riots in Wisconsin during the Civil War," WMH 2 (March 1919):334-37, and Frederick Hale, "The Americanization of a Danish Immigrant in Wisconsin, 1847-1872,"

WMH 64 (Spring 1981):202-15.
31. William F. Whyte, "Chronicles of Early Watertown," WMH 4 (1921):297.
32. Luebke, Ethnic Voters, p. 88.
33. William B. Hesseltine, "Lincoln's Problems in
Wisconsin," WMH 48 (Spring 1965):187-95, esp. 194.
34. Lynn I. Schoonover, "A History of the Civil War
Draft in Wisconsin," unpublished M.A. thesis, University of Wisconsin, 1915.
35. "Edward Salomon," in The National Cyclopedia of American Biography (New York, 1904), 12:75,
and Frank Klement, "The Soldier Vote in Wisconsin
during the Civil War," WMH 28 (September 1944):37-47.
36. Current, History of Wisconsin, p. 333, and
William W. Winterbotham, "Memoirs of a Civil War
Sleuth," WMH 19 (December 1937-March 1936):131-60, 276-
93.
37. Current, History of Wisconsin, p. 333; "Letters
of the Late Archbishop Michael Heiss," Salesianium 11
(April 1916):19-22; and "Letter of Joseph Salzmann to
the Ludwigmissionsverein (Munich), Oct., 3, 1864,"
Salesianium 42 (January 1947):19-25.
38. Current, History of Wisconsin, p. 335 footnote
50.
39. Schafer, "Who Elected Lincoln?" and Wilhelm
Hense-Jensen, "Influence of the Germans in Wisconsin,"
Proceedings SHSW 49 (1901):144-47.

Chapter Four

1. Douglas G. Marshall, "Wisconsin's Population
Changes and Prospects 1900-1963," Research Bulletin 241
(March 1963):22-23; William J. Schereck, "Collecting
Wisconsin Ethnic Material," WMH 39 (Summer 1956):263-
65.
2. Robert C. Nesbit, Wisconsin: A History (Madison: University of Wisconsin Press, 1973), p. 346;
Harry H. Heming, The Catholic Church in Wisconsin
(Madison: Wisconsin State Council Knights of Columbus,
1976), pp. 60 ff., 125; and Current, History of Wisconsin, pp. 287, 547.
3. Richard Jensen, The Winning of the Midwest: Social and Political Conflict, 1888-1896
(Chicago: University of Chicago Press, 1971), pp. 58-88.
4. Paul Kleppner, The Cross of Culture (New York:
Free Press, 1970), p. 158.

5. Statistics for the year 1893 show 279 Catholic schools with 44,669 pupils in them. The German Wisconsin Lutheran Synod had 149 schools with 9,000 pupils, the Missouri Synod had 107 schools with 8,500 pupils, and seven other synods, including the Scandinavians, had another 63 schools with 2,464 pupils. Nesbit, _Wisconsin_, p. 354. Many authors have discussed the Bennett Law in Wisconsin. Useful sources are Louise Phelps Kellogg, "The Bennett Law in Wisconsin," _WMH_ 2 (September 1918):3-25; William F. Whyte, "The Bennett Law Campaign in Wisconsin," _WMH_ 10 (June 1927):363-90; Robert J. Ulrich, "The Bennett Law of 1889: Education and Politics in Wisconsin," unpublished Ph.D dissertation, University of Wisconsin, 1965; Paul Kleppner, "The Politics of Change in the Midwest: The 1890s in Historical and Behavioral Perspective," unpublished Ph.D. dissertation, University of Pittsburgh, 1967, especially pp. 241-64; Roger E. Wyman, "Wisconsin Ethnic Groups and the Election of 1890," _WMH_ 51 (Summer 1968):269-93; Roger E. Wyman, "Voting Behavior in the Progressive Era: Wisconsin as a Case Study," unpublished Ph.D. dissertation, University of Wisconsin, 1970; and Donald L. Kinzer, "The Political Uses of Anti-Catholicism: Michigan and Wisconsin, 1890-1894," _Michigan History_ 39 (1955):312-26.

6. William D. Hoard, in January 10, 1889, _Messages_, p. 17.

7. "Wisconsin Bishops Protest the Bennett Law," _Social Justice Review_ 31 (December 1940 and January 1941):282-84, 318-20. As the situation obtained in La Crosse, see Gerald Edward Fisher, _Dusk Is My Dawn: The First Hundred Years, Diocese of La Crosse_ (La Crosse: n.p., 1969), pp. 45-58.

8. Peter Leon Johnson, D.D., "The Antecedents of St. Francis Seminary in Milwaukee," _WMH_ 40 (Autumn 1956):39-44.

9. "Wisconsin Bishops Protest," pp. 319-20.

10. Kellogg, "The Bennett Law," pp. 11 ff. Some German Americans argued that there was no necessity of learning English, since many communities of the state used only German and the language was supposedly universally understood. Prudent Americanizers also recognized the value of the German press in teaching American life and traditions to the non-English-speaking German immigrants.

11. La Vern J. Rippley, "German Assimilation: The

Effect of the 1871 Victory on American-Germanica," in
Germany and America: Essays on International Relations
and Immigration, ed. Hans L. Trefousse (New York:
Columbia University Press, 1980), pp. 122-37.
        12. Quoted in Kellogg, "The Bennett Law," 15.
        13. Ibid., p. 22.
        14. Amerika (St. Louis), September 27, 1921.
        15. Lloyd Hustevdt, Rasmus Bjorn Anderson,
Pioneer Scholar (Northfield, Minn.:   Norwegian-American
Historical Association, 1966), esp. pp. 215-18.
        16. Frank C. Nelson, "The School Controversy
among Norwegian Immigrants," Norwegian-American Studies
26 (Northfield, Minn.:   Norwegian American Historical
Association, 1974), pp. 206-19.
        17. Information about Wall's activities is in the
William F. Vilas papers, Wisconsin State Historical
Society. Wyman, "Voting Behavior," pp. 80 ff.
        18. Whyte, "Bennett Law," p. 386.
        19. Karel D. Bicha, "Karel Jonas of Racine:
'First Czech in America,'" WMH 63 (Winter 1979-
1980):122-40, esp. 134.
        20. Wyman, "Voting Behavior," p. 85 ff. Election
returns are in the Wisconsin Blue Book. Begun in 1862,
the Blue Books appeared annually until 1883 and bian-
nually from 1885.
        21. John C. Spooner to H. M. Ketchin, November
18, 1890.
        22. Wyman, "Voting Behavior," footnote 47, p.
981.
        23. Ibid., p. 99.
        24. Ibid., p. 105.
        25. Wilhelm Hense-Jensen, Wisconsin's Deutsh-
Amerikaner bis zum Schluss des neunzehnten Jahrhunderts
(Milwaukee: Germania, 1900), 1:226 ff., and La Vern J.
Rippley, "The German-American Normal Schools," in Erich
A. Albrecht and J. Anthony Burzle, eds., Germanica-
Americana 1976 (Lawrence, Kansas: Max Kade Document
and Research Center, 1977), pp. 63-71.
        26. Herman J. Deutsch, "Yankee-Teuton Rivalry in
Wisconsin Politics in the Seventies," WMH 14 (March
1931):262-82, and (June 1931):403-18, esp. 409.
        27. George M. Stephenson, "Nativism in the
Forties and Fifties, with Special Reference to the
Mississippi Valley," Mississippi Valley Historical
Review 9 (1922):189-202; Ellis B. Usher, "Puritan
Influence in Wisconsin," Proceedings SHSW (1899), pp.

117-28.

28. Hense-Jensen, Wisconsin's Deutsch-Amerikaner, 1:166.

29. Quoted from the Milwaukee Daily Sentinel, June 6, 1873, p. 8, by Deutsch, "Yankee-Teuton," p. 271.

30. Quoted in ibid., p. 281.

31. Ibid., p. 410 footnote 17.

32. Dr. O. W. Wright to the editor of the Milwaukee Daily News, May 10, 1874, p. 3, as cited in ibid., p. 413.

33. Herman J. Deutsch, "Disintegrating Forces in Wisconsin Politics of the Early Seventies: The Liberal Republican Movement," WMH 15 (December 1931):168-81, esp. 171, 180. See also his "Disintegrating Forces in Wisconsin Politics of the Early Seventies: The Ground Swell of 1873," WMH 15 (March 1932):282-96.

34. See Paul Kleppner, The Cross of Culture (New York: Free Press, 1970), pp. 40, 47-55, 70.

35. John Luchsinger, "The Planting of the Swiss Colony at New Glarus, Wis.," Collections SHSW 12 (1892):335-82; Henry E. Jacobs, A History of the Evangelical Lutheran Church in the United States (New York: Christian Literature Company, 1893), pp. 406-31; Kate A. Everest Levi, "Early Lutheran Immigration to Wisconsin," Transactions WASAL 8 (1888-1891):289-98; "How Wisconsin Came by Its Large German Element," Collections SHSW 12 (1892):299-334; and "Geographic Origins of German Immigration to Wisconsin," Collections SHSW 14 (1898):341-93.

36. Sister M. Justile McDonald, The Irish in Wisconsin in the Nineteeth Century (Washington, D.C.: Catholic University Press, 1954), pp. 150 ff., esp. 192, and Kleppner, Cross, p. 55.

37. Colman J. Barry, The Catholic Church and German Americans (Milwaukee: Bruce, 1953), and John J. Meng, "Cahenslyism: The First Stage, 1883-1891," Catholic Historical Review 31 (January 1946):389-413, and "Cahenslyism: The Second Chapter, 1891-1910," ibid. 32 (October 1946):302-40.

38. Reverend J. A. Burns, C.S.C., The Growth and Development of the Catholic School System in the United States (New York: Benziger Brothers, 1912), pp. 258 ff., 299 ff.

39. Berenice Cooper, "Die Freien Gemeinden in Wisconsin," Transactions WASAL 53 (1964):53-69. See

also Dale J. Donnelly, "The Low German Dialect of Sauk County, Wisconsin: Phonology and Morphology" (Ph.D. dissertation, University of Wisconsin, 1969).

40. I am indebted for this general thesis to Paul Kleppner. For a specific example of a local study, cf. Ann M. Legreid and David Ward, "Religious Schism and the Development of Rural Immigrant Communities: Norwegian Lutherans in Western Wisconsin, 1880-1905," Upper Midwest History 2 (1982):13-29.

41. Gerald Marsden, "Patriotic Societies and American Labor: The American Protective Association in Wisconsin," WMH 41 (Summer 1958):287-94.

42. Wyman, "Voting Behavior," p. 136, and John Higham, Strangers in the Land: Patterns of American Nativism (New York: Atheneum, 1963), p. 83.

43. O. Fritjof Ander, "The Swedish-American Press and the American Protective Association," Church History 6 (June 1937):165-77.

44. Additional concerns have been hinted at by Joseph Schafer, "The Yankee and the Teuton in Wisconsin," WMH 6 (1922-23):part 1, "Characteristic Attitudes toward the Land," pp. 125-45; part 2, "Distinctive Traits as Farmers," pp. 261-79; part 3, "Some Social Traits of Yankees," pp. 336-402; part 4, "Some Social Traits of the Teutons," 7 (1923):3-19; part 5, "Social Harmonies and Discords," pp. 148-71, esp. 161 ff.

45. Robert M. La Follette, La Follette's Autobiography: A Personal Narrative of Political Experience, first published in 1913 (Madison: University of Wisconsin Press, 1960).

46. Stuart Dean Brandes, "Nils Haugen and the Wisconsin Progressive Movement," unpublished M.A. thesis, University of Wisconsin-Madison, 1965.

47. Ibid., pp. 40 ff. See also Nils P. Haugen, "Pioneer and Political Reminiscences," WMH 12, part 1 (September 1928):41-57; part 2 (December 1928):176-91; part 3 (March 1929):271-93; part 4 (June 1929):379-402; 13, part 5 (December 1929):121-30.

48. Ralph G. Plumb, "Emil Baensch," WMH 23 (March 1940):264-68.

49. Padriac M. Kennedy, "Lenroot, La Follette and the Campaign of 1906," WMH 42 (Spring 1959):163-74; Herbert F. Margulies, The Decline of the Progressive Movement in Wisconsin, 1890-1920 (Madison: SHSW, 1968), and his Senator Lenroot of Wisconsin (Columbia: University of Missouri Press, 1977).

50. Herbert F. Margulies, "The Background of the La Follette-McGovern Schism," WMH 40 (Autumn 1956):21-29.

Chapter Five

1. Robert S. Maxwell, Emanuel L. Philipp: Wisconsin Stalwart (Madison: SHSW, 1959).
2. Rev. J. A. Burns, C.S.C., The Growth and Development of the Catholic School System in the United States (New York: Benziger Brothers, 1912), pp. 299-302, quotation pp. 299-300.
3. Ibid., pp. 325, 326, 327.
4. Merle Curti and Vernon Carstensen, The University of Wisconsin: A History, 1848-1925, 2 vols. (Madison: University of Wisconsin Press, 1949). See also Lorentz H. Adolfson, "A Half-Century of University Extension," WMH 40 (Winter 1956-57):99-106.
5. Frank J. Woerdehoff, "Dr. Charles McCarthy´s Role in Revitalizing the University Extension Program," WMH 40 (August 1956):13-18, and his "Dr. Charles McCarthy: Planner of the Wisconsin System of Vocational Adult Education," WMH 41 (Summer 1958):270-74. Charles McCarthy, The Wisconsin Idea (New York: Macmillan, 1912); Frederick C. Howe, Wisconsin: An Experiement in Democracy (New York: Charles Scribner´s Sons, 1912); and Marion Casey, Charles McCarthy: Librarianship and Reform (Chicago: American Library Association, 1981).
6. Albert B. Faust, The German Element in the United States (New York: Steuben Society, 1927), 2:228 ff.
7. Howe, Wisconsin, p. 4.
8. Ibid., p. 63.
9. Ibid., pp. 38-40.
10. Marvin Wachman, History of the Social Democratic Party of Milwaukee, 1897-1910 (Urbana: University of Illinois Press, 1945), pp. 62 ff.
11. Wyman, "Voting Behavior," p. 331, cites the Sheboygan Press, November 1, 1910.
12. Gerd Korman, Industrialization, Immigrants and Americanizers: The View from Milwaukee 1866-1921 (Madison: SHSW, 1967), esp. p. 50.
13. Letter of Wall to Vilas, May 18 and June 12, 1892, cited in ibid., p. 50. Footnote 19 on p. 50 details how campaigners played on ethnic animosities.
14. Letter dated August 13, 1914, cited by Wyman, "Ethnic Behavior," p. 333.

15. Milwaukee Sentinel, April 2, 1900, cited by Bayrd Still, Milwaukee (Madison: SHSW, 1965), p. 308.

16. Here and below, Robert Griffith, "Prelude to Insurgency: Irvine L. Lenroot and the Republican Primary of 1908," WMH 49 (Autumn 1965):16-28, esp. 20-21.

17. U.S. Census for 1910, pp. 1081 ff., and for 1920, p. 1141.

18. Donald E. Pienkos, "The Polish Americans in Milwaukee Politics," in Angela T. Pienkos, ed., Ethnic Politics in Urban America: The Polish Experience in Four Cities (Chicago: Polish American Historical Association, 1978), pp. 66-91, and Still, Milwaukee, pp. 312-15.

19. Gerd Korman, "Political Loyalties, Immigrant Traditions, and Reform: The Wisconsin German-American Press and Progressivism," WMH 40 (Spring 1957):161-68, esp. 163.

20. Germania Abendpost, April 2, 1909, in Korman, "Loyalties," p. 164.

21. Germania Abendpost, November 4, 1912.

22. Wyman, "Voting Behavior," pp. 343 ff.

23. Taylor, Marathon, Shawano, Kewaunee, Manitowoc, Sheboygan, Green Lake, Ozaukee, Dodge, Washington, Milwaukee, and Jefferson.

24. Wyman in "Voting Behavior" presents data, pp. 379 ff.

25. Still, Milwaukee, p. 126.

26 Wachman, History, pp. 52-53, Korman, Industrialization, p. 115.

27. Wyman, "Voting Behavior," pp. 393 ff.; Still, Milwaukee p. 304; Wachman, History, pp. 39-40.

28. Milwaukee Journal, September 7, 1906, and Herbert F. Margulies, Decline of the Progressive Movement in Wisconsin, 1890-1920 (Madison: SHSW, 1968), pp. 110-11.

29. Herbert F. Margulies, "The Decline of Wisconsin Progressivism, 1911-1914," Mid America 39 (July 1957):131-55, and Emanual L. Philipp, Political Reform in Wisconsin, edited and abridged by Stanley P. Caine and Roger E. Wyman (Madison: SHSW, 1973).

Chapter Six

1. Lee Soltow, Patterns of Wealthholding in Wisconsin since 1850 (Madison: University of Wisconsin Press, 1971), pp. 8, 35-38, 40-42.

2. Roger D. Simon, The City Building Process: Housing and Services in New Milwaukee Neighbor-

hoods 1880-1910 (Philadelphia: American Philosphical
Society, 1978), p. 19; ward map p. 2 and ethnic group
maps pp. 20-21.
        3. Ibid., p. 55. See also Justin B. Galford,
"The Foreign Born and Urban Growth in the Great Lakes,
1850-1950: A Study of Chicago, Cleveland, Detroit, and
Milwaukee," unpublished Ph.D. dissertation, New York
University, 1957; Alberto C. Meloni, "Italy invades the
Bloody Third: The Early History of Milwaukee's Ital-
ians," Messenger MCHS 25 (March 1969):34-46; and Salva-
tore J. Tagliavia, "Italians in Milwaukee," unpublished
M.A. thesis, St. Francis Seminary (Milwaukee), 1945.
        4. Carl H. Chrislock, Ethnicity Challenged:
The Upper Midwest Norwegian-American Experince in World
War I (Northfield, Minn.: Norwegian-American Historical Association, 1981), pp. 7 ff, quotation p. 14.
        5. The 1910 United States Census, p. 1082, and
tables in Ellis Baker Usher, Wisconsin: Its Story
and Biography 1848-1913 (Chicago: Lewis Publishing,
1914), pp. 64-65. See also Guy-Harold Smith, "Notes on
the Distribution of the Foreign Born Scandinavians in
Wisconsin in 1905," WMH 14 (June 1931):419-36.
        6. George M. Stephenson, "The Mind of the Scandi-
navian-Immigrant," Norwegian-American Studies and
Records 4 (1929):68.
        7. Richard J. Fapso, Norwegian in Wisconsin
(Madison: SHSW, 1977), pp. 29-30.
        8. E. Clifford Nelson, "The Union Movement among
Norwegian-American Lutherans from 1880 to 1917," unpublished Ph.D. dissertation, Yale University, 1952.
        9. Karl B. Raitz and Cotton Mather, "Norwegians
and Tobacco in Western Wisconsin," Annals, Association
of American Geographers 61 (1971):684-96.
        10. Jon M. Wefald, A Voice of Protest: Nor-
wegians in American Politics, 1890-1917 (Northfield,
Minn.: Norwegian-American Historical Association,
1971), pp. 4-5, and O. B. Grimley, The New Norway: A
People with the Spirit of Cooperation (Oslo: J. G.
Tanum, 1939).
        11. Theodore C. Blegen, Norwegian Migration to
America: The American Transition (Northfield, Minn.:
The Norwegian-American Historical Association, 1940),
p. 75.
        12. Wefald, A Voice, pp. 13-17. See also David
L. Brye, "Wisconsin Scandinavians and Progressivism
1900-1950," Norwegian-American Studies 27 (1977):

163-93.
13. Odd S. Lovoll, A Folk Epic: The Bygdelag in America (Boston: Twayne Publishers, for Norwegian American Historical Association, 1975).
14. Peter A. Munch, "Segregation and Assimilation of Norwegian Settlements in Wisconsin," in Norwegian-American Studies and Records (Northfield, Minn.: Norwegian-American Historical Association, 1954), 18:102-40.
15. Oscar N. Olson, The Augustana Lutheran Church in America, 1860-1910: The Formative Period (Davenport: Augustana Book Concern, 1956). See Also Harald Runblom and Hans Norman, eds., From Sweden to America: A History of Migration (Minneapolis: University of Minnesota Press, 1976), and Frederick Hale, Swedes in Wisconsin (Madison: SHSW, 1983), a 32-page pamphlet with illustrations.
16. Fritjof Ander, "The Swedish American Press and the American Protective Association," Church History 6 (June 1937):156-79. See also in general Allan Kastrup, The Swedish Heritage in America: The Swedish Element in America and American-Swedish Relations in their Historical Perspective (St. Paul: Swedish Council of America, 1975) and Lars Ljungmark, Swedish Exodus (Carbondale, Ill.: Southern Illinois University Press, 1975).
17. Herbert F. Margulies, Senator Lenroot of Wisconsin: A Political Biography, 1900-1929 (Columbia: University of Missouri Press, 1977), p. 397.
18. Statistical tables and map by John H. Bille, "A History of the Danes in America," Transactions WASAL 11 (March 1896):1-48.
19. Thomas P. Christensen, "Danish Settlement in Wisconsin," WMH 12 (September 1928):19-40.
20. Torben Krontoft, "Factors in Assimilation: A Comparative Study," Norwegian-American Studies 26 (1974):184-205. See also Harald Ansgar Pedersen, "Acculturation among Danish and Polish Ethnic Groups in Wisconsin," unpublished Ph.D. dissertation, University of Wisconsin, 1949.
21. Frederick Hale, Danes in Wisconsin (Madison: SHSW, 1981), pp. 30-31, an illustrated 32-page pamphlet.
22. Wyman, "Voting Behavior," p. 669.
23. John I. Kolehmainen and George W. Hill, Haven in the Woods: The Story of the Finns in Wisconsin

(Madison: SHSW, 1951), rev. ed. 1965, under cover map
and charts; see also John I. Kolehmainen, "The Finns of
Wisconsin," WMH 27 (June 1944):391-99.

24. Richard W. E. Perrin, "Log Sauna and the
Finnish Farmstead: Transplanted Architectural Idioms
in Northern Wisconsin," WMH 44 (Summer 1961):284-86,
and Mark Knipping, Finns in Wisconsin (Madison: SHSW,
1977), p. 27.

25. Conan Bryant Eaton, "The Icelanders in Wisconsin," WMH 56 (Autumn, 1972):2-20, maps and illustrations, and also Harry K. White, "The Icelanders on
Washington Island," Collections SHSW 14 (1898):215-39.

26. "The Holland Immigrants" and "The Belgian
Immigrants," in Leo Rummel, History of the Catholic
Church in Wisconsin (Madison: Knights of Columbus,
1976), pp. 105-9.

27. Henry S. Lucas, Netherlanders in America:
Dutch Immigration to the United States and Canada, 1789-
1950 (Ann Arbor: University of Michigan Press, 1955),
chapter 2, and Gerald F. De Jong, The Dutch in America 1609-1974 (Boston: Twayne, 1976).

28. Henry S. Lucas, ed., Dutch Immigrant Memoirs
and Related Writings, 2 vols. (Assen, Netherlands: Van
Gorcum, 1955), 2:129-39, 91-109, 110-28, 151-74.

29. Hjalmar Holand, Wisconsin's Belgian Community
(Sturgeon Bay: Door County Historical Society, 1933);
Lee W. Metzner, "The Belgians in the North County," WMH
26 (March 1943):280-88; and Anton Jarstad, "The Melting
Pot in Northeastern Wisconsin," WMH 26 (June 1943):426-
32.

30. Xavier Martin, "The Belgians of Northeast
Wisconsin," Collections SHSW 13 (1895):175-396, esp.
383-84.

31. Karel D. Bicha, "The Czechs in Wisconsin
History," WMH 53 (Spring 1970):194-203.

32. Glen L. Taggert, "Czechs of Wisconsin as a
Culture Type," unpublished Ph.D. dissertation, University of Wisconsin, 1947, and Nan Mashek, "Bohemian
Farmers of Wisconsin," Charities 13 (December
1904):211-14.

33. J. J. Vlach, "Our Bohemian Population," Proceedings SHSW (Madison: State Printer, 1902), pp. 159-
62.

34. Karel D. Bicha, "Karel Jonas of Racine:
First Czech in America," WMH 63 (Winter 1979-80):122-
40, esp. 134, 140.

35. Albert Hart Sanford, "Polish People of Portage County," Proceedings SHSW 55 (1907):159-88.

36. J. W. S. Tomkiewicz, "Polanders in Wisconsin," in Proceedings SHSW, 1901 pp. 148-52.

37. Wilfred L. Be Beau, "A German Immigrant Farmer Pioneers in Northern Wisconsin," WMH 38 (Summer 1955):239-44.

38. Korman, Industrialization, Immigrants and Americanizers, pp. 61-84.

39. Joseph A. Wytrwal, America's Polish Heritage: Social History of the Poles in America (Detroit: Endurance Press, 1961), and Wyman, "Voting Behavior," p. 720.

40. Bayrd Still, Milwaukee pp. 268 ff.; Thaddeus Borun, We, the Milwaukee Poles, (Milwaukee: Nowiny, 1946); and Joseph A. Litzow, "Poles in Milwaukee, 1906 to 1909," unpublished M.A. thesis, St. Francis Seminary (Milwaukee), 1943.

41. Anthony J. Kuzniewski, "Milwaukee's Poles, 1866-1918: The Rise and Fall of a Model Community," Milwaukee History 1 (1978):13-24.

42. Anthony J. Kuzniewski, Faith and Fatherland: The Polish Church War in Wisconsin 1896-1918 (Notre Dame: Notre Dame University Press, 1980); M. J. Madaj, "The Polish Immigrant, the American Catholic Hierarchy, and Father Wenceslaus Kruszka," Polish American Studies 26 (January-June 1969):16-29; and Thomas I. Monzell, "The Catholic Church and the Americanization of the Polish Immigrant," ibid., pp. 1-15.

43. McDonald, Irish in Wisconsin, and ibid., "The Irish of the North Country," WMH 40 (Winter 1956-67):126-32.

44. John Paul von Grueningen, ed., The Swiss in the United States (Madison: Swiss-American Historical Society, 1940), pp. 31 ff.; Leo Schelbert, ed., New Glarus 1945-1970: The Making of a Swiss American Town (Glarus: Tschudi, 1970); Dieter Brunnschweiler, New Glarus, Wisconsin: Gründung, Entwicklung and heutiger Zustand einer Schweizerkolonie im amerikanischen Mittelwesten (Zurich: Flutern, 1954); and John Luchsinger, "The Swiss Colony of New Glarus," Collections SHSW 8 (1879):411-39.

45. Kate Asaphine Everest, "How Wisconsin Came by Its Large German Element," Collections SHSW 12 (1892):299-334, and ibid. (Kate Everest Levi), "Geographical Origin of German Immigration to Wisconsin,"

Collection SHSW 14 (1898):341-93. See also Clifford
Nelson, German-American Political Behavior-in Nebras-
ka and Wisconsin, 1916-1920 (Lincoln: University of
Nebraska Press, 1972); the pamhplet by Richard H. Zeit-
lin, Germans in Wisconsin (Madison: SHSW, 1977), 30
pp. with map and illustrations; M. Walter Dundore, "The
Saga of the Pennsylvania Germans in Wisconsin," Penn-
sylvania German Folklore Society 19 (1954):56-66; and
Roe-Merrill Secrist Heffner, "German Settlements in
Wisconsin,"Bulletin of the American Council of Learned
Societies 34 (1942), 19-26.
        46. Joseph Schafer, Four Wisconsin Counties,
Prairie and Forest (Madison: SHSW, 1927); his The Win-
nebago-Horicon Basin (Madison: SHSW, 1937); his A
History of Agriculture in Wisconsin (Madison: SHSW,
1922); and Lester W. J. Seifert, "Some German Contri-
butions to Wisconsin Life," Yearbook of German-American
Studies 18 (Lawrence, Kans.: SGAS, 1983), pp. 173-83.
        47. Schafer points this out frequently. Township
agricultural statistics were given in the Wisconsin
State Census 1905 (Madison: State Printer, 1906), part 2.
        48. Carl Wittke, Refugees of Revolution: The
German Forty-Eighters in America (Philadelphia:
University of Pennsylvania Press, 1952; reprinted by
Greenwood Press, Westport, Conn., 1970), and Marcus L.
Hansen, "The Revolution of 1848 and German Emigration,"
Journal of Economic and Business History 2 (August
1930):630-58.
        49. La Vern J. Rippley, "The German-American
Normal Schools," in Erich A. Albrecht and J. Anthony
Burzle, eds., Germanica Americana 1976 (Lawrence, Kan-
sas: Max Kade Document and Research Center, 1977), pp.
63-71.
        50. Hildegard Binder Johnson, "Adjustment to the
United States," in A. E. Zucker, ed., The Forty-Eight-
ers: Political Refugees of the German Revolution (New
York: Columbia University Press, 1950), pp. 43-78.
See also Jürgen Eichhoff, "Deutsche Sprache in Wiscon-
sin," Deutsch als Muttersprache in den Vereinigten
Staaten, Teil I:IV (Wiesbaden: Steiner, 1978), 65-75.
        51. Philip Gleason, The Conservative Reformers:
German-American Catholics and the Social Order (Notre
Dame: University of Notre Dame Press, 1968), and Col-
man J. Barry, The Catholic Church and German Americans
(Milwaukee: Bruce, 1953).
        52. Rippley, "German Assimilation," in Germany

and America, pp. 122–37.

53. Wyman, "Voting Behavior," pp. 540–41.

54. Philip Gleason, "An Immigrant Group's Interest in Progressive Reform: The Case of the German-American Catholics," *American Historical Review* 72 (December 1967):367–79.

55. Wyman, "Voting Behavior," p. 563.

56. Ibid., p. 585.

Chapter Seven

1. Quoted in Clifford L. Nelson, *German American Political Behavior in Nebraska and Wisconsin 1916–1920* (Lincoln: University of Nebraska Press, 1972), p. 7.

2. Frederick C. Luebke, *Bonds of Loyalty: German Americans and World War I* (Dekalb: Northern Illinois University Press, 1974), p. 141. See also Louis L. Gerson, *The Hyphenate in Recent American Politics and Diplomacy* (Lawrence: University of Kansas Press, 1964).

3. Statistics in *Harvard Encyclopedia of Ethnic Groups,* ed. Stephen Thernstrom (Cambridge, Mass.: Harvard University Press, 1980), pp. 791, 1047 ff.; *The Catholic Encyclopedia* (1911), 12:210.

4. Dean Essliger, "American-German and Irish Attitudes Toward Neutrality, 1914–1917, a Study of Catholic Minorities," *Catholic Historical Review* 53 (1967):194–216.

5. Jean L. Berres, "Local Aspects of the Campaign for Americanism: *The Milwaukee Journal,* in World War I," unpublished Ph.D. dissertation, Southern Illinois University, Carbondale, 1977, pp. 1 ff.

6. Charles August Nelson, "Progressivism and Loyalty in Wisconsin Politics, 1912–1918," unpublished M.A. thesis, University of Wisconsin, 1961.

7. Monroe Billington, "The Gore Resolution of 1916," *Mid-America* 47 (April 1965):89–98.

8. Quoted in David L. Brye, *Wisconsin Voting Patterns in the Twentieth Century 1900–1950* (New York: Garland Publishing, 1979), p. 245. See also Padraic Kennedy, "La Follette's Foreign Policy: From Imperialism to Anti-Imperialism," *WMH* 46 (Summer 1963):287–93.

9. Luebke, *Bonds of Loyalty,* pp. 83–111.

10. George Wagner, "A Voice from Germany," *WMH* 2 (December 1918):149–57.

11. Max Heinrici, ed., *Das Buch der Deutschen in*

Amerika (Philadelphia: Walther's Buckruckerei, 1909).
    12. Milwaukee Journal, August 29, 1914, p. 3;
November 14, 1914, p. 1.
    13. Milwaukee Journal, June 4, 1915, p. 10; June
28, 1915, p. 2.
    14. Milwaukee Journal, October 16, 1916, p. 9.
    15. Milwaukee Journal, March 8, 1916, p. 14.
    16. United States Congress, Senate Committee on
the Judiciary, Hearings on the National German-American
Alliance (65th Congress, 2d session, 1918), p. 266.
    17. Clifton James Child, The German-American in
Politics 1914-1917 (Madison: University of Wisconsin
Press, 1939), pp. 2, 35, 37.
    18. Hexamer, in Luebke, Bonds of Loyalty, p. 100;
Bruncken, in Child, German-Americans, p. 40.
    19. John M. Work, "The First World War," WMH 41
(Autumn 1957):32-44.
    20. Still, Milwaukee, p. 285.
    21. Sally M. Miller, Victor Berger and the Prom-
ise of Constructive Socialism 1910-1920 (Westport,
Conn.: Greenwood Press, 1973), especially pp. 22-23;
Edward J. Muzik, "Victor L. Berger: Congress and the
Red Scare," WMH 47 (Summer 1964):309-18; Roderick Nash,
"Victor L. Berger: Making Marx Respectable," ibid.,
pp. 301-8; Frederick I. Olson, "Victor Berger: Social-
ist Congressman," WASAL 58 (1970):27-38, and his "The
Socialist Party and the Unions in Milwaukee, 1900-1912,
WMH 64 (Winter 1960-61):110-16. See also Marvin
Wachman, History of the Social-Democratic Party of Mil-
waukee 1897-1910 (Urbana: University of Illinois
Press, 1945).
    22. Robert C. Reinders, "Daniel W. Hoan and the
Milwaukee Socialist Party during the First World War,"
WMH 36 (Autumn 1952):48-55.
    23. William F. Raney, Wisconsin, A Story of Prog-
ress (Appleton: Perrin, 1963), p. 382, and Miller,
Victor Berger, pp. 165 ff.
    24. Reinders, "Daniel Hoan," p. 54; Sister Mary
Antoinette Henke, O.S.M., "World War I: Dissent and
Discord in Milwaukee," unpublished M.S. thesis, Loyola
University, Chicago, 1966.
    25. Clifton Child, The German-Americans in Poli-
tics, 1914-1917 (Madison: University of Wisconsin
Press, 1939), p. 162, and Karen Falk, "Public Opinion
in Wisconsin During World War I," WMH 25 (June
1942):389-407, esp. 395.

26. Samuel Hopkins Adams, "Invaded America: Wisconsin Joins the War," Everybody's Magazine 38 (January 1981):28-33.

27. H. C. Peterson and Gilbert C. Fite, Opponents of War 1917-1918 (Madison: University of Wisconsin Press, 1957), pp. 208-234.

28. Miller, Victor Berger, p. 205.

29. Muzik, "Victor Berger," pp. 316-17.

30. Olson, "Victor Berger," p. 27.

31. Articles appeared in Atlantic Monthly, Century, Everybody's Magazine, Forum, Nation, New Republic, North American Review, Outlook, and World's Work, not to mention major newspapers. The writings of Gustavus Ohlinger, The German Conspiracy in American Education (New York: George H. Doran, 1919), and Ernest L. Meyer, "Hey Yellowbacks": The War Diary of a Conscientious Objector (New York: John Day, 1930), were typical.

32. Reported in Falk, "Public Opinion in Wisconsin" p. 389. See also James Weinstein, "Anti-War Sentiment and the Socialist Party, 1917-1918," Political Science Quarterly 74 (June 1959):215-39.

33. The letter was reprinted as "Prussianizing Wisconsin, La-Follette's Magazine, January 1919, pp. 6-8.

34. Robert S. Maxwell, Emanuel L. Philipp, Wisconsin Stalwart (Madison: SHSW, 1959).

35. Brye, Wisconsin Voting Patterns, pp. 250 ff.

36. Esslinger, "American-German and Irish Attitudes," p. 206.

37. Milwaukee Journal, November 14, 1914, p. 1.

38. Philip Gleason, The Conservative Reformers (Notre Dame: University of Notre Dame Press, 1968), pp. 159 ff.

39. Brye, Wisconsin Voting Patterns, p. 257.

40. Milwaukee Journal, October 1, 1916, and Nelson, German-American Political Behavior, p. 17.

41. "Letters of Paul O. Husting Concerning the Present Crisis," WMH 1 (December 1917):388-416. See also Lawrence James Martin, "Opposition to Conscription in Wisconsin, 1917-1918," unpublished M.S. thesis, University of Wisconsin, 1952.

42. Seward W. Livermore, Politics Is Adjourned, Woodrow Wilson and the War Congress, 1916-1918 (Middletown, Conn.: Wesleyan University Press, 1966), pp. 117-21, and Milwaukee Sentinel, March 27, 1918.

43. Milwaukee Journal, April 3, 1918; Nelson, Ger-

man-American Political Behavior, pp. 36-39; and Brye,
Voting Patterns, p. 246.

44. Herbert F. Margulies, Senator Lenroot of Wisconsin, A Political Biography, 1900-1929 (Columbia: University of Missouri Press, 1977), pp. 170, 186, 233,
396.

45. Ibid., p. 247, and Herbert F. Margulies, "The La
Follette-Philipp Alliance of 1918," WMH 38 (Summer
1955):248-49.

46. Berres, "Local Aspects," pp. 53-54.

47. Ibid., p. 124.

48. Mark Sullivan, Our Times, vol. 5, Over
Here 1914-1918 (New York: Scribner's, 1933), p. 333.

49. Milwaukee Journal, February 2, 1918, p. 4.

50. Ibid., February 24, 1918, part 2, p. 2.

51. Klueter and Lorence, Woodlot and Ballot Box, p.
272.

52. Charles E. Strickland, "American Aid to Germany,
1919-1921," WMH 45 (Summer 1962):256-70; Baraboo Weekly News, June 13, 1918; and Baraboo News Republic, May
5, 1983.

53. Milwaukee Journal, June 15, 1918, p. 12, and
September 13, 1918, p. 2.

54. Ibid., December 22, 1918, part 2, p. 1.

55. Ibid., December 29, 1918, p. 14.

56. Quoted by Adams, "Wisconsin Joins the War," p.
31.

57. Lorin Lee Cary, "The Wisconsin Loyalty Legion,
1917-1918," WMH 53 (Autumn 1969):33-50, esp. 39.

58. Milwaukee Journal, September 10, 1917, and
October 9, 1917, urged the Legion to become more
active.

59. Quotation from Adams, "Wisconsin Joins the War,"
pp. 82-84.

60. John D. Stevens, "When Sedition Laws Were Enforced: Wisconsin in World War I," WASAL 58 (1970):39-
60.

61. Madison Capital Times, January 3, 4, 1918, and
John Dean Stevens, "Suppression of Expression in Wisconsin during World War I," unpublished Ph.D. dissertation, University of Wisconsin, Madison, 1967, p. 57.

62. Irvine L. Lenroot, "The War Loyalty of Wisconsin," 59 (June 1918):695-702.

63. Carl Wittke, "American Germans in Two World
Wars," WMH 27 (1943):6-16.

64. Thirteenth United States Census, III 1073-1074.

65. Stevens, "Suppression," pp. 44 ff., and Lawrence James Martin, "Opposition to Conscription in Wisconsin 1917-1918," unpublished M.S. thesis, University of Wisconsin, 1952.

66. Stevens, "Suppression," pp. 145-57.

67. Child, The German-Americans, p. 173.

68. Berres, "Local Aspects," pp. 211-14.

69. Stevens, "Suppression," pp. 179-90.

70. David A. Shannon, "The World, the War, and Wisconsin: 1914-1918," Messenger MCHS 22 (March 1966):43-46, esp. 45. See also Errol W. Stevens, "Heartland Socialism: The Socialist Party of America in Four Midwestern Communities," unpublished Ph.D. dissertation, 1978, Indiana University, especially chapter 2, pp. 26-59.

71. Shannon, Ibid., p. 47, and Brye, Voting Patterns, 262-63.

Chapter Eight

1. Wallace H. Moore, "The Conflict Concerning the German Language and German Propaganda in the Public Secondary Schools of the United States," unpublished Ph.D. dissertation, Stanford University, 1937, pp. 84-99.

2. Jack W. Rodgers, "The Foreign Language in Nebraska, 1918-1923," Nebraska History 39 (March 1958):1-22, esp. 17.

3. J. Q. Emery, state superintendent, Laws of Wisconsin Relating to Common Schools, High and Normal Schools and to the State University (Madison: State Printer, 1898), pp. 43-44.

4. Capital Times, February 3 and March 21, 1919, and Madison Democrat, February 28 and March 21, 1919.

5. Milwaukee Sentinel, March 22, 1919.

6. Wisconsin News, March 26, 1923.

7. Capital Times, May 9, 1923.

8. Sample articles are by H. M. Kallen, "Politics, Profits, and Patriotism in Wisconsin," Nation 106 (March 7, 1918):257-59, and Percy E. Davidson, "German Language Legislation and the Spirit of American Education," Schools and Society 11 (March 13, 1920):301-10.

9. Wisconsin Blue Book, 1921, p. 435.

10. Korman, Industrialization, p. 164. See also Edward George Hartmann, The Movement to Americanize the Immigrant (New York: AMS, 1967), pp. 13-37.

11. Wisconsin Blue Book, 1921, pp. 440 ff. Four-

teenth Federal Census, Population, pp. 1135-39.

12. Anthony J. Kuzniewski, Faith and Fatherland, and his "Milwaukee's Poles, 1866-1918: The Rise and Fall of Model Community," Milwaukee History 1 (1978):13-24.

13. Milwaukee County Council of Defense, Official Bulletin, February 2, 1918, p. 2, quoted in Korman, Industrialization, p. 183.

14. Ibid., pp. 190 ff.

15. Alfred E. Koenig, Committee Chairman, Proceedings of the Second Minnesota State Americanization Conference at Minneapolis, Minnesota May 19, 1920 (Minneapolis: Minneapolis Council of Americanization, 1920).

16. John A. Lapp, "Bogus Propaganda: Dollar Mark Shows in Attempts to Control Americanization Program," National Catholic War Council Bulletin 1 (June, July 1920):9-10, quotation p. 10.

17. Frederick A. Sweet, "Putting Over a Civic Education Program," National Catholic War Council Bulletin 1 (August 1920):10-11. See also Thomas I. Monzell, "The Catholic Church and the Americanization of the Polish Immigrant," Polish American Studies 26 (January-June 1969):1-15.

18. WMH 3 (1919-1920):89, 92, 326, 500-501.

19. Carl H. Chrislock, The Progressive Era 1899-1918 (St. Paul: Minnesota Historical Society, 1971), pp. 145 ff., and Theodore Saloutos, "The Expansion and Decline of the Nonpartisan League in the Western Middle West, 1917-1921," Agricultural History 20 (October 1946):235-52.

20. James J. Lorence, "The Ethnic Impact of Wilson's War: The German-American in Marathon County, 1912-1916," Transactions WASAL 66 (1978):113-23. See also his "Dynamite for the Brain: The Growth and Decline of Socialism in Central and Lakeshore Wisconsin 1910-1920," WMH 66 (Summer, 1983):251-73.

21. Brye, Voting Patterns, pp. 259 ff.

22. Samuel Lubell, The Future of American Politics (New York: Harper, 1955; 3d ed., 1965), p. 134, and R. A. Burchell, "Did the Irish and German Voters Desert the Democrats in 1920? A Tentative Statistical Answer," Journal of American Studies 6 (August 1972):153-64.

23. John B. Duff, "German-Americans and the Peace, 1918-1920," American Jewish Historical Quarterly 59 (January 1970):424-44, esp. 441; quotation 438.

24. Ibid., p. 440.

25. Herbert F. Margulies, "Irvine L. Lenroot and the Republican Vice-Presidential Nomination of 1920," WMH 61 (Autumn 1977):21-31.

26. Brye, Voting Patterns, pp. 262 ff. See also Herbert F. Margulies, The Decline of the Progressive Movement in Wisconsin (Madison: SHSW, 1968), pp. 278 ff.

27. Herbert F. Margulies, "The Election of 1920 in Wisconsin: The Return to `Normalcy´ Reappraised," WMH 41 (Autumn 1957):15-22.

28. Brye, Voting Patterns, pp. 275 ff.

29. Scott D. Johnston, "Wisconsin Socialists and the Conference for Progressive Political Action," WMH 37 (Winter 1954):96-100.

30. James H. Shideler, "The La Follette Progressive Party Campaign of 1924," WMH 33 (June 1950):444-57.

31. Alan R. Havig, "A Disputed Legacy: Roosevelt Progressives and the La Follette Campaign of 1924," Mid-America 53 (January 1971):44-64.

32. Padraic Colum Kennedy, "La Follette and the Russians," Mid-America 53 (July 1971):190-208.

33. Duncan Macrae and James Neldrum, "Critical Elections in Illinois: 1888-1958," American Political Science Review 54 (September 1960):669-83, esp. 677, and Bruce Stave, "The La Follette Revolution and the Pittsburgh Vote, 1932," Mid-America 49 (October 1967):244-51.

34. Andrew R. Baggaley, "Religious Influence on Wisconsin Voting, 1828-1960," American Political Science Review 56 (May 1962):66-70.

35. William Ogburn and Neil Talbot, "A Measurement of the Factors in the Presidential Election of 1928," Social Forces 7 (December 1929):175-83, and Paul A. Carter, "The Campaign of 1928 Re-Examined: A Study in Political Folklore," WMH 46 (Summer 1963):263-72.

36. Brye, Voting Patterns, p. 308.

37. Joseph Schafer, "Prohibition in Early Wisconsin," WMH 8 (March 1925):281-99.

38. William Francis Raney, Wisconsin: A Story of Progress (Appleton: Perrin Press, 1963), pp. 316-24.

39. Clifton James Child, The German-Americans in Politics, 1914-1917 (Madison: University of Wisconsin Press, 1939), pp. 10 ff.

40. "James John Blaine," National Cyclopedia of American Biography (New York: James T. White, 1937), 26:280-81.

41. Brye, Wisconsin Voting Patterns, p. 310.
42. Baggaley, "Religious Influences," 66-70.
43. Nesbit, Wisconsin, pp. 466-67, and Norman F. Weaver, "The Knights of the Ku Klux Klan in Wisconsin, Indiana, Ohio and Michigan," Ph.D. dissertation, University of Wisconsin, 1954.
44. Lucile Kane, "Settling the Wisconsin Cutovers," WMH 40 (Winter 1956-1957):91-98.
45. Theodore Saloutos, "The Greeks of Milwaukee," WMH 53 (Spring 1970):175-93.
46. Theodore Saloutos, "Growing Up in the Greek Community of Milwaukee," Messenger MCHS 29 (1973):46-60.
47. Strickland, "American Aid," p. 257.
48. La Vern J. Rippley, "Gift Cows for Germany," North Dakota History 40 (Summer 1973):4-15, and ibid., "American Milk Cows for Germany: A Sequel," North Dakota History 44 (Summer 1977):15-23.

Chapter Nine

1. James I. Clark, Wisconsin meets the Great Depression (Madison: SHSW, 1956).
2. Richard M. Bernard, Marital Assimilation in Wisconsin 1850-1920 (Minneapolis: University of Minnesota Press, 1980).
3. Robert and Maryo Gard, My Land, My Home, My Wisconsin (Milwaukee: Milwaukee Journal, 1978).
4. Henry M. Pelling, "The Rise and Decline of Socialism in Milwaukee," Bulletin of the International Institute for Social History 10 (1955):91-103, quotation on 99, and Donald Pienkos, "Politics, Religion, and Change in Polish Milwaukee, 1900-1930," WMH 61 (Spring 1978):179-209.
5. Nesbit, Wisconsin, p. 493.
6. Edward M. Coffman and Paul H. Hass, eds., "With MacArthur in the Pacific: A Memoir by Philip F. La Follette," WMH 64 (Winter 1980-81):83-106.
7. Brye, Voting Patterns, pp. 317-18, and Harold Gosnell and Morris Cohen, "Progressive Politics: Wisconsin an Example," American Political Science Review 34 (October 1940):920-35.
8. Brye, Voting Patterns, p. 318.
9. Klueter and Lorence, Woodlot and Ballot Box, pp. 334-35.
10. David O. Powell, "The Union Party of 1936: Campaign Tactics and Issues," Mid-America 46 (April

1946):126-41, esp. 134.

11. Samuel Lubell, The Future of American Politics, 3d rev. ed. (New York: Harper & Row, 1965), p. 143.

12. Louis H. Bean et al., "Nationalities and 1944," Public Opinion Quarterly 7 (Fall 1944):368-75.

13. La Vern J. Rippley, The German-Americans (Boston: Twayne, 1976), pp. 196-213. See also Sander A. Diamond, The Nazi Movement in the United States 1924-1941 (Ithaca: Cornell University Press, 1974).

14. Leland V. Bell, In Hitler's Shadow (Port Washington, N.Y.: Kennikat, 1973), p. 27.

15. Details are available on a microfilm of clippings about Bund activities in the Milwaukee County Historical Society.

16. Samuel Lubell, "Who Really Elected Truman?" Saturday Evening Post, January 22, 1949, pp. 15 ff.

17. Brye, Voting Patterns, p. 334.

18. Michael O'Brien, McCarthy and McCarthyism in Wisconsin (Columbia: University of Missouri Press, 1980), Thomas C. Reeves, The Life and Times of Joe McCarthy: A Biography, (New York: Stein & Day, 1982), and William Bragg Ewald, Jr., Who Killed Joe McCarthy? (New York: Simon & Shuster, 1984).

19. Patrick J. Maney, "Young Bob" La Follette: A Biography of Robert M. La Follette, Jr., 1895-1953 (Columbia: University of Missouri Press, 1978), p. 287.

20. Michale O'Brien, "Young Joe McCarthy, 1908-1944," WMH 63 (Spring 1980):179-232.

21. Klueter and Lorence, Woodlot and Ballot Box, pp. 365-66.

22. Louis L. Gerson, The Hyphenate in Recent American Politics and Diplomacy (Lawrence: University of Kansas Press, 1964), pp. 187 ff.

23. Quotation by Maney, "Young Bob," p. 307. See also Robert M. La Follette, Jr., "Turn the Light on Communism," Collier's 119 (February 8, 1947):22, 73-74, and David A. Shannon, "Was McCarthy a Political Heir of La Follette," WMH 45 (Autumn 1961):3-9.

24. Michael J. O'Brien, "The Anti-McCarthy Campaign in Wisconsin, 1951-1952," WMH 56 (Winter 1972-1973):91-108, esp. 95.

25. Howard B. Schonberger, "The General and the Presidency," WMH 57 (Spring 1974):201-19.

26. Robert W. Griffith, Jr., "The General and the Senator: Republican Politics and the 1952 Campaign in

Wisconsin," WMH 54 (Autumn 1970):23-29, and his Poli-
tics of Fear: Joseph R. McCarthy and the Senate (Lex-
ington: University of Kentucky Press, 1970).
    27. Richard M. Fried, Men Against McCarthy (New
York: Columbia University Press, 1976), p. 232, and
Sharon Coady, "The Wisconsin Press and Joseph McCarthy:
A Case Study," unpublished M.A. thesis, University of
Wisconsin, 1956.
    28. Louis H. Bean, Influence in the 1954 Mid-Term
Elections (Washington, D.C.: Public Affairs Institute,
1954), pp. 18-23.
    29. Lubell, The Future, p. 153.
    30. David P. Thelen and Ester S. Thelen, "Joe Must
Go: The Movement to Recall Senator Joseph R.
McCarthy," WMH 49 (Spring 1966):185-209, Michael
O'Brien, "The Anti-McCarthy Campaign in Wisconsin 1951-
1952," WMH 56 (Winter 1972-1973):91-108, and David M.
Oshinsky, "Wisconsin Labor and the Campaign of 1952,"
ibid., 109-118.
    31. O'Brien, McCarthy, pp. 203 ff.
    32. Wisconsin State Journal, May 3, 1957.

Chapter Ten

    1. John H. Fenton, Midwest Politics (New York:
Holt, Rinehart & Winston, 1966), pp. 62-74, table p.
70, and Richard H. Haney, "The Rise of Wisconsin's New
Democrats: A Political Realignment in the Mid-Twen-
tieth Century," WMH 58 (Winter 1974-1975):91-106.
    2. David W. Adamany, "The 1960 Election in Wiscon-
sin," unpublished M.S. thesis, University of Wisconsin,
1963, and Jane Catherine Hendra, "The 1960 Democratic
Campaign in Wisconsin," unpublished M.S. thesis, Uni-
versity of Wisconsin, 1961.
    3. Quoted in Adamany, "The 1960 Election," p. 98.
    4. Richard C. Haney, "Wallace in Wisconsin: The
Presidential Primary in 1964," WMH 61 (Summer
1978):259-78.
    5. Charles A. Ward, "The Serbian and Croatian Com-
munities in Milwaukee," General Linguistics 16 (Summer,
Fall 1976):161-65. See also Timothy P. Maga, "Diplomat
Among Kings: John Cudahy and Leopold III," WMH 67
(Winter 1983-1984):83-98.
    6. Marie Prisland, "The Slovenians, Most Recent
American Immigrants," WMH 33 (March 1950):265-80.
    7. Nelson Lichtenstein, ed., Political Pro-

files: The Johnson Years (New York: Facts on File, 1976), p. 239.
8. Statistical tables in Pienkos, "Politics, Religion, and Change," pp. 189-91.
9. Roger D. Simon, The City-Building Process: Housing and Services in New Milwaukee Neighborhoods 1880-1910 (Philadelphia: American Philosophical Society, 1978), pp. 19-20. See also his "The Expansion of an Industrial City: Milwaukee, 1880-1910," unpublished Ph.D. dissertation, University of Wisconsin, 1971; Gwen Schultz, "Evolution of the Areal Patterns of German and Polish Settlement in Milwaukee," Erdkunde 10 (1956):136-41; and Victor Greene, For God and Country (Madison: SHSW, 1975), pp. 55 ff.
10. Simon, City-Building, p. 56. See also Roger D. Simon, "Housing and Services in an Immigrant Neighborhood: Milwaukee's Ward 14," Journal of Urban History 2 (August 1976):435-57.
11. Pienkos, "Politics," p. 192, and Eugene Miller, "Leo Krzycki: Polish American Labor Leader," Polish American Studies 33 (Autumn 1976):52-64.
12. Pienkos, "Politics," p. 194. See also Alexander Syski, "Reverend Waclaw Kruszka: The Nestor of Polish Historians in America," Polish American Studies 1 (1944):62-70.
13. Time, April 17, 1964, p. 37.
14. "Wisconsin," in Richard N. Scammon, ed., America Votes 1964, vol. 6 (Washington, DC: Governmental Affairs Institute, 1966), pp. 451-62.
15. Louise W. Holborn, The International Refugee Organization (New York: Oxford University Press, 1956), p. 367.
16. Joseph B. Schechtman, The Refugee in the World: Displacement and Integration (New York: Barnes, 1963); Alfred de Zayas, Nemesis at Potsdam (Boston: Routledge & K. Paul, 1977).
17. Juris Veidemanis, "Social Change: Major Value-Systems of Latvians at Home, as Refugees, and as Immigrants," unpublished Ph.D. dissertation, University of Wisconsin, 1961, and his "Latvian Settlers in Wisconsin: A Comparative View," WMH 45 (Summer 1962):251-55.
18. Juris Veidemanis, "Two Generations of Mental Isolation: Latvians in Northern Wisconsin," Wisconsin Sociologist, June 1960, pp. 1-23, and Justin B. Galford, "The Foreign Born and Urban Growth in the Great Lakes, 1850-1950: A Study of Chicago, Cleveland, De-

troit, and Milwaukee," unpublished Ph.D. dissertation, New York University, 1957, esp. p. 337.

19. Ward, "The Serbian and Croatian Communities," pp. 154 ff.

20. Anton Kremling, ed., Die Donauschwaben in den Vereinigten Staaten von Amerika (Cleveland: Wächter & Anzeiger, 1977), pp. 115-27, 183 ff. and in general Jacob Steigerwald, Donauschwäbische Gedankenskizzen aus USA--Reflections of Danube Swabians in America (Winona: Translation & Interpretation Service, 1983).

21. Kathleen Conzen, "The Germans," in Stephan Thernstrom, ed., Harvard Encyclopedia of Ethnic Groups (Cambridge, Mass.: Harvard University Press, 1980), pp. 405-25.

22. Fred Stare, "Wisconsin's Canning Industry, Past and Present," WMH 36 (Autumn 1952):34-38.

23. John Huber, "Migratory Agricultural Workers in Wisconsin," unpublished M.A. thesis, University of Wisconsin, 1967.

24. Doris P. Slesinger and Eileen Muirragni, "Migrant Agricultural Labor in Wisconsin: A Short History" (Madison: Institute for Research on Poverty, 1979), p. 5.

25. William H. Metzler and Frederick O. Sargent, Migratory Farmworkers in the Midcontinent Streams (Washington, D.C.: United States Department of Agriculture Research Service, 1960).

26. "Fact Sheet on Out of State Workers in Wisconsin, 1978," of the Wisconsin State Employment Service.

27. Christobal S. Berry-Caban, "A Survey of the Puerto Rican Community on Milwaukee's Northeast Side in 1976" (Milwaukee: Urban Observatory, University of Wisconsin-Milwaukee), 50 pp. typescript, ERIC Document Center.

28. Alexandro Portes, "Dilemmas of a Golden Exile: Integration of Cuban Refugee Families in Milwaukee," American Sociological Review 34 (August 1969):505-18.

29. Lyle and Magdalene Shannon, Minority Migrants in the Urban Community. Mexican-American and Negro Adjustment to Industrial Society (Beverly Hills: Sagre Publications, 1973).

Selected Bibliography

1. Miscellaneous
Hill, George. "Wisconsin State Census--Studies for
    1905." Unpublished study originally entitled
    "Ethnic Backrounds in Wisconsin," completed by the
    Department of Rural Sociology, University of Wiscon-
    sin, 1937-1940. Available at the State Historical
    Society of Wisconsin.
Roesler, John S. Papers. One Box, map. State
    Historical Society of Wisconsin Study undertaken by
    correspondence in 1890.

2. Books
Anderson, Harry H., ed. German-American Pioneers in
    Wisconsin and Michigan, The Frank-Kerler Let-
    ters, 1849-1864. Translated by Margaret Wolff.
    Milwaukee: Milwaukee County Historical Society,
    1971.
Anderson-Sannes, Barbara. Alma on the Mississip-
    pi 1848-1832. Alma, Wisconsin: Alma Historical
    Society. 1980.
Annual Report of the Emigration Commission of the State
    of Wisconsin for the Years 1853-1884.
Anuta, Michael J. East Pussians From Russia. Men-
    ominee, Mich.: privately published by the author,
    1979.
Bernard, Richard M. The Melting Pot and the Altar:
    Marital Assimilation in Early Twentieth-Century
    Wisconsin. Minneapolis: University of Minnesota
    Press, 1980.
Borun, Thaddeus. We, the Milwaukee Poles. Milwaukee:
    Nowiny, 1946.
Byre, David L. Wisconsin Voting Patterns in the Twen-
    tieth Century, 1900-1950. New York: Garland Pub-
    lishing, 1979.
Conzen, Kathleen Neils. Immigrant Milwaukee, 1836-
    1860. Cambridge: Harvard University Press, 1976.
Current, Richard N. The History of Wisconsin: The
    Civil War Era, 1848-1873. Madison: SHSW, 1976.
Curti, Merle. The Making of an American Community.

Stanford: Standord University Press, 1959; reprint-
ed 1969.
Greene, Victor.   For God and Country: The Rise of
Polish and Lithuanian Ethnic Consciousness in America, 1860-1910.   Madison: SHSW, 1975.
Heming, Harry.   The Catholic Church in Wisconsin.   Mil-
waukee: Catholic Historical Publishing, 1895-1898.
Hense-Jensen, Wilhelm.   Wisconsin's Deutsch-Amerikaner
bis zum Schluss des neunzehnten Jahrhunderts, 1 and
2.   Milwaukee: Germania, 1900, 1902.
Holmes, Fred L.   Old World Wisconsin.   Eau Claire: E.
M. Hale, 1944.
Jensen, Richard.   The Winning of the Midwest: Social
and Political Conflict, 1888-1896.   Chicago: Uni-
versity of Chicago Press, 1971.
Kleppner, Paul.   The Cross of Culture (New York: The
Free Press, 1970).
Kloss, Heinz.   Atlas of German-American Settlements.
Marburg: N. G. Elwert, 1974.
Klueter, Howard R., and Lorence, James J.   Woodlot and
Ballot Box, Marathon County in the Twentieth Century.
Wausau: Marathon County Historical Society, 1977.
Kolehmainen, John I., and Hill, George W.   Haven in
the Woods: The Story of the Finns in Wisconsin.
Madison: SHSW, 1965.
Korman, Gerd.   Industrialization, Immigrants and Ameri-
canizers: The View from Milwaukee 1866-1921.   Mad-
ison: SHSW, 1967.
Kuzniewski, Anthony J.   Faith and Fatherland: The
Polish Church War in Wisconsin, 1896-1918.   Notre
Dame: University of Notre Dame Press, 1980.
Lovoll, Odd S.   A Folk Epic: The Bygdelag in America.
Boston: Twayne, for the Norwegian American Histor-
isal Association, 1975.
McDonald, M. Jistile.   History of the Irish in Wiscon-
sin in the Nineteenth Century.   Washington, D.C.:
Catholic University Press, 1954.
Mather, Cotton.   Upper Coulee Country.   Prescott, Wis.:
Trimbelle Press, 1975.
Miller, Sally M.   Victor Berger and the Promise of
Constructive Socialism 1910-1920.   Westport, Conn.:
Greenwood Press, 1973.
Nelson, Clifford L.   German-American Political Behavior
in Nebraska and Wisconsin 1916-1920.   Lincoln: Uni-
versity of Nebraska Press, 1972.
Nesbit, Robert C.   Wisconsin: A History.   Madison:

University of Wisconsin Press, 1973).

O'Brien, Michael J. McCarthy and McCarthyism in Wisconsin. Columbia: University of Missouri Press, 1980.

Perrin, Richard W. E. Wisconsin Architecture. Washington, D.C.: Department of the Interior, 1965.

Raney, William Francis. Wisconsin: A Story of Progress. Appleton: Perrin Press, 1963.

Rippley, La Vern J. The German-Americans. Boston: Twayne, 1976.

Rummel, Reverend Leo, Ord. Praem. History of the Catholic Church in Wisconsin. Madison: Wisconsin State Council of Knights of Columbus, 1976.

Schafer, Joseph. Wisconsin Domesday Book, General Series 1: A History of Agriculture in Wisconsin. Madison: SHSW, 1922.

___. Wisconsin Domesday Book, General Series 2: Four Wisconsin Counties, Prairie and Forest. Madison: SHSW, 1927.

___. Wisconsin Domesday Book, General Series 3: The Wisconsin Lead Region. Madison: SHSW, 1932.

___. Wisconsin Domesday Book, General Series 4: The Winnebago-Horicon Basin. Madison: SHSW, 1937.

Schelbert, Leo, ed. New Glarus 1845-1970, the Making of a Swiss-American Town. Glarus: Tschudi, 1970.

Simon, Roger D. The City-Building Process: Housing and Services in New Milwaukee Neighborhoods 1880-1910. Philadelphia: American Philosophical Society, 1978.

Still, Bayrd. Milwaukee, the History of a City. Madison: SHSW, 1948.

Wisconsin Blue Books. From 1862 to present.

Zeitlin, Richard H. Germans in Wisconsin. Madison: SHSW, 1977.

3. Articles

Anderson, Harry H. "Early Scandinavian Settlement in Milwaukee County." Messenger, MCHS 25 (March 1969:2-19.

___. "Norwegian Shipbuilding in Early Milwaukee." Milwaukee History 1 (1978):81-104.

Bicha, Karel D. "The Czechs in Wisconsin History." WMH 53 (Spring 1970):194-203.

___. "Karel Jonas of Racine: First Czech in America!" WMH 63 (Winter 1979-80):122-40.

Blegen, Theodore C. "The Competition of the North-

western States for Immigrants." WMH 3 (1919–
1920):3–29.

Bruncken, Ernst. "German Political Refugees in the
United States during the Period from 1815–1860."
Deutsch-Amerikanische Geschichtsblätter 3
(1903):33–48; 4 (1905):33–59.

Brye, David L. "Wisconsin Scandinavians and Progressivism, 1900–1950." Norwegian-American Studies 27
(1977):163–93.

Buenker, John D. "Immigration and Ethnic Groups." In
John A. Neuenschwander, ed. Kenosha County in the
Twentieth Century: A Topical History. Kenosha:
County Bicentennial Commission, 1976, pp. 1–49.

Cary, Lorin Lee. "The Wisconsin Loyalty Legion, 1917–
1918." WMH 53 (Autumn 1969):33–50.

Cooper, Bernice. "Die Freien Gemeinden in Wisconsin."
Transactions, WASAL 53 (1964):53–69.

Conzen, Kathleen Neils. "Patterns of Residence in
Early Milwaukee." In Leo F. Schnore, ed. Urban History: Quantitative Explorations by American Historians.
Princeton: Princeton University Press, 1975, pp.
145–83.

Copeland, Louis Albert. "The Cornish in Southwest
Wisconsin." Collections, SHSW 14 (1898):301–34.

Deutsch, Herman J. "Yankee-Teuton Rivalry in Wisconsin
Politics in the Seventies." WMH 14 (March
1931):262–82.

_____. "Christian Morals and Political Attitude." WMH
14 (June 1931):403–18.

_____. "Disintegrating Forces in Wisconsin Politics of
the Early Seventies: The Liberal Republican Movement." WMH 15 (December 1931):168–81.

_____. "Disintegrating Forces in Wisconsin Politics of
the Early Seventies: The Ground Swell of 1873."
WMH 15 (March 1932):282–96.

Eaton, Conan Bryant. "The Icelanders in Wisconsin."
WMH 56 (Autumn 1972):2–20.

Eichhoff, Jürgen. "German in Wisconsin." In Glenn G.
Gilbert, ed. The German Language in America. Austin: University of Texas Press, 1971, pp. 43–57.

Everest, Kate Asaphine (Levi). "How Wisconsin Came by
Its Large German Element." Collections, SHSW 12
(1892):299–334.

Hale, Frederick. "The Americanization of Danish
Immigrants in Wisconsin, 1847–1872." WMH 64 (Spring
1981):202–15.

Jarsatad, Anton. "The Melting Pot in Northeastern Wisconsin." WMH 26 (June 1943):426-32.

Karsten, John H. "A Half Century of Dutch Settlement in Wisconsin, 1847-1897." In Henry S. Lucas, ed. Dutch Immigrant Memoirs and Related Writings. Assen, Netherlands: Van Gorcum, 1955, pp. 129-39.

Kellogg, Louis Phelps. "The Bennett Law in Wisconsin." WMH 2 (September 1918):3-25.

Kolehmainen, John I. "The Finns of Wisconsin." WMH 27 (June 1944):391-99.

Kuzniewski, Anthony J. "Milwaukee's Poles, 1866-1918: The Rise and Fall of a Model Community." Milwaukee History 1 (1978):13-24.

Larsen, Lawrence H. "Draft Riot in Wisconsin, 1862." Civil War History 7 (December 1961):421-527.

Lenroot, Irvine L. "The War Loyalty of Wisconsin." Forum 59 (June 1918):695-702.

Levi, Kate A. Everest. "Geographical Origins of German Immigration to Wisconsin." Collections, SHSW 14 (1898):341-93.

Luchsinger, John. "The Planting of the Swiss Colony at New Glarus, Wisconsin." Collections, SHSW 12 (1892):335-82.

McDonald, M. Justile. "The Irish of the North Country." WMH 40 (Winter 1956-57):126-32.

Madja, M. J. "The Polish Immigrant, the American Hierarchy, and Father Wenceslaus Kruszka." Polish American Studies 26 (January-June 1969):16-29.

Martin, Xavier. "The Belgians of Northeast Wisconsin." Collections, SHSW 13 (1895):375-96.

Meloni, Alberto C. "Italy Invades the Bloody Third: The Early History of Milwaukee's Italians." Messenger, MCHS 25 (March 1969):34-46.

Metzner, Lee Weilep. "The Belgians in the North Country." WMH 26 (March 1943):280-88.

Munch, Peter A. "Segregation and Assimilation of Norwegian Settlements in Wisconsin." Norwegian-American Studies and Records 18 (Northfield, Minn.: NAHA, 1975):102-40.

Muzik, Edward J. "Victor L. Berger: Congress and the Red Scare." WMH 47 (Summer 1964):309-18.

Nash, Roderick. "Victor L. Berger: Making Marx Respectable." WMH 47 (Summer 1964):301-8.

Ostergren Robert C. "Geographic Perspectives on the History of Settlement in the Upper Midwest." Upper Midwest History 1 (1982):14-29.

Perrin, Richard W. E. "Log Sauna and the Finnish
  Farmstead: Transplanted Architectural Idioms in
  Northern Wisconsin." WMH 44 (Summer 1961):284-86.
Pienkos, Donald E. "The Polish Americans in Milwaukee
  Politics." In Angela T. Pienkos, ed. Ethnic Poli-
  tics in Urban America: The Polish Experience in
  Four Cities. Chicago: Polish American Historical
  Association, 1978, pp. 66-91.
____. "Politics, Religion, and Change in Polish Milwau-
  kee, 1900-1930." WMH 61 (Spring 1978):179-209.
Prisland, Marie. "The Slovenians, Most Recent American
  Immigrants." WMH 33 (March 1950):265-80.
Raitz, Karl B., and Mather, Cotton. "Norwegians and
  Tobacco in Western Wisconsin." Annals of the Asso-
  ciation of American Geographers 61 (1971):684-96.
Rippley, La Vern J. "American Milk Cows for Germany: A
  Sequel." North Dakota History 44 (Summer 1977):15-
  23.
Saloutos, Theodore. "The Greeks of Milwaukee." WMH 53
  (Spring 1970):175-93.
____. "Growing up in the Greek Community of Milwaukee."
  Messenger, MCHS 29 (1973):46-60.
Sanford, Albert Hart. "Polish People of Portage
  County." Proceedings, SHSW 55 (1907):259-88.
Schafer, Joseph. "Christian Traugott Ficker's Advice
  to Emigrants." WMH 25 (December 1941):217-36;
  (March 1942):331-55; and (June 1942):456-75.
____. "The Yankee and the Teuton in Wisconsin." A
  series in the WMH 6 (1922-23). Part 1: "Charac-
  teristic Attitudes Toward the Land," pp. 125-45;
  part 2: "Distinctive Traits as Farmers," pp. 261-
  79; part 3: "Some Traits of Yankees," pp. 386-402;
  part 4: "Some Social Traits of the Teutons." 7
  (1923):3-19; part 5: "Social Harmonies and Discords," pp. 148-71.
Schereck, William J. "The Peoples of Wisconsin."
  Typewritten script in the State Historical Society
  of Wisconsin. A 1956 radio braodcast.
Sienkaniec, Ladislas J., O.F.M. "The Poles of Upper
  North Wisconsin." WMH 39 (Spring 1956):195-98.
Simon, Roger D. "Housing and Services in an Immigrant
  Neighborhood: Milwaukee's Ward 14." Journal of Ur-
  ban Histoy 2 (August 1976):435-57.
Smith, Guy-Harold. "Notes on the Distribution of the
  Foreign Born Scandinavians in Wisconsin in 1905."
  WMH 14 (June 1931):419-36.

____. "Notes on the Distribution of the German Born in Wisconsin in 1905." WMH 13 (December 1929):107-20.

Stevens, John D. "When Sedition Laws Were Enforced: Wisconsin in World War I." Transactions, WASAL 58 (1970):39-60.

Tomkiewicz, J. W. S. "Polanders in Wisconsin." In Proceedings, SHSW, 1901 (Madison: State Printer, 1902), pp. 148-52.

Veidemanis, Juris. "Latvian Settlers in Wisconsin: A Comparative View." WMH 45 (Summer 1962):251-55.

____. "Two Generations of Mental Isolation: Latvians in Northern Wisconsin." Wisconsin Sociologist (June 1960):1-23.

Vlach, J. J. "Our Bohemian Population." Proceedings, SHSW, 1901 (Madison: State Printer, 1902), pp. 159-62.

Ward, Charles A. "The Serbian and Croatian Communities in Milwaukee." General Linguistics 16 (Summer, Fall 1976):151-65.

Whyte, William F. "The Bennett Law Campaign in Wisconsin." WMH 10 (June 1927):363-90.

Wyman, Roger E. "Wisconsin Ethnic Groups and the Election of 1890." WMH 51 (Summer 1968):269-93.

4. Dissertations and Theses

Berres, Jean L. "Local Aspects of the Campaign for Americanism: The Milwaukee Journal in World War I." Ph.D. dissertation, Southern Illinois University, Carbondale, 1977.

Brandes, Stuart Dean. "Nils Naugen and the Wisconsin Progressive Movement." M.A. thesis, University of Wisconsin, 1965.

Galford, Justin B. "The Foreign Born and Urban Growth in the Great Lakes, 1850-1950: A Study of Chicago, Cleveland, Detroit, and Milwaukee." Ph.D. dissertation, New York University, 1957.

Kuyper, Susan Jean. "The Americanization of German Immigrants: Language, Religion, and Schools in Nineteenth Century Rural Wisconsin." Ph.D. Dissertation, University of Wisconsin, 1980.

Martin, Lawrence James. "Opposition to Conscription in Wisconsin, 1917-1918." M.S. thesis, University of Wisconsin, 1952.

Mayer, Jonathan David. "The Journey-to-Work, Ethnicity, and Occupation in Milwaukee, 1860-1900." Ph.D. dissertation, University of Michigan, 1977.

Meyer, Mary D. "The Germans in Wisconsin and the Civil War: Their Attitude Toward the Union, the Republicans, Slavery, and Lincoln." M.S. thesis, Catholic University of America, 1937.

Nelson, Charles August. "Progressivism and Loyalty in Wisconsin Politics, 1912-1918." M.A. thesis, University of Wisconsin, 1961.

Nokkentvedt, Christian. "From Danish Parishes to Midwestern America, 1837-1921: A Case Study of Danes in Racine, Wisconsin." Ph.D. dissertation in progress, University of Illinois-Chicago Circle.

Overmoehle, Sister M. Hedwigis. "The Anti-Clerical Activities of the Forty-Eighters in Wisconsin 1848-1860." Ph.D. dissertation, St. Louis University, 1941.

Pedersen, Harald Ansgar. "Acculturation among Danish and Polish Ethnic Groups." Ph.D. dissertation, University of Wisconsin, 1949.

Simon, Roger D. "The Expansion of an Industrial City: Milwaukee, 1880-1910." Ph.D. dissertation, University of Wisconsin, 1971.

Slocum, Walter Lucius, "Ethnic Stocks as Culture Types in Rural Wisconsin: A Study of Differential Native American, German and Norwegian Influence on Certain Aspects of Man-Land Adjustment in Rural Localities." Ph.D. dissertation, University of Wisconsin, 1940.

Stevens, John Dean. "Suppression of Expression in Wisconsin During World War I." Ph.D. dissertation, University of Wisconsin, 1967.

Sutherland, Laura Elizabeth. "The Immigrant Family in the City: Milwaukee's Poles, 1880-1905." M.A. thesis, University of Wisconsin-Milwaukee, 1974.

Taggert, Glen L. "Czechs of Wisconsin as a Culture Type." Ph.D. dissertation, University of Wisconsin, 1947.

Ulrich, Robert J. "The Bennett Law of 1889: Education and Politics in Wisconsin." Ph.D. dissertation, University of Wisconsin, 1965.

Veidemanis, Juris. "Social Change: Major Value Systems of Latvians at Home as Refugees, and as Immigrants." Ph.D. dissertation, University of Wisconsin, 1961.

Wyman, Roger E. "Voting Behavior in the Progressive Era: Wisconsin as a Case Study." Ph.D. dissertation, University of Wisconsin, 1970.

Index

DATE DUE